BRITISH BATTLESHIP
VS
ITALIAN BATTLESHIP

The Mediterranean 1940–41

MARK STILLE

OSPREY PUBLISHING
Bloomsbury Publishing Plc
PO Box 883, Oxford, OX1 9PL, UK
1385 Broadway, 5th Floor, New York, NY 10018, USA
E-mail: info@ospreypublishing.com
www.ospreypublishing.com

OSPREY is a trademark of Osprey Publishing Ltd

First published in Great Britain in 2020

A catalogue record for this book is available from the British Library.

ISBN: PB 9781472832269; eBook 9781472832276;
ePDF 9781472832283; XML 9781472832290

20 21 22 23 24   10 9 8 7 6 5 4 3 2 1

Maps by www.bounford.com
Index by Rob Munro
Typeset by PDQ Digital Media Solutions, Bungay, UK
Printed and bound in India by Replika Press Private Ltd.

Osprey Publishing supports the Woodland Trust, the UK's leading woodland
conservation charity.

To find out more about our authors and books visit
www.ospreypublishing.com. Here you will find extracts, author interviews,
details of forthcoming events and the option to sign up for our newsletter.

Author's note

The author would like to extend his most sincere gratitude to Maurizio Brescia
who provided most of the photographs for this book and undertook a very
thorough review of the text. Keith Allen also reviewed the text and saved the
author from several unforced errors.

Editor's note

In most cases imperial measurements, including nautical miles (NM), knots
(kn) and long tons, have been used in this book. For ease of comparison please
refer to the following conversion table:

1 NM = 1.85km
1yd = 0.9m
1ft = 0.3m
1in = 2.54cm/25.4mm
1kn = 1.85km/h
1 long ton = 1.02 metric tonnes
1lb = 0.45kg

Front cover, above: At the battle of Calabria, only *Warspite* with its
modernized 15in twin turrets had the ability to engage the Italian battle line.
This is the view as *Warspite*'s 15in/42 Mk I guns engage *Giulio Cesare*.
Warspite's salvoes are tight, and they soon hit their target at 26,000yd, the
longest hit ever recorded by a battleship.
Front cover, below: *Vittorio Veneto*, the lead ship in Italy's most modern class of
battleships, never had an opportunity to engage a British battleship. The
closest it came was at the battle of Cape Matapan in which *Vittorio Veneto* and
three British battleships were present, but did not exchange fire. In this view,
Vittorio Veneto is firing a broadside at a British light cruiser. The guns in all
three 15in triple turrets are at high elevation to engage the target 25,000yd
away. On this occasion, the Italian battleship fire was observed to be accurate,
but due to the salvo-dispersion problem no hits were scored.
Title-page photograph: View looking aft from the bow of *Conte di Cavour*,
taken after the ship's 1933–37 reconstruction. (NH 86139 courtesy of the
Naval History and Heritage Command)

Artist's note

Readers may care to note that the original paintings from which the
battlescene artwork and cover views for this book were prepared are available
for private sale. All reproduction copyright whatsoever is retained by the
publishers. All enquiries should be addressed to:

p.wright1@btinternet.com

The publishers regret that they can enter into no correspondence upon
this matter.

CONTENTS

Introduction   4

Chronology   8

Design and Development   10

The Strategic Situation   25

Technical Specifications   29

The Combatants   44

Combat   52

Analysis   70

Aftermath   75

Bibliography   79

Index   80

INTRODUCTION

The battle for control of the Mediterranean Sea was the longest campaign involving naval, air and ground forces of World War II. At various stages, it involved the navies of the United Kingdom, the United States, France, Italy and Germany. Although World War II had been under way since 1 September 1939, hostilities in the Mediterranean did not begin until Italy entered the war on 10 June 1940. Just 12 days later, France signed an armistice with Germany and dropped out of the Allied powers facing Germany and Italy. This left the United Kingdom to carry the fight alone against the Axis in the Mediterranean. Initially, Italy fought largely alone in the Mediterranean but as its fortunes waned, Germany was forced to play a greater role. Italy's Regia Marina (Royal Navy) was the predominant Axis naval force in the Mediterranean until Italy signed an armistice with the Allied powers on 3 September 1943 (made public five days later) and duly defected from the Axis. Despite myth, the Regia Marina fought hard during the naval war in the Mediterranean and on several occasions more than held its own against the British Royal Navy.

The United Kingdom decided to contest control of the Mediterranean for several reasons. The primary driver was the important sea lines of communications (SLOCs) which ran through the Mediterranean Sea from the United Kingdom to its colonial possessions in India and the Far East. If the sea lanes through the Mediterranean were closed, the British would be forced to use the Cape of Good Hope route around Africa, a total distance of 12,000 miles. This route quadrupled shipping requirements compared to the Mediterranean route and had strategic implications for Allied capabilities and plans worldwide. In reality, though, the Mediterranean was the only place where British forces could fight against the Axis with any hope of success. The Royal Navy entered the war as the strongest navy in Europe and considered the Regia Marina to be a weak opponent which would be quickly crushed. Once the Regia

Marina was defeated, the British would have the option of seizing Italy's Libya colony or attacking anywhere along Europe's southern periphery.

British hopes of quickly defeating the Regia Marina and seizing Libya were frustrated by the stubborn resistance of the Italians and the intervention of the Germans who contributed ground forces which restored the Axis position in Libya and air forces which helped the Axis to strengthen its hold upon the Central Mediterranean. Control of this area allowed the Axis to supply its forces in Libya and closed off the Mediterranean to British shipping. It also made it increasingly difficult for the British to supply the island of Malta. Even during the early stages of the naval war in the Mediterranean, both sides focused on convoy operations in the Central Mediterranean which served as a trigger for several large naval encounters.

Dating from the mid-1930s, this photograph shows the Queen Elizabeth-class battleship *Barham* after its 1931–34 modernization. (NH 63077 courtesy of the Naval History and Heritage Command)

This view of *Conte di Cavour* at Taranto in 1938 after the completion of its rebuilding shows the port-side 4.7in secondary battery twin turrets and the forward 3.9in twin turret for anti-aircraft protection. The device on top of the superstructure is the main-battery rangefinder. (M. Brescia Collection)

On 10 June 1940, when Italy entered World War II, the naval balance favoured the Allies. Following the withdrawal of France from the war, however, the naval balance between the Royal Navy and the Regia Marina was more even, with the former holding the edge in large ships and the latter in all other categories.

The naval balance in the Mediterranean, June 1940

Ship type	Royal Navy	Regia Marina	Ship type	Royal Navy	Regia Marina
Carrier	2	0	Light cruiser	7	14
Battleship	4	2	Destroyer	31	59
Battlecruiser	1	0	Submarine	12	113
Heavy cruiser	0	7			

Warspite in Malta's Grand Harbour in autumn 1938 after completion of the battleship's 1934–37 reconstruction. Note the massive bridge structure and the aviation facilities amidships with a double-ended aircraft catapult and space for two floatplanes. The rebuilt *Warspite* was a major player in the early naval war in the Mediterranean. (M. Brescia Collection)

The Regia Marina was not ready for the naval war in the Mediterranean; it only had two battleships in service, though it expected to have another two modernized and two new battleships enter service within a matter of months. Until they did so, however, the Royal Navy had an edge in large ships. On top of this, the Royal Navy operated aircraft carriers while the Regia Marina had none. The immediate availability of naval air power operating from the decks of aircraft carriers serving with the British battle fleet was to prove a key factor in the battles to come. The Regia Marina possessed a considerable edge in cruisers, destroyers and submarines, but this could prove irrelevant in a fleet action.

Both navies adhered to the traditional concepts of sea control which placed the battle fleet and its most powerful component, the battleship, at the centre of operations. Sea control could only be gained and maintained by a balanced battle fleet which was composed of several important components. Cruisers were used by both

sides for scouting, and the Regia Marina used its heavy cruisers in the battle line to make up for its lack of battleships. Destroyers were necessary for screening and to conduct torpedo attacks on the enemy battle line. The Royal Navy used aircraft carriers to extend its striking range to cripple enemy ships so that they could be brought within range of the battle fleet. Nevertheless, the centrepiece of the battle fleet was the battleship. Only the battleship had the combination of striking power and protection required to defeat another battleship. The 'big guns' of the battleship were the final arbiter of victory at sea.

While both sides accepted the primacy of the battleship, they did not plan to employ their battleships in the same manner. The Royal Navy sought a quick decision at sea and was aggressive in its employment of the battle fleet. The Regia Marina did not shirk from a clash of battle fleets but sought to accept battle only under advantageous conditions. Because it could not replace its losses, and because control of the Central Mediterranean was underpinned by a fleet of battleships, the Regia Marina had to maintain a fleet-in-being and was therefore much more cautious in the tactical employment of its battle fleet.

The British and Italian battle fleets first clashed soon after Italy entered the war. The resulting engagement – the battle of Calabria on 9 July 1940 – was one of the largest naval battles of the entire war, but because it proved brief and indecisive it is virtually unknown today. Subsequent opportunities for British and Italian battleships to engage each other again were rare, though both battle fleets were active and often came within close proximity of each other. Despite the few instances of direct engagement, the battleships of the two navies played a key role in every major naval engagement in the Mediterranean during 1940 and 1941.

CHRONOLOGY

1914

May	*Giulio Cesare* is completed.
December	*Queen Elizabeth*, lead battleship of five, is completed.

1915

April	*Conte di Cavour*, lead battleship of three, is completed.
April	*Warspite* is completed.
May	*Caio Duilio*, lead battleship of two, is completed.
September	*Barham* is completed.

1916

February	*Malaya* and *Valiant* are completed.
March	*Andrea Doria* is completed.
May	*Royal Sovereign*, lead battleship of five, is completed, along with *Revenge* and *Royal Oak*.
December	*Resolution* is completed.

1917

October	*Ramillies* is completed.

1927

August	*Nelson*, lead battleship of two, is completed.
December	*Rodney* is completed.

1937

June	*Conte di Cavour* and *Warspite* are both recommissioned after modernization.
October	*Giulio Cesare* is recommissioned after rebuilding.

1939

November	*Valiant* completes modernization.

1940

May	*Vittorio Veneto* and *Littorio* are completed.
10 June	Italy enters World War II.
3 July	The British Force H attacks the French fleet at Mers-el-Kébir.
9 July	Three British battleships face two Italian battleships at the battle of Calabria; *Giulio Cesare* is damaged and the Italian battle fleet breaks off the action.
15 July	*Caio Duilio* is recommissioned after rebuilding.
6 September	The British reinforce the Mediterranean Fleet with the battleship *Valiant* and the aircraft carrier *Formidable*. The Italian battle fleet attempts to intercept with five battleships, but fails to make contact.
26 October	*Andrea Doria* is recommissioned after rebuilding.
11–12 November	British carrier aircraft attack the Italian battle fleet at Taranto. *Conte di Cavour* is heavily damaged and never returns to service; *Littorio* and *Andrea Doria* are damaged, but return to service.
27 November	The Italian battle fleet sorties to engage Force H off south-western Sardinia. The British battleship *Ramillies* and battlecruiser *Renown* fight an indecisive action with *Vittorio Veneto* and *Giulio Cesare* at the battle of Cape Spartivento.
December	*King George V*, lead battleship of five, is completed.

1941

31 January *Queen Elizabeth* completes extensive modernization.

9 February Force H, with one battleship, one battlecruiser and one aircraft carrier, bombards Genoa; led by three battleships, the Italian battle fleet puts to sea but fails to intercept.

26–29 March At the battle of Cape Matapan the Italian battle fleet, led by *Vittorio Veneto*, attempts to attack British convoys in the Eastern Mediterranean. After an indecisive gunnery action south of Crete, British carrier aircraft damage *Vittorio Veneto*. The battleship escapes, but three Italian heavy cruisers and two destroyers are sunk.

22–26 August Force H lays mines off Livorno; led by *Vittorio Veneto* and *Littorio*, the Italian battle fleet puts to sea but fails to intercept.

1 October A British operation to send a large convoy to Malta from Gibraltar, escorted by three battleships and an aircraft carrier, ends; an Italian battle fleet led by *Vittorio Veneto* and *Littorio* puts to sea, but fails to intercept.

25 November The British battleship *Barham* is sunk by *U-331*.

18 December At the first battle of Sirte, the Italian battle fleet with *Littorio*, *Giulio Cesare* and *Andrea Doria* fights an inconclusive engagement with a British cruiser–destroyer force to cover an Axis convoy headed to Libya.

19 December Italian manned torpedo craft heavily damage *Queen Elizabeth* and *Valiant* in Alexandria harbour.

1942

22 March In the second battle of Sirte, the Italian battle fleet, led by *Littorio*, attacks the escort of a British convoy headed for Malta. A long-range gunnery duel delays the convoy long enough so that all four merchant ships are sunk by air attack.

June *Roma* is completed.

12–16 June The British mount a major relief for Malta with convoys from Gibraltar and Alexandria. The Italian battle fleet moves against the eastern convoy with *Vittorio Veneto* and *Littorio*; the convoy is forced to retreat to Alexandria.

10–15 August In Operation *Pedestal*, part of a major British convoy gets through to Malta; the Italian battle fleet is unable to intervene because of a lack of fuel oil.

8 November In Operation *Torch*, Allied forces land in Vichy North Africa.

1943

May Axis forces in Tunisia surrender.

July In Operation *Husky*, Allied forces land on Sicily.

8 September An armistice between Italy and the Allied powers is announced.

10–11 September Much of the Italian battle fleet arrives at Malta to be interned.

Rebuilding of *Andrea Doria* began at Trieste in late 1937 (as shown in this view) and lasted until October 1940. The result was a battleship of limited capabilities which was outmatched by British battleships operating in the Mediterranean. (M. Brescia Collection)

DESIGN AND DEVELOPMENT

THE ROYAL NAVY'S BATTLESHIP FORCE

The Royal Navy entered World War II with a battleship force almost entirely built during World War I. All of the ships had been modernized between the wars, some extensively so, but the Royal Navy's battle fleet went into the naval war in the Mediterranean with definite operational limitations. The nature of the Royal Navy's battleship force was further shaped by the terms of the Washington Naval Treaty of 1922 which limited the size of the force and prevented new construction except for the two Nelson-class battleships, *Nelson* and *Rodney*, both of which were completed in 1927. The British were slow to re-arm as the threat of Nazi Germany emerged, however, and it was not until 1937 that the five battleships of the new King George V class were laid down. The lead ship of the class, *King George V*, was not completed until December 1940.

The Royal Navy's battleship force was stretched thin by 10 June 1940 when Italy entered the war. The primary threat to the United Kingdom and its SLOCs was the Kriegsmarine (German Navy). The Germans used their small battle fleet to lead the invasion of Norway in April 1940 and to raid British SLOCs in the North Atlantic. This required the Royal Navy to keep its most modern battleships in the North Atlantic. It also forced the Royal Navy to devote some of its least capable and slowest battleships to protect convoys. The stresses of fighting the Germans increased when the battleship *Bismarck* was completed in August 1940. *Tirpitz*, the second of the

Bismarck-class battleships, joined the Kriegsmarine fleet in February 1942; both battleships were more powerful than any single British battleship. As a matter of course, the British considered it necessary to use two of their most modern battleships to counter a single Bismarck-class battleship.

In late 1941 the Japanese looked increasingly likely to enter World War II. The British did not plan to send a battle fleet to the Far East until months after the outbreak of war, but this was quickly changed when Churchill decided to send a small force with the battlecruiser *Repulse* and the battleship *Prince of Wales* to the Far East as a deterrent against Japanese expansion, followed by a larger battle fleet comprised primarily of Royal Sovereign-class battleships. This obviously left fewer resources available to the Royal Navy to counter the Axis forces in the Mediterranean.

Before Italy entered the war in June 1940, the Royal Navy's Mediterranean Fleet was brought up to strength. The backbone was formed by the five Queen Elizabeth-class battleships, considered more powerful than the four oldest Italian battleships. Royal Sovereign-class battleships were also used in the Mediterranean when the British thought more battleships were necessary to keep an edge on the Italian battle fleet, but for the most part the slow speed of these ships confined them to Atlantic convoy escort duties or other special missions. The two Nelson-class battleships were mostly kept in home waters, as were the just-commissioning King George V-class battleships.

THE QUEEN ELIZABETH CLASS

The Queen Elizabeth class – *Queen Elizabeth*, *Warspite*, *Valiant*, *Barham* and *Malaya* – was conceived during the dreadnought-building race in the years preceding World War I. The first modern British battleship, *Dreadnought*, and the next several classes of British battleships carried 12in guns. The British then went to a 13.5in main battery with the Orion class in the 1909 Naval Programme. In the 1912 Naval Programme, Winston Churchill, as First Lord of the Admiralty, pushed for the adoption of a 15in main battery as a hedge against a similar move by other naval powers. In addition to

This photograph shows *Warspite* in its original configuration from 1917. The five Queen Elizabeth-class battleships were the most powerful in the world at the time with a fine balance of protection, firepower and speed. The year before, on 31 May, *Warspite* had taken 15 hits from large-calibre German shells at the battle of Jutland but was able to keep fighting. (M. Brescia Collection)

Barham pictured in 1937 with other battleships of the Home Fleet. *Barham* was the least modernized of the five Queen Elizabeth-class battleships, but saw heavy service in the Mediterranean before being lost on 25 November 1941 to torpedoes launched by *U-331*. (M. Brescia Collection)

the increase in firepower, the British decided to incorporate a major increase in propulsive power. To achieve the design speed of 25kn, 24 boilers were needed.

The main battery was composed of the new 15in/42 Mk I gun, all eight of which were placed on the centreline in four twin turrets. The secondary battery, which was intended for defence against torpedo boats, was composed of 16 6in Mk XII single guns mounted in casemates, but it was quickly determined that the after four guns were worthless in heavy seas. Two of the four guns were removed and the other two were moved to better positions.

Armour on the Queen Elizabeth class totalled 29 per cent of the design displacement. With this, designers were able to provide a 13in waterline armour belt with 6in armoured bulkheads to enclose the area within the main belt. Barbette armour was a maximum of 10in thick. Horizontal protection was distributed over four different decks and totalled as much as 7in in some areas. Underwater protection was weak, however, as was common for all warships of the period, with only a 2in torpedo bulkhead.

The Queen Elizabeth-class battleships went to a full oil-fired system, the first battleships to do so. Four turbines drove the four shafts to achieve the desired 75,000shp. On trials, the 25kn design speed was not achieved, but the 24kn that was recorded made them some of the fastest battleships of the era. In addition to unmatched firepower and speed, these battleships possessed considerable protection; and their combination of firepower, speed and protection made them well-balanced

ships. In fact, they were the first 'fast battleships' ever designed which became the norm for designers of post-Washington Naval Treaty battleships built in the years immediately preceding World War II.

Because the Washington Naval Treaty prohibited new battleship construction, the Royal Navy was forced to modernize its existing battleships. In the case of the Queen Elizabeth class this reconstruction was significant. Details are provided later in this book.

Valiant shown off Gibraltar in 1935–36 after completion of its first modernization. The battleship received a new fire-control system and aviation facilities on the quarterdeck, and had its two stacks trunked into one. (M. Brescia Collection)

THE ROYAL SOVEREIGN CLASS

The battleships of the 1913 Naval Programme became the Royal Sovereign class, four of which – *Revenge, Royal Sovereign, Royal Oak* and *Resolution* – were completed between February and December 1916 and the fifth, *Ramillies*, in September 1917. The five ships possessed broadly similar capabilities to those of the preceding Queen Elizabeth class with the salient exception of reduced speed. For this reason, they were viewed as a step backwards from the very successful Queen Elizabeth class; and because they received very limited modernizations between the wars and saw their service speed drop below the original 23kn, by the beginning of World War II they were second-line units.

In terms of firepower, the Royal Sovereigns class was virtually unchanged from the Queen Elizabeth class with a main battery of eight 15in/42 Mk I guns and a slightly smaller secondary battery of 14 6in Mk XII guns in casemates.

Protection was on the same scale as that of the Queen Elizabeth class. The total weight of armour was 31.7 per cent of design displacement. The main belt was a maximum of 13in thick which covered the area between the forward and aft 15in twin turrets. At the end of the belt were 6in transverse armoured bulkheads.

Ramillies, final ship of the Royal Sovereign class, shown here on trials in 1917. Despite their heavy armament, the Royal Sovereign-class battleships were always seen as a step backwards from the very successful preceding Queen Elizabeth class because of their lower maximum speed. (Library of Congress)

Horizontal protection again featured the inefficient distribution of armour over four decks, but was significant over key areas.

Underwater protection remained a weakness. *Ramillies* was completed with shallow anti-torpedo bulges and *Revenge* and *Resolution* were fitted with the same before the end of World War I. *Royal Sovereign* received its anti-torpedo bulges in a refit begun in 1920 and *Royal Oak* was fitted with anti-torpedo bulges during its 1922–24 refit. All five ships had their vital areas covered by an anti-torpedo bulkhead 1–1.5in thick. This underwater protection proved inadequate during World War II, however.

Speed was not a priority design consideration and the original design speed was only 21kn. After the success of the oil-fired Queen Elizabeth class, it was planned that the Royal Sovereign class would revert to mixed oil and coal firing as a hedge against the possibility that World War I would disrupt oil supplies. In late 1914, the design was changed to oil-firing only and maximum speed was raised to 23kn. Eighteen boilers drove the four turbines and generated a total of 40,000shp.

THE NELSON CLASS

As mentioned earlier, the two battleships of the Nelson class – *Nelson* and *Rodney* – were kept in home waters during the early part of World War II to counter the threat of the Kriegsmarine. They did not see service in the Mediterranean until July 1941 when *Nelson* was assigned to escort a convoy to Malta. In September that year, both battleships formed part of the escort for a large Malta convoy during which *Nelson* was hit by a single torpedo dropped from a Regia Aeronautica (Italian Air Force) torpedo bomber. The torpedo hit forward of the forward-most 16in triple turret and caused severe flooding which required repairs at Malta. Neither ship had the opportunity to engage its Italian counterparts despite extensive Mediterranean service in 1942 and 1943.

The origin of the design for the Nelson class came from the requirement to match the Japanese and American navies which already had battleships armed with 16in guns in service following World War I. Because of the existing Japanese and American battleships, the Washington Naval Treaty permitted the British to build two similar

Royal Sovereign in 1938–39 steaming in column with other battleships and cruisers of the Home Fleet. By the start of World War II, the Royal Sovereign-class battleships were obsolescent and were assigned secondary duties for most of the conflict. (M. Brescia Collection)

battleships. The design had to conform to the treaty's 35,000-ton limit for battleships, so there was an inevitable compromise in the struggle to fit a heavy armament, heavy protection and high speed into a single hull. The result was a truncated-looking design which uniquely placed all three main-battery triple turrets forward of the superstructure to reduce weight by decreasing the length of the hull which required armour. The designers succeeded in building a battleship with an unparalleled armament of nine 16in/45 Mk I guns, a high standard of protection and an acceptable top speed of 23kn.

A Nelson-class battleship leads a major portion of the Royal Navy's capital ships in manoeuvres between the wars. In a navy wedded to the big gun, the two Nelson-class battleships were important assets because they carried the fleet's only 16in guns. (NH 50918 courtesy of the Naval History and Heritage Command)

The main battery was built around the new 16in/45 Mk I gun which fired a 2,048lb shell at very high velocity, resulting in increased barrel wear and decreased accuracy. The triple turret itself had a series of problems that were never solved. Twelve 6in Mk XII guns comprised the secondary battery, all mounted in twin mounts and placed aft.

Protective armour represented 29.3 per cent of the standard displacement. The main belt was a maximum of 14in deep over the magazines and 13in elsewhere. Barbette armour was a maximum of 15in thick with the armour of the 16in turret face being 16in thick. Horizontal protection featured a main armoured deck with a maximum of 6.25in over the magazines, 4.25in over the steering gear and 3.75in over the machinery spaces. *Nelson* received additional horizontal armour during a 1937 refit. Underwater protection was designed to defeat the effect of a 750lb mine or torpedo warhead through a combination of a 1.5in anti-torpedo bulkhead, an internal anti-torpedo bulge between the belt and the outer hull, and a water-filled buoyancy chamber.

Because of the specified weight limitations, machinery was limited to that necessary to develop 46,000shp, which was sufficient for 23.5kn. Although this speed may have been good enough to keep up with Royal Navy's other battleships, it was inferior to that of almost all other foreign battleships.

THE KING GEORGE V CLASS

The final class of British battleships to see service in the Mediterranean during the war was the five-ship King George V class; but only one of the ships, *Prince of Wales*, saw action in the Mediterranean while escorting a convoy to Malta during September 1941. Because they were the Royal Navy's most modern battleships, they were usually held in home waters to maintain the desired 2:1 advantage over *Bismarck* and *Tirpitz*.

The lead ship of the class was laid down in January 1937, while treaty limitations were technically still in force, so the design was still based on the 35,000-ton limit and a self-imposed limit of a 14in main battery. The British decided not to take advantage of escalator clauses which permitted battleships of up to 45,000 tons fitted with 16in guns so as not to delay the completion of the new ships. Despite these limitations, the ships which entered service possessed a good balance of firepower, protection and speed.

The main battery consisted of ten 14in Mk VII guns in two quadruple turrets and a single twin turret. The guns were smaller than those on other navies' battleships of the period but proved successful in service. However, the complex loading equipment in the quadruple turrets caused problems throughout World War II. The secondary battery dispensed with the antiquated concept of separate secondary and anti-aircraft batteries by fitting 16 5.25in Mk I dual-purpose guns in eight twin turrets.

The protection scheme was designed to protect the vitals of the ship from 15in shells. This was judged sufficient because the largest German and Italian battleships mounted 15in guns. The main belt consisted of 15in of armour and was enclosed with transverse armoured bulkheads of 10–12in. Horizontal protection was a maximum of 6in over the magazine and 5in over the machinery spaces. Torpedo protection depended on an internal anti-torpedo bulge featuring three layers of plating which created two vacant spaces and a central space filled with water.

Each King George V-class battleship was fitted with eight boilers with superheaters that could produce 100,000shp on four shafts – enough to produce a top speed of 28kn. This was a dramatic improvement for a British battleship but still inferior to the top speeds of the latest German and Italian battleships.

This is a view of *Prince of Wales* after completion in early 1941. Note the large bridge structure, similar to that fitted on the modernized Queen Elizabeth-class battleships, the twin stacks and the aviation facilities between and the 14in quadruple turret forward. (80-G-190724 courtesy of the Naval History and Heritage Command)

THE REGIA MARINA'S BATTLESHIP FORCE

After World War I, Italy experienced severe economic difficulties, which meant that it was unable to build up to the 175,000 tons of battleships allocated to it by the Washington Naval Treaty. For most of the 1920s, the Regia Marina's battleship force consisted of the unique *Dante Alighieri*, the two surviving ships of the Conte di Cavour class and two Caio Duilio-class ships. No new battleship construction was undertaken due to the poor economic conditions and the fact that the Regia Marina's rival, France's Marine nationale, also made no effort to build up to France's allowed 175,000 tons allocation. With its limited naval budget during the 1920s, Italy decided to build 10,000-ton cruisers and use them as surrogate capital ships. In 1928, *Dante Alighieri* was scrapped, and the two Conte di Cavour-class ships were placed in reserve.

France laid down the first of two 26,500-ton Dunkerque-class battleships armed with eight 13in guns in 1932. Germany responded with two ships of the Scharnhorst class. Italy was forced to respond because France was seen as the most likely naval

adversary, and began design work on what became the Vittorio Veneto class. This new class was much larger than the treaty displacement of 35,000 tons; in fact, the new ships came in at over 40,000 tons, but this was of no concern to the Italian government. As a stop-gap measure until the new battleships could be completed, modernization of the four older Italian battleships commenced.

THE CONTE DI CAVOUR CLASS

The three-ship Conte di Cavour class – *Conte di Cavour*, *Giulio Cesare* and *Leonardo da Vinci* – was designed in 1908 but not completed until April 1915. By then they were already inferior to battleships already in service with the other naval powers of the day (except the French) because the three Italian ships were lacking in protection, firepower and, to a lesser extent, speed. The design of the Conte di Cavour class confirmed the Italian preference for speed over protection and a continued acceptance of a smaller main battery because Italian industry was incapable of building guns larger than 12in diameter.

When completed, the Conte di Cavour class ships mounted a main battery of 13 British-designed but Italian-built 12in/46 guns fitted in a unique combination of three triple turrets and two twin turrets. This was an inferior arrangement, however, because one of the triple turrets was placed amidships which gave it limited firing arcs on both beams. The secondary battery was composed of 18 single 4.7in/50 guns, also designed in the United Kingdom but built in Italy, all mounted in casemates.

Protection of the Conte di Cavour-class ships was a definite improvement over that of the preceding *Dante Alighieri*, but was greatly inferior to that of British, German, American and Japanese ships of the same period. The main belt was 10in thick and covered the area between the main-gun turrets. Horizontal armour was composed of a main deck of 1in, sloping to 1.5in on the deck edges, and a middle deck with just over another 1in of armour. The turret barbettes and conning tower were covered by

Giulio Cesare conducted a port visit to the Mediterranean Fleet's main base at Malta in June 1938. Despite an extensive rebuild in 1933–37, *Giulio Cesare* was no match against the British battleships of the period. (NH 86591 courtesy of the Naval History and Heritage Command)

19

11in of armour. There was no dedicated underwater protection when the three ships of the class were completed.

The propulsion system of mixed-firing boilers and three sets of turbines produced only 31,000shp, sufficient to drive the ships at a top speed of 21.5kn.

As mentioned above, the two surviving ships of the class (*Leonardo da Vinci* was sunk by a magazine explosion on 2 August 1916, salvaged in 1919 and scrapped in 1923) were modernized before World War II. Details are provided later in this book.

THE CAIO DUILIO CLASS

The two ships of the Caio Duilio class, *Caio Duilio* and *Andrea Doria*, were laid down in early 1912 and completed in 1915 and 1916 respectively. In almost all respects, they were repeats of the proceeding Conte di Cavour class. The main battery was identical, but the secondary battery was improved with the fitting of 16 6in/45 guns, again all in casemates. Protection differed only slightly; the main armour belt was still 10in thick and the heaviest protection of 11in was placed on the turret barbettes, the turret faces and the conning tower. Propulsion again employed a combination of coal and oil-fired boilers which developed 32,000shp and a top speed of 21.5kn. The two Caio Duilio-class ships also received extensive modernization before the start of World War II, details of which are outlined later in this book.

This is a Caio Duilio-class battleship during World War I. The appearance of the two ships of this class was almost identical to that of the preceding Conte di Cavour class. Both ships possessed a heavy broadside, as evident in this view, but the main guns were only 12in in diameter meaning they were outgunned by all other modern battleships of the day. (M. Brescia Collection)

THE VITTORIO VENETO CLASS

The design genesis of what became the Regia Marina's final class of battleships was a long one. In 1931, France announced construction of the new Dunkerque class of battleship which drove the Italians to respond in kind. The original design work resulted in an orthodox ship of 35,000 tons armed with six 16in guns in three twin turrets and a speed of 28–29kn, but this design was rejected in favour of a larger ship with a main battery of nine 15in/50 guns in three triple turrets. The Italians wanted to move up to a 16in gun but the design and production of such a gun would have delayed construction of the new class. The 15in/50 gun had already been designed for a previously cancelled battleship design which meant construction of the new class could begin much sooner.

The keels for the first two ships, *Vittorio Veneto* and *Littorio*, were both laid down on 28 October 1934. Construction took until May 1940, which meant that the ships were still working up when Italy entered World War II in June 1940. Two more ships, *Impero* and *Roma*, were laid down in May and September 1938, respectively, by which time Italy was no longer bound by any naval treaty limitations. Construction of *Roma* was completed on 14 June 1942, but *Impero* was never completed.

The final design for the Vittorio Veneto class produced a well-balanced ship with above-average firepower, good protection and above-average speed. It is important to

This is *Littorio* running trials in December 1939. Much equipment has yet to be fitted and the bow was later modified to address a severe vibration problem. (M. Brescia Collection)

note that the success of Italian designers was largely attributable to the fact that Italian naval authorities permitted the ships to exceed 40,000 tons, well over the naval treaty limit of 35,000 tons. It was not just the Italians who experienced difficulties in producing a balanced design with a good combination of firepower, protection and speed on a 35,000-ton hull. American, British and French battleship designers also exceeded the 35,000-ton limit, but not with the same blatant disregard and not by the same amount.

The main battery was composed of the Italian-designed 15in/50 gun, the first gun of that size fitted on any Italian battleship. The nine guns were fitted on three triple turrets and were the dominating feature of what was a very attractive ship. Two turrets were placed forward and the third aft; the latter turret overlooked the quarterdeck where the aircraft catapult was located. This arrangement protected the aircraft on the quarterdeck from blast damage from the main guns. Each triple turret weighed 1,570 tons, as much as most destroyers of the day, and was heavily protected with face armour of 14in and side and roof armour 8in thick.

Italian designers considered a heavy secondary armament to be necessary for defence against torpedo attack from the large fleet of French destroyers. However, they continued the inefficient practice of providing separate batteries to contend with enemy surface ships and air attack. The secondary battery against surface

Vittorio Veneto was completed in May 1940 but had not finished trials by the time Italy entered World War II on 10 June 1940. This is a view of the ship running trials. Note the superstructure with the two rangefinders on top and the clearance of the aft 15in triple turret over the quarterdeck where the aircraft catapult was fitted. (M. Brescia Collection)

attack was composed of 12 6in L/55 guns fitted in four triple turrets, two on each beam. A battery of 12 3.5in/50 single mounts was provided for long-range anti-aircraft protection.

The protective scheme for the new class was slightly inferior to that of other contemporary foreign battleship designs, though the Italian designers were confident that it provided adequate protection against enemy battleship gunfire. The main belt was relatively thin and shallow and consisted of 11in of armour with a 2.75in outer plate. Italian designers did not fully employ the 'all or nothing' concept in which armour was only placed over vital areas with non-vital areas being left unprotected, because forward of the armoured citadel the side armour was reduced to just over 5in; no side armour was fitted aft of the armoured citadel.

Horizontal protection was heavy for a battleship designed in 1932, before the threat of air attack was fully appreciated. Protection over the machinery spaces was just over 6.5in thick, tapering to just over 6in outboard. Magazine protection was an impressive 6.5–8.5in. The turret barbettes were covered by a not-so-impressive 5.9in of armour. The conning tower was unlike that of foreign designs; on the Vittorio Veneto class the entire bridge tower was provided with some level of armoured protection, the most armour being placed on the levels on which the captain's and admiral's bridges and fire-control stations were located.

The Italians devised an elaborate underwater protection scheme which was named after its designer, Umberto Pugliese. The Pugliese system was also placed on the four older Regia Marina battleships during their extensive modernization, but their smaller beams meant that the system could not be fitted in full, so the Vittorio Veneto-class ships were the only Italian battleships to receive the entire system. The system was designed to provide protection against an explosion of 770lb of TNT. To provide this level of protection Pugliese designed a multi-layered system consisting of an angled exterior belt covering the bulged lower hull and two interior longitudinal bulkheads. There was a semi-circular space between the longitudinal bulkheads and the outer belt armour included a cylinder that was designed to act as a shock absorber. This cylinder was filled with fuel oil, water or a mixture of both and had an empty cylinder placed within it. The force of an underwater explosion was designed to hydraulically crush the cylinder to dissipate the force of the explosion. This system was not always successful under wartime conditions, however, because it suffered from two defects. One was caused by a manufacturing issue when rivets had to be used instead of welding and the rivets were unable to handle the explosive stresses placed on the seams. The other defect which reduced the effectiveness of the system was the desire to maintain the required hull form for high speed, which meant that the maximum diameter of the hollow cylinder could not be maintained throughout the entire length of the area covering the armoured citadel.

The propulsion system was designed to achieve a top speed of 30kn. This required 130,000shp which called for eight boilers in four boiler rooms to drive the four sets of turbines. Under trial conditions in 1939, *Vittorio Veneto* and *Littorio* developed greater than their design power and reached over 31kn even with a full displacement of over 41,000 tons. Under wartime conditions, both ships were still able to make 29kn.

This is *Roma* in the summer of 1942 after completion that June. The primary difference between *Roma* and the two previous ships in the Vittorio Veneto class was the increased height of the bow. *Roma* joined the Italian battle fleet too late to have any realistic opportunity to engage the British and was sunk on 9 September 1943 after being struck by a Fritz X radio-controlled glide bomb dropped by a Luftwaffe Do 217 bomber while en route to Malta for internment after the declaration of an armistice between Italy and the Allied powers. (M. Brescia Collection)

BATTLESHIP DESIGN COMPARISON

The battleships available to both the Royal Navy and Regia Marina at the start of the naval war in the Mediterranean dated from World War I. Both navies carried out extensive modernization of their dated battleships, but the results were quite different. The difference stemmed from the fact that the Royal Navy's Queen Elizabeth-class battleship was a fundamentally better ship and was better able to take modernization. Most importantly, these ships were armed with 15in/42 guns, which made them formidable offensive platforms and gave the Royal Navy five battleships with greater firepower than the modernized Italian battleships with their 12.6in/44 guns. The Queen Elizabeth-class ships were also better protected and enjoyed a larger zone of immunity to the Italian 12.6in/44 guns than the modernized Italian battleships had against the British 15in/42 guns. The advantages enjoyed by the British battleships were obvious, but just as obvious was the Italian battleships' advantage in speed which allowed the Regia Marina to select when and for how long it wanted to engage in a gunnery duel with the Royal Navy's more powerful battleships. This speed advantage was important because the Regia Marina was under orders to avoid engagements unless its battleships enjoyed a clear superiority. It also placed a premium on the ability of torpedo bombers operating from the Royal Navy's aircraft carriers to damage the Regia Marina's battleships to the extent that they could not disengage and escape from the Royal Navy's battle line.

The arrival of the Vittorio Veneto-class battleships altered the equation. These ships possessed slightly better firepower and protection compared to that of the Queen Elizabeth-class battleships. In addition, they still enjoyed a clear speed advantage which permitted the Regia Marina to dictate the terms of an engagement. Now victory depended on other, less obvious, factors than comparing the size of a battleship's guns and the thickness of its armour. These factors included the abilities of the task-force commander, the training of a battleship's crew, the fire-control systems used by each navy, main-gun salvo dispersion, the presence of radar and the effects of air power. All these factors combined to play a role in determining the winner of an engagement involving battleships.

THE STRATEGIC SITUATION

THE BRITISH SITUATION

In June 1940, the naval situation in the Mediterranean was turned on its head. Italy entered World War II on the 10th, just in time for Italian dictator Benito Mussolini to attack France before that country surrendered to Germany. When France surrendered on 22 June, the entire French fleet was removed from the Allied order of battle. The Royal Navy now had to bear the naval war against Italy alone. The British had the advantage of controlling both ends of the Mediterranean, but naval operations became a major drain on British resources.

The Mediterranean Fleet was one of the Royal Navy's principal commands. Its main base was at Malta with secondary bases at Alexandria in Egypt and Gibraltar on the southern coast of Spain. At the start of the naval war in the Mediterranean, the Mediterranean Fleet had a strength of four battleships (*Warspite*, *Malaya*, *Royal Sovereign* and *Ramillies*), one aircraft carrier (*Eagle*), six light cruisers and 21 destroyers. The fleet was commanded by Vice-Admiral (later Admiral) Sir Andrew Cunningham who had extensive experience in the Mediterranean. The Admiralty in London was known to meddle in fleet operations, but in the traditions of the Royal Navy the local commander was expected to exercise aggressive control of his forces. The entry of Italy into the war forced the Mediterranean Fleet to abandon Malta as its primary base because it was practically devoid of air defences and was located only a short distance from Axis air bases on Sicily. The bulk of the Mediterranean Fleet was moved to

Alexandria where maintenance facilities were inadequate. British submarines continued to operate from Malta, however, and a surface force was briefly moved to the island in late 1941 to attack Italian convoys moving to Libya.

France's surrender left a naval void in the Western Mediterranean which had to be filled. The Admiralty's response was to create Force H under Vice-Admiral Sir James Somerville and base it at Gibraltar. This was a small but balanced force with the usual composition of an aircraft carrier, one or two battleships or battlecruisers and several light cruisers and destroyers. From Gibraltar, Force H operated in the Eastern Atlantic or Western Mediterranean. Because most convoys headed for Malta came from the west, Force H was a major factor in Mediterranean operations. The Admiralty reinforced Force H as and when required to enable it to escort convoys to Malta.

The Mediterranean Fleet had a multitude of missions at the start of the naval war in the Mediterranean. Among these were the requirement to bring the Regia Marina to battle whenever and wherever possible; to protect the movement of reinforcements to the fleet and other garrisons in the Mediterranean; to gain control of the Eastern Mediterranean to protect Egypt, Palestine and Cyprus; to attack Italian SLOCs to Libya and to interrupt Italian trade with ports on the Black Sea.

THE ITALIAN SITUATION

While the traditional enemy of the Regia Marina was France's Marine nationale, in the 1930s an aggressive Italian foreign policy created the conditions whereby war with the United Kingdom was inevitable. Mussolini took his expansionist foreign policy to the next level when he declared war on the United Kingdom and France on 10 June 1940, when it seemed that Germany was on the verge of defeating France. Despite warnings from his service chiefs that the Italian military was not ready for war, Mussolini entered World War II with the expectation of gaining easy spoils in the peace negotiations after what he believed would be a short conflict. The war would also be a way to reduce Italy's vulnerability to economic strangulation by the United Kingdom and for Italy to become the pre-eminent Mediterranean power.

Mussolini's belief that the war would be short had profound implications for the Regia Marina and its operational conduct. Despite the fact that it was the most ready of Italy's armed forces, the Regia Marina lacked the means to conduct a prolonged war successfully. Losses to the fleet, especially battleships, could not be replaced by Italy's weak shipbuilding industry. Given the presumption of a short war, and the inability to replace losses, Italian naval planners were loath to risk the fleet. In fact, the need to maintain the fleet was an overriding requirement from a strategic point of view because it underpinned Italy's status as a major Mediterranean power, while from an operational perspective the mere existence of the battle fleet exerted control over the Central Mediterranean. All this made Italian naval planners cautious, but this should not be confused with an unwillingness to fight on the part of the Regia Marina.

The Regia Marina had several primary missions foremost of which was the requirement to exert control over the Central Mediterranean. This would prevent the movement of British naval forces and shipping through the area and would allow the maintenance of communications with Libya in North Africa and the Balkans. The convoy routes from Italy to Libya had to be protected; failure to do so meant that any attempt to defend the colony was doomed.

The Regia Marina's war plan, issued on 29 May 1940, was conservative. It envisaged offensive operations in the Central Mediterranean whereby the Strait of Sicily would be blockaded. Only light forces would operate in the Western and Eastern Mediterranean to harass British SLOCs. Italian SLOCs to Libya and Albania had to be protected. The battle fleet would be used, but only under conditions of equal or superior strength. Submarine and air operations were to be co-ordinated with the surface fleet. The war plan called for the battle fleet to be used against the Royal Navy's Mediterranean Fleet before the latter could be reinforced in a battle fought close to friendly bases.

Even in this strategically defensive construct, the Regia Marina intended to employ its battle fleet against the Mediterranean Fleet. By fighting near friendly bases, and with the assistance of submarine and air forces, favourable conditions for an engagement could be created. Should favourable conditions not exist, the battle fleet would not be risked. The Regia Marina did not intend to commit heavy units in the Western and Eastern Mediterranean; when it did conduct a major operation into the Eastern Mediterranean the result was a disaster.

As the naval war in the Mediterranean dragged on, the Regia Marina continued to adhere to these sensible guidelines. As far as the battleships were concerned, the Regia Marina employed them aggressively on the operational level to achieve their primary missions until fuel shortages became crippling. However, the aggressive commitment of battleships on the operational level did not translate to comparable aggression at the tactical level for the reasons already discussed. At the start of the naval war in the Mediterranean, with only the two Conte di Cavour-class battleships available, the battle fleet was employed more conservatively. Only when the other battleships – especially those of the new Vittorio Veneto class – entered service would the opportunity to seek battle under favourable circumstances exist. In any event, it is incorrect to believe that the Regia Marina's battle fleet hid in harbour during the war.

Italian naval operations were controlled by supreme naval headquarters called Supermarina. The Regia Marina's chief-of-staff, Ammiraglio d'Armata Domenico Cavagnari, commanded Supermarina but it was his deputy, Ammiraglio di Squadra

Odoardo Somigli, who supervised the fleet's routine operations. In December 1940, Ammiraglio di Squadra Arturo Riccardi and Ammiraglio di Squadra Inigo Campioni assumed the roles of commander and deputy, respectively. This change of command reduced the degree of centralized control exercised by Supermarina, but throughout the naval war in the Mediterranean Supermarina discouraged tactical commanders from exercising any real degree of initiative. The fact that Supermarina liked to intervene in every aspect of naval operations was bad enough; even worse was the slowness of the staff to formulate orders, which meant that by the time it issued orders they were time-late and out of touch with the realities at sea.

In 1928, the fleet had been divided into two fleets (*squadre*). The 1ª Squadra was based at La Spezia in northern Italy and the 2ª Squadra at Taranto in southern Italy. It was intended to combine the two *squadre* into a single *squadra* with a single commander, but at the start of the naval war in the Mediterranean they still both existed. The 1ª Squadra included both of the operational battleships, three heavy cruisers, five light cruisers and six destroyer divisions with a total of 24 destroyers. The 2ª Squadra consisted of four heavy cruisers, six light cruisers and four destroyer divisions with another 16 destroyers. The large submarine force was under an independent *squadra*. A number of regional naval commands were allocated a small number of old destroyers, a large number of torpedo boats and other small combatants.

The two *squadre* were united for the first time at the battle of Calabria (known as the battle of Punta Stilo in Italy) on 9 July 1940. The *squadre* continued to operate independently until 9 December 1940 when they were combined into a single force. On 12 January 1942, the two-*squadre* system was brought back but both *squadre* were now under the control of a single entity known as the Forze Navali ('Naval Forces'). In January 1943, all the Regia Marina's battleships were gathered into the 1ª Squadra and all of its cruisers into the 2ª Squadra. Only three months later, the post of Comando in Capo delle Forte Navali da Battaglia ('Commander-in-Chief, Naval Battle Forces') was established which again united the two *squadre*.

TECHNICAL SPECIFICATIONS

CONTRASTING DOCTRINE

The Royal Navy's 1939 fighting instructions recognized the big guns of the battleship as the fleet's key weapon. Battleships were to concentrate fire on a few targets to score early in any engagement. The tactical objective was to achieve the maximum volume of fire in order to overwhelm the enemy. Decisive results could only be achieved if the battleships closed to within 12,000–16,000yd of the enemy, and Royal Navy battleships were modernized with additional horizontal protection to permit them to survive the run-in to the desired engagement range. Night fighting was encouraged if the enemy showed signs of weakness or if it was considered possible to reach a decisive conclusion under cover of darkness. It was even encouraged to accept action between battleships at night if the day action had not achieved decisive results. In the 1930s the British worked to improve their night-fighting tactics and training, including the use of battleships' gunnery. In comparison, other navies emphasized the use of torpedoes at night or else eschewed night combat altogether.

The Regia Marina intended to fight its battles at extended ranges; in fact, most naval battles in the Mediterranean were fought in daylight with good visibility which facilitated this doctrine. Several factors shaped the Italian desire to fight at extended ranges. Foremost was the superior range of Italian guns which gave them the ability to engage at ranges beyond those of their enemies. Another key factor was the superior speed of all Italian battleships over their British counterparts. Theoretically, this permitted the Regia Marina to keep the action at extended range. It also gave the Regia Marina the ability to choose whether and when to break off an action. Finally, and with the exception of the modern battleships, the rebuilt Italian battleships possessed inferior protection compared to that of British battleships, which made the Regia Marina reluctant to close the engagement range to a point where Royal Navy heavy ships were more likely to deal punishing blows.

Italian doctrine for surface action called for fire to be opened at long range. Gunnery was conducted in a deliberate manner with fire being adjusted after each salvo. Once the proper range had been found, the target would be engaged with rapid fire to inflict maximum damage. After the enemy force had been attrited, decisive combat at short range would ensue. Obviously, this doctrine hinged on accuracy at long range. In the pre-radar era, however, it was difficult for any World War II navy to demonstrate consistent accuracy at extended range, but the Regia Marina was as good as any other navy in this respect.

The Regia Marina had made little preparation for night fighting and, if given a choice, preferred to end an action when darkness fell. This certainly held true for its battleships, which were not to be risked at night. This placed the Regia Marina at a severe disadvantage against the Royal Navy, which stressed night fighting.

BRITISH BATTLESHIPS

Only the battleships of the Queen Elizabeth and Royal Sovereign classes are examined in detail because these were the only battleships employed in the engagements covered in this book.

The five ships of the Queen Elizabeth class were modernized to various degrees before the start of World War II. Three ships of the class (*Queen Elizabeth*, *Warspite* and *Valiant*) were essentially rebuilt; the other two (*Barham* and *Malaya*) received much less work. The main effect of the reconstruction work was to increase protection; speed and main-gun firepower were left essentially unchanged.

Modernization began in 1924 when *Warspite* went into the yards. In this first phase, the ship received anti-torpedo bulges which extended to within 90ft of the bow and stern and additional anti-aircraft guns. In 1934, *Warspite* returned to Portsmouth for reconstruction which entailed the removal of the superstructure and the gutting of the hull. The propulsion system was replaced with six new boilers and direct-drive turbines which brought maximum output to 80,000shp. With the increased displacement following modernization, speed was recorded as 23.8kn on trials. Horizontal protection against bombs or plunging fire was improved with an armoured deck forward of 3in, 5.5in over the magazines and 3.5in over the machinery spaces.

Warspite's main battery remained as before with eight 15in/42 Mk I guns in four twin turrets. The turrets were modified to increase the guns' elevation to 30 degrees which increased their maximum range by almost 7,000yd. The secondary battery was reduced to eight 6in Mk XII guns in casemates. Anti-aircraft protection was greatly augmented by a mix of four 4in twin mounts, two eight-barrel 2-pounder pom-poms and additional .5in machine guns atop two of the main-battery twin turrets.

WARSPITE

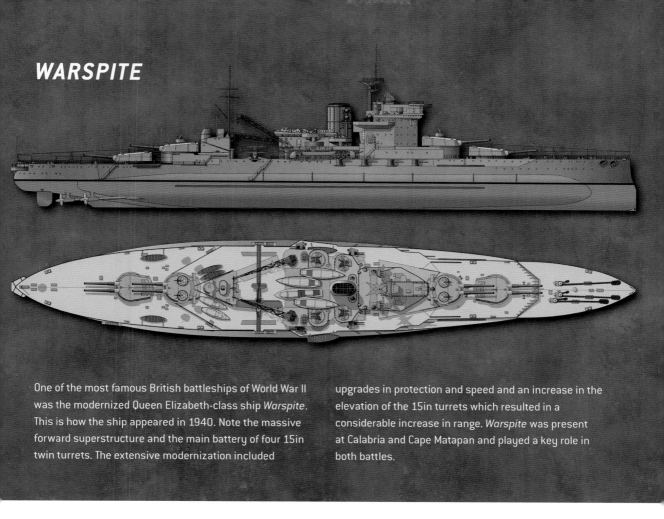

One of the most famous British battleships of World War II was the modernized Queen Elizabeth-class ship *Warspite*. This is how the ship appeared in 1940. Note the massive forward superstructure and the main battery of four 15in twin turrets. The extensive modernization included upgrades in protection and speed and an increase in the elevation of the 15in turrets which resulted in a considerable increase in range. *Warspite* was present at Calabria and Cape Matapan and played a key role in both battles.

Queen Elizabeth and *Valiant* were also rebuilt along similar lines to each other. During 1926–27, *Queen Elizabeth* received anti-torpedo bulges and an additional four 4in anti-aircraft guns. Beginning in 1937, the ship underwent a major reconstruction. New boilers and turbines were fitted, bringing total output to 80,000shp and top speed to 24kn. Protection was increased to that fitted on *Warspite*. The four-turret, eight-gun main-battery arrangement was retained but the elevation of the 15in/42 Mk I guns was increased to 30 degrees. The entire secondary battery of 16 6in guns was replaced with 20 4.5in dual-purpose guns in ten twin turrets. In addition to the 4.5in guns, four eight-barrel 2-pounder pom-poms and four quintuple .5in machine guns were fitted for anti-aircraft work. *Valiant*'s modernization and appearance was very similar to that of *Queen Elizabeth*.

Valiant pictured after completion of its reconstruction at Devonport Dockyard, 1937–39. The battleship emerged with new machinery, a new bridge structure, increased elevation for the four 15in twin turrets and a secondary battery composed of 20 4.5in Mk I dual-purpose guns in ten twin turrets as evident in this view. Note also the amidships aviation facilities. In December 1939, *Valiant* received a Type 279 early-warning radar. (NH 97486 courtesy of the Naval History and Heritage Command)

Warspite was the first of three Queen Elizabeth-class battleships to undergo major modernization as shown here in the early 1930s. The bridge structure was reworked (giving the battleship a much heavier appearance) to provide adequate room for more complex fire-control equipment, searchlights and command staff. The two stacks have also been trunked into one.
(M. Brescia Collection)

Queen Elizabeth-class specifications (1940)	
Displacement (standard)	*Queen Elizabeth* and *Valiant* 31,795 tons; *Warspite* 31,315 tons; *Malaya* and *Barham* 27,940 tons
Dimensions	Length (overall) 643ft 9in; beam 104ft; draft variable from 29ft to 34ft
Machinery	*Queen Elizabeth* and *Valiant* eight boilers and four turbines producing 80,000shp; *Warspite* six boilers and four turbines producing 80,000shp; *Malaya* and *Barham* 24 boilers and four turbines producing 56,000shp
Speed	*Queen Elizabeth*, *Valiant*, *Malaya* and *Barham* 24kn; *Warspite* 23.5kn
Bunkerage/range	*Queen Elizabeth* and *Valiant* 3,393 tons; *Warspite* 3,501 tons for 5,830NM; *Malaya* and *Barham* 3,300 tons for 8,600NM at 12kn
Protection	Main belt 13in; main deck 1–5in; conning tower 11in; barbette 10in; main turret face 13in
Main battery	Eight 15in/42 Mk I guns in four twin turrets
Secondary battery	*Queen Elizabeth* and *Valiant* 20 4.5in Mk I in twin turrets; *Warspite* eight 6in Mk XII in casemates; *Malaya* and *Barham* 14 6in Mk XII in casemates
Anti-aircraft battery	Four eight-barrel 2-pdr mounts; four quad .50in machine guns
Crew	1,124 men

In contrast, *Malaya* received only moderate modernization. During 1927–29, the battleship was fitted with anti-torpedo bulges and given new anti-aircraft guns. The main modernization took place in 1934–36, during which *Malaya* received additional horizontal armour and a modern anti-aircraft fit in which the single 4in anti-aircraft gun mounts were replaced by twin mounts and two eight-barrel 2-pounder pom-poms and two quadruple .5in machine guns were added. The four-turret, eight-gun main battery and 14-gun secondary battery and the ship's machinery were not upgraded.

RAMILLIES

Ramillies was completed in 1917 and marginally modernized between the wars. These views show the battleship as it appeared in 1940. Ramillies' primary attribute was its powerful main battery of eight 15in/42 Mk I guns, as evident in the four twin turrets shown here.

Barham was the least modernized ship of the class. The principal modernization took place in 1931–34 during which time it was fitted with anti-torpedo bulges, received a limited anti-aircraft upgrade in the form of two eight-barrel 2-pounder pom-poms and two quadruple .5in machine guns, and was fitted with additional armour over the magazines and 6in casemates. The four-turret, eight-gun main battery, 14-gun secondary battery and the ship's machinery were not upgraded.

All five Queen Elizabeth-class ships were fitted with double-ended aircraft catapults before the war and radar soon after the outbreak of war.

Royal Sovereign in 'dazzle' camouflage, c.1940. (Arkivi/Getty Images)

Royal Sovereign-class specifications (1940)	
Displacement (full, class average)	31,560 tons
Dimensions	Length (overall) 620ft 7in; beam 88ft 6in (*Ramillies* 101ft 6in); draught 33ft 7in under full load conditions
Machinery	18 boilers and four turbines producing 40,000shp
Speed	20kn by 1939
Range	7,000NM at 10kn
Protection	Main belt 13in; main deck 1–4in (*Royal Oak* 1–6in); conning tower 11in; barbette 4–10in; main turret face 13in
Main battery	Eight 15in/42 Mk I guns in four twin turrets
Secondary battery	12 6in Mk XII in casemates
Anti-aircraft battery	Eight 4in Mk XVI in four twin mounts; two eight-barrel 2-pdr mounts; two quad .50in machine guns
Crew	1,146 men

Although *Royal Sovereign* and *Royal Oak* received anti-torpedo bulges in the 1920s, the five ships of the Royal Sovereign class did not receive any significant modifications before the start of World War II. Most importantly, the propulsion systems of these ships were never upgraded, which left them increasingly unable to keep up with the other ships of the battle line. More than anything, this lack of speed condemned them to second-line status. The five ships were built with a substantial level of protection, but with one exception this was never improved. *Royal Oak* was the only ship of the class to receive a significant upgrade to its protection, receiving 4in of armour over the magazines and 2.5in over the machinery during a 1934–36 modernization.

Armament of this class was largely unaltered before the war. The four 15in twin turrets did not receive the modification required to increase their elevation to 30 degrees, which meant they possessed less range than the modified turrets of the Queen Elizabeth class. All five Royal Sovereign-class battleships entered World War II with 12 6in casemate guns. Their anti-aircraft batteries were increased to four 4in twin mounts supplemented by a pair of eight-barrel 2-pounders and a pair of quadruple .5in machine guns. *Royal Oak*, lost on 14 October 1939 after being torpedoed by *U-47*, retained its four underwater torpedo tubes.

ITALIAN BATTLESHIPS

Between the wars, the Italians were aware of the protection and firepower deficiencies of the Conte di Cavour-class battleships. What resulted was an exercise in false economy. The decision was made not just to modernize the two ships, which would have resulted in only marginal capability improvements, but to rebuild them in what was the most extensive battleship rebuild project carried out by any navy between the wars. The work was so extensive that only 40 per cent of the original ship was left.

The rationale for such a costly project was that the two battleships would provide a temporary counter to the new French Dunkerque class until the Vittorio Veneto class entered service. The entire undertaking was ill-considered because the result was a battleship with marginal capabilities compared to foreign battleships and also because it drained resources which could have been better spent getting the Vittorio Veneto class ready for service before the start of the war.

This beam view of *Giulio Cesare* in 1940 gives a good view of the ship's configuration after reconstruction. Note the absence of the amidships 12in triple turret, the new forward superstructure, the re-located stacks and the presence of new secondary and anti-aircraft batteries. (M. Brescia Collection)

The rebuild work commenced in 1933 and did improve the capabilities of the Conte di Cavour class in all areas. Protection was upgraded in the form of an additional 3,227 tons of armour, most of which went into the ships' horizontal protection which went from 1in to just over 3in over the machinery spaces and 4in over the magazines. Underwater protection was addressed with the fitting of the Pugliese system. On the Conte di Cavour class this included the addition of a hollow curved bulkhead up to 2in thick in front of a 1in-thick torpedo bulkhead. The space in between was filled with hollow cylinders designed to absorb the energy of a torpedo or mine explosion.

Conte di Cavour-class specifications (June 1940)

Displacement	Standard 26,140 tons; full load 29,032 tons
Dimensions	Length (overall) 611ft 7in; beam 92ft 10in; draught 30ft
Machinery	Eight boilers and two turbines producing 75,000shp (93,000shp on trials)
Speed	28kn
Range	2,472 tons of oil provided a range of 6,400NM at 13kn
Protection	Main belt 9.8in; main deck 3.1in over the machinery and 3.9in over the magazines; conning tower 10.2in; barbette 11in; main turret face 11in
Main battery	Ten 12.6in/44 guns in two triple and two twin turrets
Secondary battery	12 4.7in/50 in six twin turrets
Anti-aircraft battery	Eight 3.9in/47 in four twin turrets; eight 37mm/54 in four twin mounts; 16 20mm/65 machine guns in eight twin mounts
Crew	1,236 men

Speed was increased considerably by fitting a new bow that added 33ft to the ships' overall length and the replacement of the original machinery. The old boilers were replaced with eight superheated boilers. New turbines were also installed which increased power to 75,000shp; on trials, the ships developed over 93,000shp. Even with a greater displacement after modernization, the greater power increased the top speed to over 28kn.

The main and secondary batteries of both ships were changed. The 12in triple turret amidships was removed which reduced the main battery to ten guns in two triple and two twin turrets. The guns were re-bored and their calibre increased to 12.6in, which allowed for the firing of a heavier 1,157lb shell. Elevation of the turrets was increased to 27 degrees which produced a maximum range of 31,280yd. A new secondary battery was fitted consisting of six 4.7in twin turrets and four 3.9in/47 twin anti-aircraft guns in shielded mountings.

The apparent success of the Conte di Cavour-class rebuild, completed in 1937, prompted the Regia Marina to give the same treatment to the two ships of the Caio Duilio class. Work on both ships began in April 1937 and the project largely mirrored the rebuild of the Conte di Cavour class.

Caio Duilio-class specifications (1940 modernization)	
Displacement	*Caio Duilio*: standard 26,434 tons; full load 29,391 tons; *Andrea Doria*: standard 25,924 tons; full load 28,882 tons
Dimensions	Length (overall) 613ft 3in; beam 91ft 11in; draught 33ft 10in
Machinery	Eight boilers and two turbines producing 75,000shp
Speed	27kn
Range	6,400NM at 13kn with a maximum bunkerage of 2,550 tons
Protection	Main belt 9.8in; main deck 3.1in over the machinery and 3.9in over the magazines; conning tower 10.2in; barbette 11in; main turret face 11in
Main battery	Ten 12.6in/44 guns in two triple and two twin turrets
Secondary battery	12 5.3in/45 in four triple turrets
Anti-aircraft battery	Ten 3.5in/50 in ten single mounts; 15 37mm/54 in six triple and three single mounts; 12 20mm/65 machine guns in twin mounts
Crew	1,485 men

The protective scheme was augmented to the same extent as on the Conte di Cavour class. This included underwater protection because both ships were also fitted with the Pugliese system. It should be noted, however, that neither class had enough space to install the entire Pugliese system.

The original propulsion system was replaced with an eight-boiler, two-shaft configuration which developed 75,000shp. The ships' hull form was improved by the addition of a 36ft-long bow section which included a bulbous foot. Despite the increase in displacement after the rebuild, the ships' top speed rose to 27kn.

GIULIO CESARE

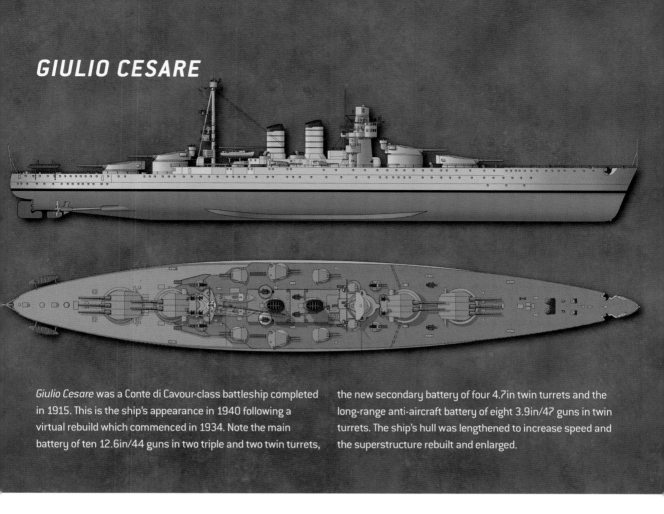

Giulio Cesare was a Conte di Cavour-class battleship completed in 1915. This is the ship's appearance in 1940 following a virtual rebuild which commenced in 1934. Note the main battery of ten 12.6in/44 guns in two triple and two twin turrets, the new secondary battery of four 4.7in twin turrets and the long-range anti-aircraft battery of eight 3.9in/47 guns in twin turrets. The ship's hull was lengthened to increase speed and the superstructure rebuilt and enlarged.

The modernization of the main battery was identical to that on the Conte di Cavour class. The 12in triple turret amidships was removed and the remaining four turrets were arranged in pairs fore and aft with the twin turret placed in a superfiring position over the triple turret. The main-gun calibre was increased to 12.6in which fired a heavier shell with better penetrating power.

This fine view of *Andrea Doria* in 1940 shows the differences from the rebuilt Conte di Cavour class. In comparison, the Caio Duilio class had a larger forward superstructure, larger and more powerful secondary and anti-aircraft batteries, and did not have a tripod mainmast aft. (M. Brescia Collection)

Vittorio Veneto in 1940, soon after completion. (NH 47564 courtesy of the Naval History and Heritage Command)

Vittorio Veneto-class specifications (upon completion)	
Displacement	Standard 40,516 tons; full load 45,029 tons
Dimensions	Length (overall) 780ft; beam 108ft 1in; draught 34ft 4in
Machinery	Eight boilers and four turbines producing 130,000shp (134,000–139,000shp on trials)
Speed	29kn
Range	4,580NM at 16kn
Protection:	Main belt 13.8in; main deck 6.7in over the machinery spaces and 8.6in over the magazines; conning tower 8.1in; barbette 13.8in; main turret face 13.8in
Main battery	Nine 15in/50 guns in three triple turrets
Secondary battery	12 6in/55 in four triple turrets
Anti-aircraft battery	12 3.5in/50 in single mounts; 20 37mm/54 in eight twin and four single mounts; 20 20mm/65 machine guns in twin mounts
Crew	1,830–1,960

The main difference between the Conte di Cavour and Caio Duilio classes after their rebuilds was their secondary batteries. The new Caio Duilio class featured a much heavier secondary battery with four 5.3in triple turrets located two per side alongside the rebuilt forward superstructure. The long-range anti-aircraft battery was significantly augmented and consisted of ten 3.5in/50 guns in single mounts. These were enclosed and fully stabilized, but the stabilization system proved unsuccessful and was removed in 1942. *Caio Duilio* returned to service in July 1940 and *Andrea Doria* in October 1940.

VITTORIO VENETO

Vittorio Veneto was the lead ship of the final class of Italian battleships. These views show the ship in 1940 after completion. The ship projects an attractive and balanced appearance. Note the main battery of three large 15in triple turrets. The Italians continued the inefficient practice of separate secondary and anti-aircraft batteries, as clearly shown in these views.

The three ships of the Vittorio Veneto class were the epitome of Italian battleship design. They were elegant and balanced ships which gave the Regia Marina the ability to slug it out with the Royal Navy. *Vittorio Veneto* was completed in April 1940 and *Littorio* followed in May. Both ships required more fitting out and work-ups, so they were not ready for service when the naval war in the Mediterranean began. Of note, the Vittorio Veneto-class ships were the only Italian battleships to receive radar during the war. Unfortunately for the Italians, this did not occur until well into the war. *Littorio* received an experimental EC.3 *bis* radar in August 1941 and in April 1942 received an updated version. In September 1942, *Littorio* received an EC.3 *ter* radar. *Vittorio Veneto* received an EC.3 *ter* in June 1943. The third and last ship of the class, *Roma*, was not completed until June 1942 and was not ready for operations until August.

BATTLESHIP ARMAMENT

Without doubt, one of the Royal Navy's most successful gun designs was the 15in/42 Mk I main-battery gun. Noteworthy for its reliability and accuracy, this gun proved

Malaya pictured in 1935 after modernization. The ship's machinery was not modernized and the elevation of its 15in/42 Mk I main guns was not increased, which meant the range of the main battery was inferior to that of all Italian battleships. (M. Brescia Collection)

so successful that it was used on three classes of battleships and three classes of battlecruisers with little modification. The specifications in the table are for the guns aboard the Queen Elizabeth class which could be fired at 30 degrees elevation and those aboard the Royal Sovereign class which were restricted to 20 degrees elevation.

The original secondary-battery gun for both the Queen Elizabeth and Royal Sovereign classes was the 6in Mk XIII gun mounted in single casemates. Because this gun was designed to provide defence against torpedo boats, it had only a 14-degree elevation. After their extensive modernization, *Queen Elizabeth* and *Valiant* had all their casemate guns removed and replaced with the 4.5in Mk I or Mk III dual-purpose guns which fired a 55lb shell at a maximum elevation of 80 degrees.

Italian battleship main guns possessed impressive characteristics but were noteworthy for their lack of success under actual combat conditions, failing to sink a single enemy ship during the naval war in the Mediterranean. The biggest issue with these guns was their excessive salvo dispersion, which greatly hampered accuracy. The high muzzle velocity of the 15in/50 gun caused excessive barrel wear which contributed to this problem. The salvo-dispersion problem was even more prevalent for the re-bored 12.6in/44 guns mounted on the four older Italian battleships. Dispersion was also caused by excessive manufacturing tolerances, both of the guns themselves and the shells they fired.

British battleship main and secondary guns

Type	Maximum elevation	Maximum range	Rate of fire	Muzzle velocity	Shell weight
Main guns					
15in/42 Mk I	30°	33,550yd	2rd/min	2,458ft/sec	1,938lb
15in/42 Mk I	20°	26,650yd	2rd/min	2,458ft/sec	1,938lb
Secondary guns					
6in Mk XII	14°	15,660yd (at 20°)	3–4rd/min	2,807ft/sec	100lb
4.5in Mk I, Mk III	80°	20,750yd (at 45°)	12rd/min	2,449ft/sec	55lb

BRITISH BATTLESHIP FIREPOWER

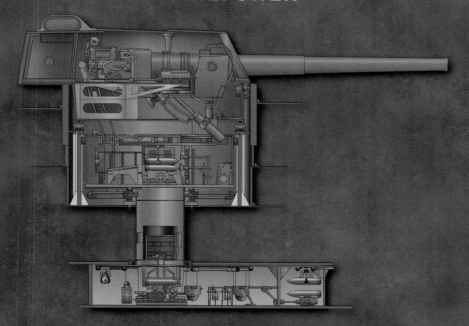

The 15in/42 Mk I gun was carried by all ships of the Queen Elizabeth and Royal Sovereign classes. It fired a 1,938lb armour-piercing shell. On the modernized Queen Elizabeth-class ships, turret elevation was increased to 30 degrees, bringing the maximum range to 33,550yd. This was greater than the 12.6in/44 guns on the older Italian battleships, but far inferior to the 46,000yd+ of the new 15in/50 guns on the Vittorio Veneto class. Unmodernized British battleships with a turret elevation of 20 degrees possessed a range of 26,650yd.

The Italians considered a heavy secondary armament essential to counter the large destroyer force possessed by France's Marine nationale. The Italians failed to develop a reliable dual-purpose gun, however, which meant their battleships employed the space- and weight-consuming design practice of fitting both a secondary battery and

This fine photograph of *Andrea Doria* in October 1940 shows the battleship after completion of its rebuilding. The main battery is trained to port and gives an impression of power. In fact, the 12.6in/44 guns were ineffective: although they possessed a long range due to their high muzzle velocity, it was at the expense of high salvo dispersion. There is no record of an Italian 12.6in/44 gun hitting an enemy target during the naval war in the Mediterranean. (M. Brescia Collection)

Italian battleship main and secondary guns					
Type	Maximum elevation	Maximum range	Rate of fire	Muzzle velocity	Shell weight
Main guns					
12.6in/44 Model 1934, Model 1936	27°	31,280yd	2rd/min	2,722ft/sec	1,155lb
15in/50 Model 1934	35°	46,216yd	1.3rd/min	2,854ft/sec	1,951lb
Secondary guns					
4.7in/50 OTO Model 1933	42°	20,779yd	6rd/min	3,117ft/sec	52lb
5.3in/45 Model 1937	45°	21,435yd	6rd/min	2,707ft/sec	72lb
6in/55 Model 1934	45°	28,150yd	4.5rd/min	2,986ft/sec	110lb

a long-range anti-aircraft battery. The 6in/55 guns on the Vittorio Veneto class also displayed a serious salvo-dispersion problem.

FIRE-CONTROL SYSTEMS

As the Royal Navy was generally short of funds between the wars, the fire-control systems aboard all existing battleships were not extensively modernized. Another reason for this low modernization priority was that the British did not consider long-range gunnery to be very effective. Coming out of World War I, British battleships were equipped with a number of 30ft and 15ft optical rangefinders, fire-control directors in their fighting tops and a fire-control table (actually a manually fed computer) which worked together to generate a fire-control solution.

Warspite was the first battleship to receive extensive fire-control modernization in the form of the Admiralty Fire Control Table (AFCT) Mk VII manually operated mechanical computer. This equipment was also fitted on the other modernized Queen Elizabeth-class battleships and it relied on the observations of the control officer and three other spotters on the ship. Data was also used from a spotting aircraft which was positioned over the ship to assess and report the target course and speed. (Spotting aircraft were used at the battle of Cape Matapan but were launched too late at the battle of Calabria.) The British combined the fire-control director and the rangefinder into what was called a director control tower (DCT) and it was integral to the AFCT. The DCT fed data to the AFCT on target course and speed which was correlated with other rangefinder readings. The AFCT calculated target bearing and the deflection needed for the battleship's turrets. The unmodernized Royal Sovereign class was fitted with two directors in the fighting top and one Dreyer Fire Control Table Mk IV.

The British had the advantage of radar, but its use was limited during the early part of the war. The Type 284 surface gunnery radar was tested on *King George V* in December 1940, but the device produced a broad beam so was only useful for determining range. Because of this, the Type 284 were nothing more than excellent rangefinders. Radar was used by *Valiant* at Cape Matapan.

ITALIAN BATTLESHIP FIREPOWER

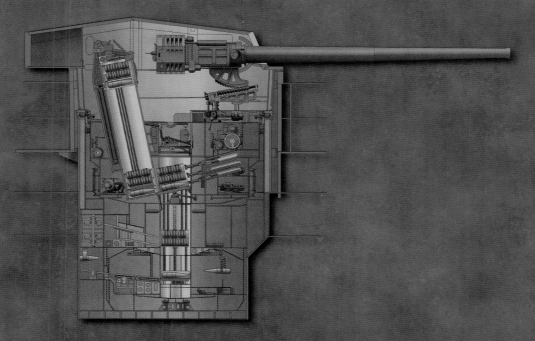

The standard main-battery gun for the four older Italian battleships was the 12.6in/44 which fired a 1,155lb shell. By increasing muzzle velocity, the maximum range of this gun was increased to 31,280yd, almost equal to that of the modernized Queen Elizabeth battleships and superior to the range of the 15in guns on unmodernized British battleships. However, the increased muzzle velocity also exacerbated the salvo-dispersion problem for the 12.6in gun.

A normal salvo by British battleships with twin 15in gun turrets was one gun from each of the four turrets. While the first gun fired, the other was being reloaded. This kept the target under continuous fire. Once the proper deflection was found, a ladder system was used to correct range. Salvoes were fired with some spread which was corrected in 400yd increments until the target was straddled. Once the target was bracketed, the guns fired for effect in the hope of gaining a hit.

Italian main-battery fire-control systems were on a par with other navies of the period. After World War I, the Italians adopted the British Barr & Stroud system. This was licence-built and fitted on the Conte di Cavour and Caio Duilio classes. Target range was calculated optically with the aid of a fire-control computer. On the Conte di Cavour and Caio Duilio classes the main-battery director was mounted above the bridge structure and contained two to four 23.6ft-long paired rangefinders. On the Vittorio Veneto and Caio Duilio classes, the director was a fixed structure above the rotating rangefinders. The rangefinders were stabilized to avoid training errors. The fire-control director transmitted data below to the plotting room where a fire-control solution was generated. The plotting table plotted five different factors: range and bearing of the target, target course, target speed and the range rate.

THE COMBATANTS

OFFICERS AND MEN

THE ROYAL NAVY

The Royal Navy was blessed with a well-trained and highly skilled officer corps. At the start of World War II, the fleet was manned largely by regular officers. An officer began his naval training at the tender age of 13. If he passed the competitive entrance exams and interview, he began training as a cadet at the Royal Naval College at Dartmouth. When he became a midshipman, his training included time on a battleship or cruiser. The educational aspect of the training was criticized as being unbalanced because it was overly technical. Supplementing the regular officers were special entry officers who entered the Royal Navy at age 18 and spent 18 months in naval training.

After being commissioned, the new sub-lieutenant was posted to the Royal Naval College at Greenwich or sent to a large ship. When promoted to lieutenant, he became a full naval officer and could remain a non-specialist officer or apply to enter a specialty which entailed another year of school. Of the specialties open to junior officers, the most highly regarded was gunnery. After eight years as a lieutenant, the officer was eligible for promotion to lieutenant commander.

At the beginning of World War II, the Royal Navy was manned by 131,000 regulars and 73,000 reservists. These were all volunteers and many already had years of service under their belts, making for a very experienced force. The pressures of war forced the Royal Navy to expand quickly and dramatically, however, until it reached a total of 783,000 men by June 1945. Most of these new additions were conscripts or short-term volunteers.

Taken in January 1938, this photograph shows the four forward 15in/42 Mk I guns of the Royal Sovereign-class battleship *Ramillies*. (Mirrorpix/Mirrorpix via Getty Images)

In peacetime, each ship of the fleet was manned by personnel from one of three home ports or 'manning divisions' based at Chatham in Kent, Portsmouth in Hampshire and Devonport (Plymouth) in Devon.

Ships were commissioned and sometimes sent to distant stations. In the case of the Mediterranean Fleet, ships were based at the fleet's main base at Malta. The base had well-developed facilities and the island provided for all the needs of the personnel on the ships based there. Because Malta was virtually undefended at the start of the naval war in the Mediterranean, the Mediterranean Fleet's primary base was moved to Alexandria in Egypt. Unlike Malta, Alexandria was not developed as a main base and had few repair or ammunition-storage facilities. Alexandria and nearby Cairo were not favoured by ships' crews as desirable locations for shore leave.

Ships remained in commission with the same crew for a prolonged period. If a ship was assigned to the Mediterranean Fleet, it was away from its home port for an extended period. If a ship was damaged or reached a point when an overhaul was required, it was usually returned to the United Kingdom where the crew could finally take some leave. When commissioned again, the ship would have a different crew, usually with a higher proportion of new and experienced personnel replacing the 'old hands' who had been transferred to other ships.

The quality of pre-war volunteers, who knew they were signing up for a life of hardship, was high because service in the Royal Navy was viewed as a prestigious career and during economically hard times, it offered secure employment. Pre-war volunteers signed up for a 12-year enlistment and started their service with the rank of ordinary seaman. Sea duty was arduous because Royal Navy ships were not designed with habitability in mind and could be assigned to overseas stations for years at a time.

Even after the start of World War II and the introduction of conscription, the Royal Navy was still imbued with a spirit of volunteerism. That was because conscripts were able to volunteer for service in the Royal Navy or Royal Air Force before ending up in the Army. As a result, until 1943, the Royal Navy had three times the number of volunteers that it needed, allowing it to select the best personnel. Volunteers had to have good eyesight without glasses and have good teeth.

As an enlisted man gained service time, he became an able seaman, leading seaman, petty officer and finally chief petty officer. The best of these men had a rare combination of leadership skills and technical abilities. They were the link between the enlisted men and the ship's officers. A leading seaman was charged to lead – an important step on the way to petty officer – but lacked the authority of a petty officer. Petty officers were granted more authority and were given separate quarters. Chief petty officers had considerable experience having spent at least five years as a leading seaman and three years as a petty officer. They enjoyed their own quarters and mess and their distinct uniform enhanced their authority. A good chief petty officer was worth his weight in gold since he possessed demonstrated leadership skills and usually possessed an area of technical expertise.

THE REGIA MARINA

The quality of officers serving in the Regia Marina was generally high because most observers considered them well-trained and motivated. The Regia Marina's Accademia Navale di Livorno was established in 1881 and was the primary pipeline for non-specialist officers. The education was technically focused. Admission to the academy was restricted and was a primary factor in shaping the officer corps' conservative and monarchical outlook. Naval officers maintained a distance from Mussolini's Fascist regime.

There were issues with the officer corps, however. Lower-ranking officers displayed aggressiveness and some degree of initiative, but this was rarely shown at higher levels. Higher-ranking officers were beholden to doctrine and the orders of their superiors. In fact, initiative was discouraged at higher levels. Vizeadmiral Eberhard Weichold, the Kriegsmarine liaison officer in Rome during 1941–43, noted that any decision by a lower-ranking officer in the Regia Marina had to be submitted to the commander of the operation for approval. Another issue was the general shortage of officers: in the Regia Marina they made up only 5.4 per cent of personnel; in the Royal Navy the total was 9.2 per cent and the British also had a stronger non-commissioned officer corps.

In June 1940, the Regia Marina numbered 168,800 men – a marked growth from the force of 4,180 officers and 70,500 enlisted personnel before the start of mobilization in September 1939. The enlisted force was made up of a mix of volunteers serving four-year enlistments and conscripts who served for two years. At the start of the war, 53 per cent of the enlisted force was composed of volunteers. The quality of Regia Marina enlisted personnel was high compared to that of Italy's other two armed services, but there were real problems with the force. The biggest problem was the lack of technical expertise because Italy possessed a low literacy rate, a narrow educational system and a small industrial base. Running a modern warship was a complex business and the lack of qualified enlisted personnel was a handicap which shifted more of the technical burdens to the officer corps. Another problem was the social gap between officers and the enlisted force, which was a detriment to morale.

Ammiraglio d'Armata Ferdinando di Savoia, Duke of Genoa, decorates a sailor of the Regia Marina in Piazza San Marco, Venice, on 10 June 1942. (Mondadori Portfolio via Getty Images)

Whatever issues the enlisted force had, the Regia Marina fought well during the naval war in the Mediterranean. Wartime propaganda created by the Royal Navy depicted the Regia Marina as being afraid to fight and not technically proficient in modern naval war; but, as this book shows, the Italians were not afraid to fight, though the fleet was used with caution. Morale within the Regia Marina never cracked, even in the extreme example in April–May 1943 when light units escorted convoys to Axis forces in Tunisia through sea lanes so dangerous they were called the 'Route of Death'. It is important to note that as the Italian military disintegrated with the acceptance of the armistice agreed with the Allied powers in September 1943, the Regia Marina remained intact.

CONDITIONS OF SERVICE

THE ROYAL NAVY

Given the relatively small size of the Mediterranean Fleet and its broad operating area, the pace of operations was relentless, though less so for the battleships because they usually only put to sea as part of a major operation. The pace of operations meant officers and men were subjected to continual stress which dulled their reactions and reduced combat effectiveness. Early in the war, during the period covered by this book, combat fatigue was just beginning to be recognized as an issue. Despite the pressures of war, however, the morale of the Mediterranean Fleet remained high by all accounts. The only time when morale discernibly wavered was in May 1941, when the fleet was subjected to continual air attack during the evacuation of Commonwealth forces from Crete during 21 May–1 June. The tradition of success enjoyed by the Royal Navy helped the crews through difficult times and gave them a sense of superiority over the upstart Regia Marina.

ANDREW B. CUNNINGHAM

Andrew Browne Cunningham – known as 'ABC' – was born in Dublin in 1883 and graduated from Britannia Royal Naval College, Dartmouth in 1898. He rose quickly in rank, helped by his exploits at the Dardanelles as the commander of the destroyer *Scorpion* in World War I and in the Baltic Sea after the war when he commanded the destroyer *Seafire*. He continued his career in destroyers, taking command of destroyer flotillas in 1922 and 1923. After more education, Captain Cunningham assumed command of the battleship *Rodney* in 1930. In 1932, he gained flag rank and was appointed as commander of the Mediterranean Fleet's destroyers. At the start of World War II, he was a vice-admiral and commander of the Mediterranean Fleet. He immediately made sure the Mediterranean Fleet was at top readiness because he believed Italy would soon come into the war.

Expertise in manoeuvring warships and in night combat came into play during Cunningham's tenure as commander of the Mediterranean Fleet. He also displayed diplomatic ability by negotiating the surrender and internment of a French squadron in Alexandria harbour as opposed to the failed negotiations over the bulk of the French fleet based at Mers-el-Kébir in Algeria.

Cunningham was extremely aggressive with his fleet after the Italians entered the war. This and several statements made after major operations indicate that he held the Regia Marina in little regard. He was aggressive almost to the point of recklessness at the battle of Calabria, but the Regia Aeronautica was unable to spring the trap set by the Italians. Cunningham successfully orchestrated a number of convoys to Malta with few losses. At Cape Matapan, he finally got his battleships within range of a segment of the Italian battle fleet and inflicted a major defeat on the Regia Marina using his skill in night combat.

In the face of a new threat, the Luftwaffe, Cunningham, promoted to full admiral at the beginning of 1941, proved determined in the face of heavy losses. He kept the Mediterranean Fleet committed to the evacuation of Commonwealth forces from Crete during 21 May–1 June 1941 despite very heavy losses. He stated that stopping the evacuation was not an option given the Royal Navy's tradition of never backing down. Nevertheless, he was criticized for excessively exposing the Mediterranean Fleet

to an aerial threat that he had no means to counter, and there is some validity in this criticism.

Cunningham left the Mediterranean Fleet briefly in late 1942 and early 1943 to command the naval forces conducting Operation *Torch*, the Allied invasion of Vichy North Africa. In February 1943, shortly after his promotion to Admiral of the Fleet, he returned to the Mediterranean Fleet and had the pleasure of seeing the tide turn in the Allies' favour with the final defeat of Axis forces in North Africa in May and the invasion of Sicily in July. On 11 September, he was at Malta to see the surrender of the Italian battle fleet. The next month, he left the Mediterranean to become First Sea Lord, a post he held until May 1946 after overseeing the post-war downsizing of the Royal Navy. Showered with awards and honours in the post-war years from both home and abroad, he died in 1963 and was buried at sea off Portsmouth.

Andrew Browne Cunningham, Commander-in-Chief of the Mediterranean Fleet during World War II, *c*.1940. (Elliott & Fry/Hulton Archive/Getty Images)

Each ship had its own character. Officers and men had intense loyalty to their ship, even though their posting would only be about two years under wartime conditions. Some ships were known as 'happy' ships and their crews exhibited extraordinarily high morale. By all accounts, the battleship *Warspite* was one such ship. The large crews aboard Royal Navy battleships meant that it took longer for the dilution of wartime expansion to be felt. During 1940–41, therefore, the Mediterranean Fleet's battleships were crewed by highly experienced and highly motivated crewmen.

A battleship was commanded by a captain with his executive officer holding the rank of commander. The captain concentrated on fighting the ship while the executive officer ran the ship. Each ship was run differently, but in general wartime discipline was relaxed, even on battleships which in peacetime stressed discipline and a 'spit and polish' attitude to even the most menial tasks. In addition to the top two officers, there were two gunnery officers, a torpedo officer (who handled electrical issues), and several non-specialist officers to run the ship's six divisions. Each 15in turret had its own officer during combat and the secondary battery was run by two or three officers. The anti-aircraft battery was also overseen by an officer. Four officers were assigned responsibility for fire control.

Life at sea was busy. Battleships had larger crews and favoured two watches meaning crewmen spent four hours on watch and four off. In their off time, the officers and men had to tend to their regular job and then find time to rest. Each ship had a watch and quarter bill which divided the crew into sections for any kind of activity the ship might undertake. There were separate bills for day action, night action and many other specific functions.

THE REGIA MARINA

As a matter of course, Italian ships spent less time at sea than their British counterparts; even less so for Regia Marina battleships because they were only used for major fleet operations. From the start of the naval war in the Mediterranean until the armistice in September 1943, Italian battleships spent only 153 days at sea. When an Italian battleship sortied, the ship was at sea for an average of only 1.6 days. Nevertheless, life aboard was arduous because Italian ships were designed for short-duration missions in the Central Mediterranean and thus did not make habitability a design priority.

As a general rule, Regia Marina training was scripted and focused on basic warfare skills. Because the battleship was the centrepiece of the fleet, exercises focused on gunnery drills. Battleships and heavy cruisers (the latter considered to be part of the battle line by the Italians) concentrated on long-range gunnery because this supported existing doctrine. Training was infrequent until 1939 when the pace picked up after war broke out. Increased training brought demonstrably better gunnery results, as was demonstrated at the start of the war when Italian long-range gunnery was generally accurate but suffered from the salvo-dispersion issue (see page 40). Anti-aircraft gunnery was hampered by a lack of ammunition, with the result that during the war Italian anti-aircraft fire was generally ineffective. However, pre-war training did focus on defending the fleet from torpedo-bomber attack and this contributed to the Regia Marina's demonstrated ability to evade aerial torpedoes during the war. A major area of weakness was the lack of night-fighting training. This and a lack of equipment for night fighting (primarily radar) dictated that the Regia Marina avoid night actions altogether.

ANGELO IACHINO

Iachino was the Regia Marina's most important command figure during World War II because he commanded the Italian battle fleet from December 1940 to April 1943. He was born in 1889 and graduated from the Accademia Navale di Livorno in 1907. In World War I, he was cited for gallantry aboard the torpedo boat *66 PN* in the northern Adriatic. After the war, he commanded the gunboat *Ermanno Carlotto* in Chinese waters. In the 1930s, he took command of the light cruiser *Armando Diaz*. Promoted to *ammiraglio di squadra* in 1939, he was in command of the 2ª Squadra and led it at the battle of Cape Spartivento on 27 November 1940. After the initial failures of the battle fleet to gain success, Iachino took over command on 9 December 1940.

Iachino promised to be more aggressive than his predecessor, and he was given more leeway by Supermarina. The change by Supermarina was minor, however, and Iachino was forced to labour under the continued restriction to only engage an inferior force. He criticized Supermarina for exercising too much control which he believed undermined his authority and crushed any initiative. Nevertheless, he demonstrated a desire to get at the British; but this was crippled by the continuing inability of the Regia Marina and Regia Aeronautica to work together and the persistent late and inaccurate scouting reports provide by Italian aviators. Iachino urged that he be allowed to conduct a raid into the Aegean Sea, an idea he later rejected as unsound. Even after Cape Matapan, he was as aggressive as his orders allowed, as demonstrated by the first and second battles of Sirte during which the Regia Marina could claim some measure of success on both occasions. Iachino's greatest success was during 11–16 June 1942 in what the Italians called the *Battaglia di mezzo giugno 1942* (Battle of mid-June 1942), during which he forced a British convoy bound for Malta to return to Alexandria.

In April 1943 Iachino was replaced by Ammiraglio di Squadra Carlo Bergamini, who led the Italian battle fleet to Malta under the terms of the armistice and was killed on his flagship *Roma* on 9 September 1943. Iachino did not retire until 1954. After the war he wrote several books on the Regia Marina's war in which he placed himself in the most favourable light possible. He died in 1975.

Ammiraglio di Squadra Angelo Iachino on the bridge of the heavy cruiser *Pola* during the battle of Cape Spartivento, 27 November 1940. When Iachino took over the fleet in December 1940 he faced the same difficulties as his predecessor, which precluded him from achieving a definitive victory against the British. However, in the context of overall Italian naval strategy, he did enjoy success against British convoys headed to Malta. (Mondadori Portfolio via Getty Images)

COMBAT

Despite only having two battleships operational at the start of the naval war in the Mediterranean, the Regia Marina was eager to seek an engagement with the Royal Navy. This came with strict conditions for fleet commander Ammiraglio di Squadra Inigo Campioni, however, because he was under orders to accept an engagement only under conditions in which he held a clear superiority. Cunningham was even more anxious for a fleet action and had no curbs on his aggressive nature. To draw the Italian fleet out, he used the Malta convoys as bait, and if this failed he was prepared to threaten the Italian mainland with attack which he was sure would force the Regia Marina to give action.

THE BATTLE OF CALABRIA

Known as the battle of Punta Stilo in Italy, the first major naval engagement of the war in the Mediterranean came on 9 July 1940, less than a month after Italy declared war on the United Kingdom and France. Like most battles in the Mediterranean, it was prompted by one or both sides moving a convoy through or into the Central Mediterranean. This was the case in July 1940 when a series of naval moves in the Central Mediterranean resulted in the largest naval battle of the entire war in the Mediterranean. On 6 July, a large (by Mediterranean standards) convoy of six ships under heavy escort left Naples and headed for Benghazi in Libya. The following day, both Regia Marina fleets departed from their bases in southern Italy to intercept a convoy that Italian intelligence believed was headed to Malta. The combined strength of the two fleets was impressive – two battleships (*Conte di Cavour* and *Giulio Cesare*), six heavy cruisers, ten light cruisers and 36 destroyers.

Conte di Cavour opens fire with its main battery during the battle of Calabria. This photograph was taken from aboard *Giulio Cesare*. (NH 86586 courtesy of the Naval History and Heritage Command)

On the same day the Italian fleets put to sea, Cunningham sortied from Alexandria with the Mediterranean Fleet. The British force consisted of the battleships *Warspite* (Cunningham's flagship), *Malaya* and *Royal Sovereign*, the aircraft carrier *Eagle*, five light cruisers and 16 destroyers. Italian intelligence was correct – there were indeed two convoys headed to Malta. Cunningham was at sea to cover the convoys' transit to Malta. The next day, two Italian Z.506 seaplanes operating from Tobruk in Libya confirmed that the Mediterranean Fleet had departed Alexandria. Meanwhile, Force H departed Gibraltar on 8 July with one battlecruiser, two battleships, one aircraft carrier, three light cruisers and 11 destroyers. This was only a diversion, however, as the Italians quickly discerned. Force H conducted an air strike on Cagliari on the island of Sardinia, and took no further part in the battle.

Both sides had a general idea of the movements of the other. Cunningham assessed that the two Regia Marina fleets were at sea to cover a convoy bound for Benghazi and placed the Mediterranean Fleet between the Libyan coast and the coastal city of Taranto in southern Italy. Meanwhile the Italians had firm knowledge of the movement of the Mediterranean Fleet. On the morning of 8 July, Regia Aeronautica bombers conducted several high-level bombing attacks on the Mediterranean Fleet. In what became a pattern, the bombers were generally accurate but only gained a single hit on the bridge of the light cruiser *Gloucester*. The Italian convoy reached its destination on the evening of 8 July. The two Regia Marina fleets, operating off the Libyan coast, knew Cunningham's location from a floatplane and changed course to intercept.

Giulio Cesare in action at the battle of Calabria. (Mondadori Portfolio via Getty Images)

At this point, Supermarina intervened. Italian intelligence had assessed that Cunningham was headed for the coast of Calabria by 1200hrs on 9 July, which led Mussolini to order that the Regia Marina postpone any engagement so that the Regia Aeronautica could bomb the Mediterranean Fleet all day on the 9th.

The Italian plan fell apart when the Regia Aeronautica bombers were unable to find the Mediterranean Fleet on the morning of the 9th. Early in the afternoon, nine Fleet Air Arm Swordfish torpedo bombers from *Eagle* mounted an attack on the Italian heavy cruisers but missed with all five torpedoes. The presence of the Swordfish alerted Campioni that the Mediterranean Fleet was nearby. After Ro.43 floatplanes launched from light cruisers located the British 80 miles to the north-east, Campioni changed course to intercept. *Conte di Cavour*, *Giulio Cesare* and the six heavy cruisers were arrayed in four columns with the two battleships in the middle. Campioni was under orders to delay the engagement to allow the Regia Aeronautica to attack, to engage the Mediterranean Fleet only if it was not concentrated, and to return his heavy ships to port when darkness fell.

Cunningham was anxious to accept battle even though his fleet was strung out in three separate formations. Four light cruisers and a destroyer (Force A) formed the advance force, followed by *Warspite* and five destroyers (Force B) 10 miles back. Behind them by another 10 miles were *Malaya*, *Royal Sovereign*, *Eagle* and ten destroyers (Force C). As the British ships steamed to the west to intercept, conditions were perfect with light seas, clear skies and high visibility.

As the range closed, the screening forces of both sides made contact. The British light cruisers reported smoke on the horizon at 1447hrs and contact on two heavy

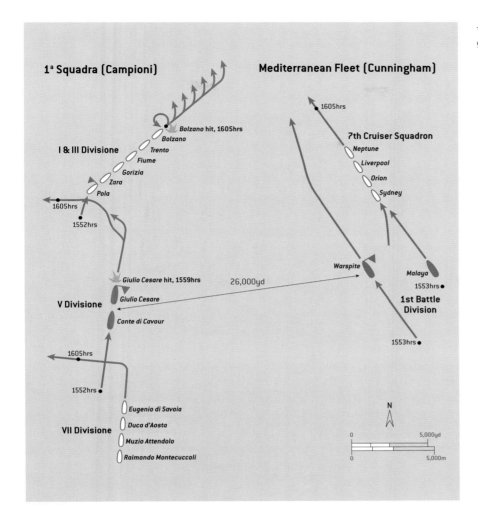

1ª Squadra (Campioni)

Mediterranean Fleet (Cunningham)

1605hrs

7th Cruiser Squadron

Bolzano hit, 1605hrs

Bolzano

I & III Divisione

Trento

Fiume

Gorizia

Zara

Pola

1605hrs

1552hrs

Neptune

Liverpool

Orion

Sydney

Giulio Cesare hit, 1559hrs

26,000yd

Warspite

Malaya

1553hrs

V Divisione

Giulio Cesare

Conte di Cavour

1st Battle Division

1553hrs

1605hrs

1552hrs

VII Divisione

Eugenio di Savoia

Duca d'Aosta

Muzio Attendolo

Raimondo Montecuccoli

N

0   5,000yd

0   5,000m

cruisers at 28,000yd at 1452hrs. At 1508hrs, the light cruiser *Neptune* reported the two Italian battleships at 30,000yd. Italian light cruisers reported contact on the Mediterranean Fleet at 1505hrs.

After performing their mission of gaining contact on the Italian battle fleet, the British light cruisers headed to the north-east. At 1512hrs, with the Italian light cruisers in pursuit, the British light cruisers changed course to the west to engage. In a gun duel between the opposing light cruisers beginning at 1520hrs, both sides shot accurately, but only *Neptune* suffered light damage. At 1526hrs, *Warspite* intervened and the Italian light cruisers turned away. The British battleship failed to score a hit with 16 salvoes.

A lull ensued from 1536hrs to 1548hrs as Cunningham regrouped. *Warspite* was steaming to the north at 15kn. *Malaya* was 3,000yd to the east, but *Royal Sovereign* was 10,000yd away from the flagship. The two Italian battleships were steaming at 25kn to the north with the six heavy cruisers in advance. With his battle line formed, Campioni was ready to open fire. He ordered *Giulio Cesare* to engage *Warspite* and *Conte di Cavour* to target *Malaya*. The battleship duel began at 1552hrs when

Giulio Cesare opened fire at almost 29,000yd. Because Cunningham had allowed his force to become separated, only *Warspite* was in range, and the British battleship replied at 1553hrs from some 26,000yd. The chances of a hit at this range were very slim.

Both sides shot accurately, and at 1600hrs, *Warspite* was forced to change course after being bracketed by *Giulio Cesare*'s 12.6in shells. The Italian heavy cruisers briefly engaged *Warspite* at 28,000yd before shifting fire to the British light cruisers. At this point, the action was developing well for the Italians. *Giulio Cesare* was shooting well, and only one of Cunningham's battleships – *Warspite* – was within range. The Italian heavy cruisers held an advantage on the British light cruisers which were facing issues with ammunition supply. All this changed when a single 15in shell from *Warspite* hit *Giulio Cesare*'s aft stack. The shell failed to penetrate into the battleship's vitals, but it did cause a large fire and created a 20ft hole in the deck. Smoke was drawn into four boiler rooms which forced them off line, which in turn brought the battleship's speed down to 18kn within three minutes. With *Giulio Cesare* on fire and the degree of damage unclear, Campioni was forced to make a decision. Knowing that he now had only a single undamaged battleship against three British battleships, he made the only sensible decision possible and ordered his battle line to turn away to the west.

A single hit from 26,000yd – the longest hit ever recorded by a battleship – had decided the battle. *Giulio Cesare* fired a total of 74 rounds, and *Conte di Cavour* 41 before ceasing fire at 1608hrs. In the space of 11 minutes, *Warspite* fired 17 salvoes, ending at 1603hrs. *Malaya* fired only three salvoes at 1608hrs, and all fell short.

The Italian fleet withdrew under cover of their destroyers. Cruisers on both sides continued to fire, and at 1605hrs the Italian heavy cruiser *Bolzano* was hit by two 6in shells and near-missed by a third but remained in action. The Italian heavy cruisers stopped firing at 1620hrs after surviving an attack by nine Swordfish from *Eagle*.

This is *Warspite* at Calabria with a salvo of Italian 12.6in shells falling astern. The shells were fired from *Giulio Cesare* from ranges up to 29,000yd. (M. Brescia Collection)

The scene on *Giulio Cesare* immediately after the direct hit by a 15in shell fired from *Warspite*. The single 15in shell-hit looked worse than it was. This is the area of the aft stack on the starboard after the fire was extinguished. The shell created a large hole in the stack and a fire which created a large amount of smoke. This was sucked into four of the eight engine boiler rooms which resulted in an immediate loss of speed, forcing Campioni to break off the battle. It was also the only hit by one battleship on another during the entire naval war in the Mediterranean. (The Print Collector/Print Collector/Getty Images)

Italian destroyers conducted four torpedo attacks to cover the withdrawal, scoring no hits, though the British reported several near-misses. British destroyers kept their distance and engaged in desultory gunnery attacks but fired no torpedoes.

The last phase of the action was almost comical. At 1645hrs, the first of the Regia Aeronautica bombers finally appeared. Seventy-six bombers attacked the Mediterranean Fleet, and another 50 mistakenly attacked Regia Marina ships. Fortunately for the Italians, none of their ships were hit. However, the efforts of the Regia Aeronautica were equally futile against Cunningham's ships. *Eagle* received the most attention but suffered only near-misses.

The battle of Calabria was indecisive, which probably explains why the action is so little known. No ships were sunk on either side and none was even heavily damaged. *Giulio Cesare* was back in action within weeks. The action has gone down as a British victory, and Cunningham declared in a report to the Admiralty in January 1941 that the action established a 'moral ascendancy' over the Italian fleet. In fact, the opposite was true. The Italians were heartened that they had engaged the Mediterranean Fleet and apparently performed well. Campioni was aggressive even to engage a superior force, and the action was only decided by a lucky hit at 26,000yd, as Cunningham himself admitted in his letter to the Admiralty. Campioni manoeuvred his force well and deserved better. He laid a trap for the British which the Regia Aeronautica bombers were unable to spring; and he manoeuvred his force well during the battle, keeping his battle line concentrated, and then was able to withdraw it safely. Cunningham's actions are hard to explain, and his force dispersion suggested that he held the Italians in little regard.

INTERLUDE BETWEEN FLEET ACTIONS

The issue of moral ascendancy was shown to be a myth when on 31 August 1940, the Italian battle fleet, now with four battleships, 13 cruisers and 39 destroyers, sortied to engage the Mediterranean Fleet which was at sea to escort a convoy to Malta. No contact was made when Cunningham passed up an opportunity to head straight for the Italian battle fleet and instead opted to sail south to provide direct support for the convoy. Campioni withdrew that evening in accordance with his orders from Supermarina to return to port if the Mediterranean Fleet was not located by dusk. Part of the British operation was to pass the battleship *Valiant*, aircraft carrier *Illustrious* and two anti-aircraft cruisers to the Mediterranean Fleet, thus providing Cunningham with a second modernized battleship.

On 7 September, the Italian battle fleet sortied again, this time to engage Force H which was reported to have left Gibraltar. The operation was entirely futile, however, because Force H headed into the Atlantic, not the Mediterranean. Most of the rest of September was quiet as the British mounted a major operation to seize Vichy-held Dakar in French West Africa. That operation too was a failure, and the battleship *Resolution* took a torpedo hit from the French submarine *Bévéziers* on the morning of the 24th. The battleship was heavily damaged, revealing the vulnerability of the Royal Sovereign-class ships to underwater damage. On 29 September, the Italian battle fleet with five battleships sortied again to strike British cruisers bound for Malta. This time, Campioni received no information from aerial reconnaissance and the interception duly failed.

With all six battleships operational, the Regia Marina possessed a clear edge over the Mediterranean Fleet. In response, Cunningham conceived a bold operation to reduce this advantage. On 11 November 1940, all six Italian battleships were riding at anchor at Taranto. The British used the opportunity to strike the Italian battle fleet with torpedoes launched by Swordfish from the aircraft carrier *Illustrious*. As part of a series of moves throughout the Mediterranean, *Illustrious* approached the heavily defended Regia Marina base and gained complete surprise. Attacking at night, the 20 Swordfish (only 12 of the aircraft were carrying torpedoes, 11 of which were launched) achieved remarkable results. Three Swordfish attacked *Conte di Cavour*, and one placed a torpedo abreast the forward superstructure. The battleship settled on the harbour bottom with its decks awash. Although re-floated eight months later, *Conte di Cavour* never returned to service. *Littorio* was attacked by four Swordfish and suffered a total of three torpedo hits; one abaft the forward turret, the second on the port quarter, and the third on the starboard bow which caused rapid flooding. Another torpedo struck *Littorio*'s stern but failed to explode. Despite this damage, the battleship was only out of action for four months. *Caio Duilio* was hit by a single torpedo which caused flooding in the forward magazine. The battleship was beached to prevent it from sinking but was returned to service by July 1941.

The raid on Taranto halved the number of operational Italian battleships available for operations. Both Churchill and Cunningham thought the shift in the naval balance was decisive, but again the Regia Marina displayed a determination to fight. This was shown only days later when on 17 November, the Italian battle fleet sortied with

Vittorio Veneto and *Giulio Cesare*, escorted by six cruisers and 14 destroyers. The objective was to intercept an outnumbered Force H which was conducting a mission to fly 12 RAF Hurricane fighters to Malta. All 12 Hurricanes aboard the aircraft carrier *Argus* were launched early so that Force H could avoid contact with the Italian battle fleet. Eight of the Hurricanes ran out of fuel before they could reach Malta and were lost along with seven of their pilots.

THE BATTLE OF CAPE SPARTIVENTO

If any more proof was needed as to the resilience of the Regia Marina, it was provided later in November 1940 when the Italians again sortied to stop Force H from getting a convoy through to Malta. This resulted in the second battleship duel of the naval war in the Mediterranean, an engagement known as the battle Capo Teulada in Italy. The engagement was precipitated by another British operation to move convoys to Malta, one from Gibraltar and one from Alexandria. Campioni led the Italian battle fleet to sea on 26 November with a force built around *Vittorio Veneto* and *Giulio Cesare*, escorted by six heavy cruisers and 14 destroyers. The Italians decided to exploit their central position and attack the convoy headed from Gibraltar because it had a much weaker escort. This convoy was escorted by Force H with the battlecruiser *Renown*, the aircraft carrier *Ark Royal*, one heavy and two light cruisers and nine destroyers. Force H was reinforced by the battleship *Ramillies*, three light cruisers and five destroyers which were transferring out of the Mediterranean Fleet. These nine ships were scheduled to rendezvous with Force H at noon on 27 November south-east of Sardinia.

Campioni was in a quandary because his inclination was to be aggressive but his orders were clear that he could only engage an inferior force. He was also burdened by the requirement to get accurate and timely air-reconnaissance reports from the Regia Aeronautica. On the morning of 27 November, he was steaming to the south-east of Cape Spartivento, the southernmost point on the island of Sardinia, waiting for intelligence. The British were in three major groups to his south and south-west. Both Campioni and the commander of Force H, Vice-Admiral James Somerville, received

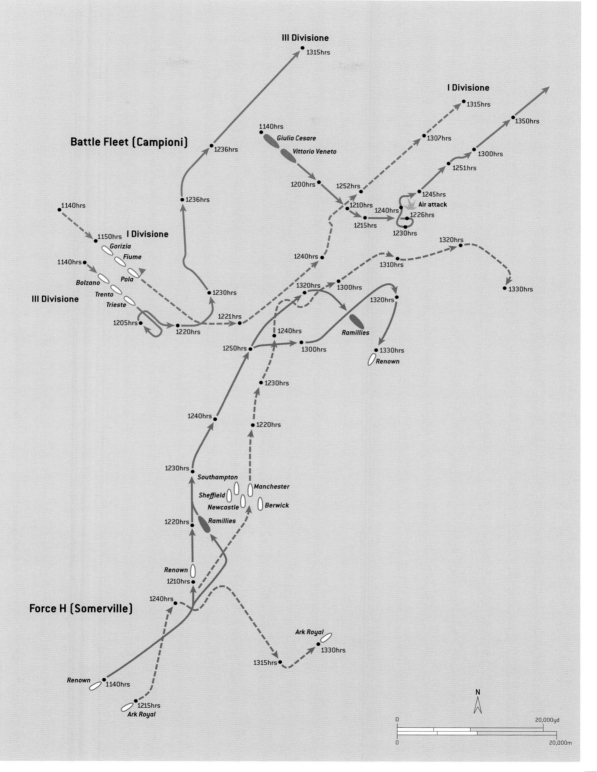

III Divisione
1315hrs

I Divisione
1315hrs
1350hrs
1307hrs
1300hrs
1251hrs

Battle Fleet (Campioni)
1236hrs
1140hrs
Giulio Cesare
Vittorio Veneto
1200hrs 1252hrs
1236hrs
1245hrs
1210hrs 1240hrs Air attack
1226hrs
1215hrs
1230hrs

1140hrs
1150hrs I Divisione
Gorizia
Fiume
1240hrs
1320hrs
1140hrs Pola
1310hrs
1330hrs
Bolzano
Trento 1230hrs
1320hrs 1300hrs
Trieste III Divisione
1320hrs
1205hrs 1221hrs
Ramillies
1220hrs
1240hrs
1250hrs 1300hrs
1330hrs
Renown
1230hrs
1240hrs
1220hrs

1240hrs
1230hrs
1220hrs

Southampton Manchester
Sheffield
Newcastle Berwick
1220hrs Ramillies

Renown
1210hrs
1240hrs

Force H (Somerville)

Ark Royal
1330hrs
1315hrs

Renown 1140hrs
1215hrs
Ark Royal

N

0   20,000yd
0   20,000m

a series of confusing air-reconnaissance reports which prevented a clean interception by either side. Neither commander was even aware of the strength of the other. Campioni even ordered his heavy-cruiser commanders not to engage at all because he was sure he did not have the clear superiority that his orders required.

Despite orders, one of the Italian heavy-cruiser divisions opened fire at 1222hrs at the British cruisers. Even at the range of 23,500yd, they scored a hit on the heavy cruiser *Berwick* which caused a fire and killed seven men. The battlecruiser *Renown* joined the action at 1224hrs with two salvoes from its 15in/42 Mk I (N) guns which fell short. *Ramillies* also sent two ranging salvoes toward the Italian heavy cruisers, but these too fell far short. The Italian heavy cruisers headed north and until 1242hrs engaged in a running gunnery duel with the pursuing British. The accuracy of this fire was generally poor except for another hit on *Berwick* at 1235hrs. *Renown* raced north to support the British light cruisers and managed to fire eight salvoes at an Italian heavy cruiser at 1245hrs at the extreme range of 30,000yd. *Ramillies* struggled to keep up with its best speed of just over 20kn.

The Italian battleships were already headed back to base as Campioni had decided to break off the action. At 1240hrs, *Vittorio Veneto* came under attack from 11 Swordfish from *Ark Royal* but successfully evaded all ten torpedoes aimed at it. The Italian battleships were sighted by *Renown* at 1250hrs. Facing a superior force of two battleships, *Renown* turned south to join with *Ramillies* but soon resumed course to the north-east when it was apparent that the Italian battleships were withdrawing. *Vittorio Veneto* finally joined the action at 1300hrs when its aft 15in triple turret engaged the British light cruisers at 32,000yd. The light cruisers quickly turned to the south-east to seek the protection of *Renown*. *Vittorio Veneto* stopped firing at 1310hrs and the Italian fleet continued unimpeded to the north-east. The British ships broke off pursuit and returned to the convoy. After both sides survived ineffective air attacks in the afternoon, the action was over.

The battle of Cape Spartivento barely qualifies as a battleship duel. The entire action was fought at extremely long range and ended in indecision. The cruisers did most of the fighting with few rounds expended by the battleships: *Ramillies* fired only two ranging salvoes and *Renown* 16 salvoes; *Vittorio Veneto* fired 19 salvoes and scored no hits. Though he never knew it, Campioni had wasted an opportunity to inflict a potential defeat on a smaller British force. Given his orders and the conflicting and inaccurate air-reconnaissance reports, however, there was never a realistic chance that he could have engaged the British and fought the battle to a successful conclusion. Somerville was condemned for his lack of aggression by Churchill, but under the circumstances, fought an intelligent battle.

December 1940 saw a change in the Regia Marina's command structure. Ammiraglio d'Armata Domenico Cavagnari was replaced as chief of staff by Ammiraglio di Squadra Arturo Riccardi. Campioni, never able to bring the British to battle successfully, was given the job as deputy chief of staff. Ammiraglio di Squadra Iachino took over as fleet commander. As the Italians were sorting themselves out, Cunningham pressed his advantage to conduct a series of operations including a battleship bombardment of Valona (Vlorë) on the south-western coast of Albania, running two convoys from Alexandria to Malta, and moving the battleship *Malaya* through the Strait of Sicily to Gibraltar. The Italians were unable to interfere with any of these operations.

Renown, shown here laid up after the war, was a battlecruiser completed in September 1916. Extensively reconstructed during 1936–39, the ship often operated as part of Force H and saw service in the Mediterranean, playing a major role in the battle of Cape Spartivento on 27 November 1940. After its reconstruction, *Renown* was powerfully armed with six 15in/42 Mk I guns in three twin turrets and 20 4.5in Mk III dual-purpose guns in twin mountings, and possessed a top speed of 29kn but retained a light scale of protection.
(M. Brescia Collection)

The Regia Marina was reduced to a single operational battleship (*Vittorio Veneto*) when a Royal Air Force bombing raid damaged *Giulio Cesare* at Naples on 8 January 1941. With only *Vittorio Veneto* operational, the Regia Marina chose not to contest the movement of two Malta convoys with heavy units. Both convoys arrived safely at Malta but the British fleet came under heavy attack on 10–11 January 1941 from newly introduced Luftwaffe aircraft based on Sicily. *Warspite* was slightly damaged, *Illustrious* was heavily damaged but survived, and a light cruiser was sunk. Almost overnight, the Central Mediterranean became an extremely dangerous place for the Royal Navy.

In February, *Giulio Cesare* and *Andrea Doria* re-joined the fleet after the completion of repairs. On 9 February, Force H bombarded Genoa with *Malaya* and *Renown*. The Italian battle fleet was waiting south-west of Sardinia in expectation of another Malta convoy. When he learned of the bombardment, Iachino headed north to intercept the two British ships with all three of his operational battleships, three heavy cruisers and ten destroyers. Bad weather hampered Italian aerial reconnaissance, however, and *Malaya* and *Renown* escaped.

THE BATTLE OF CAPE MATAPAN

The entry of Germany into the war in the Mediterranean brought pressure on the Regia Marina to be more aggressive. Iachino had the same notion and proposed a sweep into the Eastern Mediterranean to the waters around Crete to interdict Allied convoys to Greece. Riccardi was sceptical of this scheme but was forced to agree to it when the Germans promised long-range fighter cover and effective aerial reconnaissance for the Italian fleet. The sweep was named Operation *Gaudo* and commenced on the evening of 26 March. Iachino's flagship was *Vittorio Veneto*, and a total of six heavy cruisers, two light cruisers and 14 destroyers were assigned to take part in the operation. The force was divided into two with the battleship, three heavy cruisers and seven destroyers conducting a sweep south-west of Crete and the remainder of the force to sweep in the Aegean Sea north of Crete. If nothing was detected by the morning of the 28th, the entire force would return to port.

Italian success was dependent upon retaining the element of surprise and receiving the effective air support promised by the Germans; but in the event, neither happened. The British received advance warning of the operation through the decryption of Enigma intercepts and made plans for a trap. Late on 27 March, Cunningham led the Mediterranean Fleet out of Alexandria with three battleships (*Warspite*, *Valiant* and *Barham*), one aircraft carrier (*Formidable*) and four destroyers. This force was joined by four light cruisers and four destroyers already in the Aegean Sea, and five more destroyers which later left from Alexandria. The British possessed a significant firepower edge over the Italian fleet and had the even more important advantage of air power aboard *Formidable*.

It only took until just after 1200hrs on 27 March for Operation *Gaudo* to start to unravel. The appearance of a Royal Air Force Sunderland maritime-patrol aircraft and decoding of the British contact report by the signals intelligence detachment on Iachino's flagship made it apparent that the Italians no longer possessed the element of surprise. Iachino declined to cancel the operation, however, because he received a report at 1400hrs that the Mediterranean Fleet was still in port and because it looked certain that the British had not detected the presence of *Vittorio Veneto*. He hoped to gain tactical surprise against the British cruiser force he knew was operating near Crete. Supermarina also decided to let the operation proceed but cancelled the sweep into the Aegean Sea.

On the morning of 28 March, Iachino was south of the westernmost part of Crete headed east. He decided to turn back at 0700hrs if nothing had been detected by then. His luck seemed to change when an Ro.43 floatplane from *Vittorio Veneto* spotted the British light-cruiser force heading south just 40 miles from the three heavy cruisers which were leading the Italian fleet. Iachino told his cruiser commander to gain contact and then fall back on *Vittorio Veneto* which was some 10 miles behind. This plan to get the battleship within range quickly fell apart when the cruiser commander gave chase to the British light cruisers, which had decided to run to the south-east where Cunningham's battleships were located.

The Italian heavy cruisers began a slow and deliberate fire at 0812hrs. From an extreme range of almost 26,000yd, and for the next 25 minutes, they failed to score with a total of 535 8in rounds. Iachino was worried that the heavy cruisers were getting themselves into a trap and ordered his cruiser commander to break off at 0855hrs. Cunningham had every intention of springing a trap, but his battleships struggled to get into range with their best speed of 22kn. When the Italian heavy cruisers broke off and headed west, it seemed the battle was over. Cunningham's last resort was to use *Formidable*'s torpedo bombers to strike the retreating Italian heavy cruisers and slow them down to allow the British battleships to finish off any damaged ships. By 1000hrs *Formidable* had launched six Albacore torpedo bombers to do just that.

As Cunningham struggled to get his heavy ships in range, Iachino made another attempt to get *Vittorio Veneto* into the battle. At 1035hrs, the battleship reversed course with the intention of getting behind the British light cruisers. This bid failed when the battleship stumbled into the British ships at 1055hrs. Quickly determining the ships were British, *Vittorio Veneto* opened fire at 25,000yd. The first ten salvoes were very close to *Orion*; the ship suffered splinter damage, but no shell hits. As the

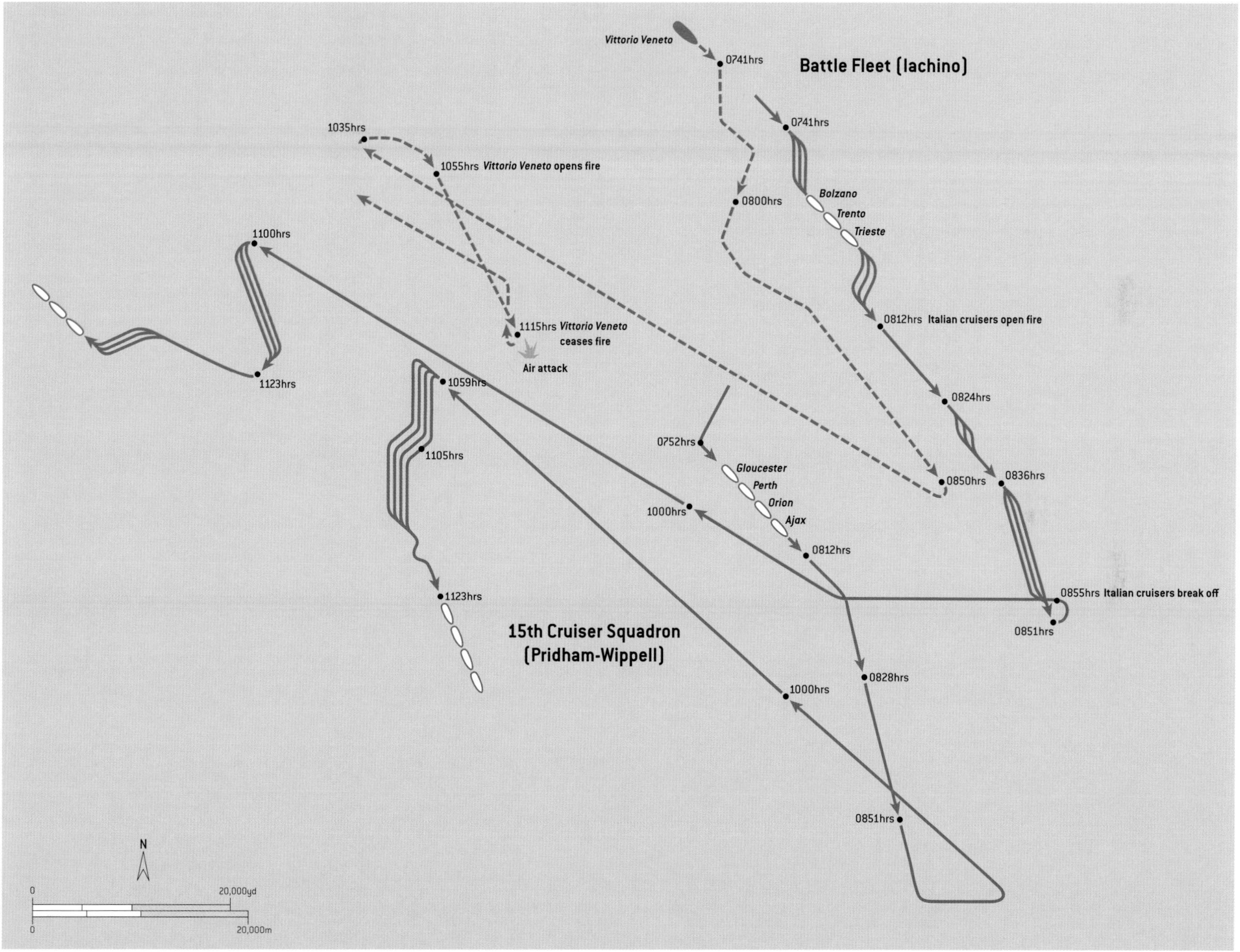

Battle Fleet (Iachino)

Vittorio Veneto

0741hrs

0741hrs

0800hrs

Bolzano
Trento
Trieste

0812hrs Italian cruisers open fire

0824hrs

0836hrs

0850hrs

0855hrs Italian cruisers break off

0851hrs

0828hrs

0812hrs

Gloucester
Perth
Orion
Ajax

0752hrs

1000hrs

1000hrs

0851hrs

1055hrs *Vittorio Veneto* opens fire

1035hrs

115hrs *Vittorio Veneto* ceases fire

Air attack

1059hrs

1105hrs

1123hrs

15th Cruiser Squadron (Pridham-Wippell)

1100hrs

1123hrs

N

0   20,000yd
0   20,000m

67

British light cruisers came under 15in gunfire, the three Italian heavy cruisers reappeared, forcing the British light cruisers to steam south-east. As the British light cruisers ran to the south-east and the safety of Cunningham's battleships, *Gloucester* was exposed to *Vittorio Veneto*'s gunners. Again, the battleship opened fire. According to a British aerial observer, the fire was accurate, even straddling the ship several times, but the salvo dispersion was too great to ensure a hit. *Gloucester* disappeared behind a smokescreen undamaged.

At 1115hrs, the slow Albacore torpedo bombers caught up with *Vittorio Veneto* and gained the proper position to attack. Iachino ordered *Vittorio Veneto* to cease fire and turn hard to starboard to evade the aerial torpedoes. This manoeuvre was successful, and all of the torpedoes missed. With this, Iachino decided to break off the action and ordered his fleet back to port. Though Iachino was unaware of it, Cunningham's battleships were only 45 miles away. With the superior speed of the Italian battleships, Iachino looked like a good bet to escape unharmed.

The only way the battle would resume was if British torpedo bombers succeeded in hitting an Italian ship and forcing it to slow down. To make this happen, the British conducted eight air attacks on the retreating Italian fleet from 1205hrs to 1950hrs. Five of these attacks were conducted by Royal Air Force Blenheim bombers; dropping from high altitude, they were unsuccessful. A small Swordfish strike from Crete also missed. However, the two strikes launched from *Formidable* changed the battle. The first at 1510hrs was directed at *Vittorio Veneto*. Of the five Albacore attacking, one placed a torpedo on the port side aft. The portside shafts were disabled, and the ship came to a temporary stop. Severe flooding ensued. Using its remaining two screws, the battleship got under way and attained 19kn. The second strike was conducted by six Albacore and four Swordfish during 1930–1950hrs as darkness fell. By now, the other three heavy cruisers from the abortive Aegean sweep had joined the Italian fleet. *Vittorio Veneto* was not hit again, but newly joined *Pola* was forced to reduce speed dramatically to avoid a collision. The heavy cruiser was hit by a torpedo which knocked out most of its boilers and the main steam line and soon drifted to a stop.

As darkness fell, neither commander had a clear grasp of the situation. Iachino was the most confused because he still had no idea that Cunningham's battleships were so close. When Iachino learned of *Pola*'s condition, he sent the other two heavy cruisers of its division to assist the stricken vessel. Iachino admitted later that if he had known anything larger than a British light cruiser was in the area, he would have ordered *Pola* scuttled. The stricken *Pola* was soon detected by radar carried on the British light cruisers. Cunningham's battleships changed course for the reported contact and the light cruisers continued to the north-west to look for the rest of the Italian fleet.

In the darkness, the radar aboard *Valiant* located *Pola* at 2210hrs some 6 miles to the south-west. Even with radar, the British were surprised when the Italian rescue force composed of the heavy cruisers *Zara* and *Fiume*, in a line ahead with four destroyers, appeared off the starboard bow of *Warspite* at 2245hrs. Cunningham immediately ordered his battleships to turn to starboard to form a column and to bring their aft turrets to bear.

The British battleships were only 3,000–4,000yd away from the surprised Italians. The two Italian heavy cruisers had their turrets trained fore and aft. With the help of radar and searchlights, the three British battleships opened fire. The range was point-

This photograph shows *Vittorio Veneto* headed into the dockyard at Taranto on 1 April 1941 after being damaged by a British aerial torpedo on 28 March during the battle of Cape Matapan. It is also an excellent close-up of the main, secondary and anti-aircraft batteries. Note the two rotating rangefinders on the bridge tower for the main battery.
(M. Brescia Collection)

blank for a 15in naval gun and the initial salvoes hit their targets. *Warspite*, the lead British battleship, targeted *Fiume* which was only 3,800yd away. Observers aboard *Warspite* stated that of the six shells of the first salvo, five hit the target. A total of 14 15in shells and 16 6in shells were fired at *Fiume*. Observing the devastation aboard the Italian heavy cruiser, *Warspite* shifted fire to the next heavy cruiser in line, *Zara*, and fired four 15in salvoes at it. *Valiant* was the second battleship in line; it also selected *Fiume* for its opening salvoes and then shifted to *Zara* for the next five salvoes. The third ship in line, *Barham*, fired at *Zara* from only 3,100yd away with several 15in shells observed to hit. The four Italian destroyers in column behind the heavy cruisers did not escape the attentions of the British. The first destroyer, *Vittorio Alfieri*, was hit and brought to a stop; the third destroyer, *Giosué Carducci*, was also struck repeatedly by the secondary batteries of the British battleships and the 4.7in guns of the escorting British destroyers. After about seven minutes, the guns of the British battleships fell silent and minutes later Cunningham ordered them to withdraw to avoid any friendly-fire incidents. The order was confusing, however, and the British light cruisers which were closing on Iachino's main body also turned back. This essentially brought the battle to an end.

The three Italian heavy cruisers, crippled by gunfire, sank of their own accord or were finished off by the British destroyers. *Fiume* went down at 2330hrs with the loss of 812 men, followed by *Zara* (sunk by a torpedo) at 0240hrs the following morning with another 783 men. The drifting *Pola* was found by British destroyers which took off part of the crew and then scuttled the heavy cruiser at 0400hrs with torpedoes with the loss of a further 328 men. The two destroyers that sank cost the lives of another 380 men.

The only good news for the Italians was the escape of the damaged *Vittorio Veneto*. As the three Italian heavy cruisers were being obliterated, *Vittorio Veneto* was some 40 miles to the west. Cunningham declined to be reckless and decided not to pursue the battleship in the face of potential air attack from Luftwaffe and Regia Aeronautica aircraft. The boldest Regia Marina naval operation of the war had ended in disaster for the Italians.

ANALYSIS

The role of the battleship in the naval war in the Mediterranean was overstated by both sides before the conflict began. The key area of contention was the Central Mediterranean. During 1940–41, after the initial engagement at Calabria when both sides were anxious for a clash, there were few occasions on which both sides had battleships in the Central Mediterranean at the same time.

Throughout the war, Force H was extremely active attacking targets on Sardinia and the Italian mainland, escorting convoys to Malta and ferrying fighter aircraft to Malta from aircraft carriers. Because Force H was usually weaker in battleships than the Mediterranean Fleet, the Italians often preferred to sortie against it rather than take on Cunningham's fleet. On several occasions, the Italian fleet had a marked firepower advantage against Force H, but a lack of effective aerial reconnaissance prevented the Italians from making contact on all but one occasion. Later in the war, convoys coming from Gibraltar were given heavy escorts of Nelson-class and King George V-class battleships which the Italians declined to engage.

Based simply on the number of occasions that its battle fleet sortied, the Regia Marina was not afraid to engage the Royal Navy. Strategically, the Italian battle fleet was employed very conservatively because it rarely ventured beyond the Central Mediterranean. Operationally, the battle fleet was employed aggressively, as the Italians sortied whenever it had a chance to engage the British. On the *tactical* level, the Italians were timid. This was due to several factors including standing orders to engage only an inferior force and their doctrine of conducting long-range gunnery duels. This translated into indecisive actions. Another crippling factor for Italian battle-fleet commanders was their having to function under a system in which effective naval–air cooperation was all but impossible. The lack of effective aerial reconnaissance was a limiting factor and, on several occasions, prevented the Regia Marina from translating

a numerical advantage into a potentially favourable tactical situation. On top of these difficulties, Italian battleships were vulnerable to air attack because land-based fighter cover was rarely delivered and their own anti-aircraft capabilities were relatively weak. The lack of shipborne radar precluded any consideration of a night engagement. Lastly, the effectiveness of Italian battleship gunnery was adversely impacted by the salvo-dispersion issue which virtually nullified the Regia Marina's most powerful weapons.

Within this framework, Italian battleships were a crucial component in what was a largely successful war waged by the Regia Marina. The Italians were able to achieve their dual primary objectives of keeping the sea lanes to Libya and the Balkans open until May 1943 while simultaneously denying the Central Mediterranean to Allied shipping until July 1943. This success is confirmed by the numbers: 98 per cent of Axis personnel were delivered safely to ports in North Africa and the Balkans together with 90 per cent of matériel.

THE BATTLES

It speaks volumes about the limited utility of battleships in the naval war in the Mediterranean that British and Italian battleships only fired at each other on one occasion during the entire conflict. This occurred at the battle of Calabria when both sides were itching for a major fleet action and before each side understood the nature of naval warfare in the Mediterranean. This action, like all three instances during which both sides had a battleship present in the same engagement, ended indecisively. The action was fought at very long range due to the Italian preference not to close to shorter range and the inability of the slower British battleships to force an action at shorter range. The action was decided by a single hit on *Giulio Cesare* delivered by *Warspite* at the improbable range of 26,000yd – the longest hit ever recorded by a battleship. The damage to the Italian battleship was not significant, but it prompted the Italian commander to break off the action.

The battle of Cape Spartivento was also fought at long range and was similarly indecisive. Despite the presence of three battleships and a battlecruiser, on no occasion

Giulio Cesare in action at the battle of Calabria, 9 July 1940. (DeAgostini/A. DAGLI ORTI/ Getty Images)

did a capital ship of one side fire on that of the opposing side. Again, the reason for this was the inability of the Italians to find the main British force and their unwillingness to close for an engagement if contact was gained. Just the presence of a slow Royal Sovereign-class battleship, which hardly played any part in the battle, encouraged the Italians to break off because it prevented them from having a superior force.

The battle of Cape Matapan ('Actions off Gavdos and Matapan' to the Italians) was the only major engagement of the naval war in the Mediterranean in which a battle was fought to a conclusion. It was also one of the few times when the British had a marked advantage in battleships, though the Italian commander remained unaware of this disturbing reality. *Vittorio Veneto* was brought into position to maul a British light-cruiser force but was failed by its inferior gunnery. Even though the Italian battleship was hit by an aerial torpedo which reduced its speed, the British were unable to bring their three Queen Elizabeth-class battleships within range. If they had been able to do so, it would have provided the only occasion on which the finest Regia Marina battleship faced the Mediterranean Fleet's most powerful battleship.

EVALUATING THE BATTLESHIPS

The Royal Navy was forced to go to war against the Regia Marina with a battle line composed of ships built before or during World War I. The backbone of the Mediterranean Fleet was provided by the Queen Elizabeth-class battleships. The British were confident that these ships were an overmatch to the older Italian battleships. To ensure this was the case, the three most modernized ships of the class – *Warspite*, *Queen Elizabeth* and *Valiant* – were deployed to the Mediterranean. The two ships of the class which received minimal modernization, *Barham* and *Malaya*, were also deployed to the Mediterranean at various points. These battleships were much superior to the older Italian battleships in terms of protection and firepower.

The 15in/42 Mk I gun was an accurate weapon, as demonstrated at the battle of Calabria, and possessed superior hitting power with its 1,938lb shell. In terms of protection, the Queen Elizabeth class was immune to penetration by the 12.6in/44 gun of the older Italian battleships at almost all ranges. The British battleships were vulnerable to underwater damage, as shown by the loss of *Barham*, but this was an issue shared by almost all battleships modernized between the wars. *Barham* was hit by three torpedoes, which would have overwhelmed the underwater protection of almost any battleship of the period.

The Royal Sovereign-class battleships played a subsidiary role in the early stages of the naval war in the Mediterranean. While they possessed the same firepower as the Queen Elizabeth class, protection, particularly underwater protection, was weaker. The key issue with both the Queen Elizabeth-class and Royal Sovereign-class battleships was their lack of speed: their superior firepower was useless unless it could be brought to bear. For the Royal Sovereign-class battleships, their lack of speed was crippling and relegated them almost always to secondary operations. On the two occasions in the Mediterranean when a battleship of this class had an opportunity to engage the Italians, their slow speed left them unable to play anything but a minimal role.

When the Vittorio Veneto-class battleships entered service, the British lost their quantitative advantage. While the Queen Elizabeth-class battleships were roughly equal in terms of firepower and protection, the new Italian battleships retained a marked speed advantage which would have allowed the Italians to dictate the terms on which any engagement was fought and whether it was fought at all. This was especially important because the Italians were reluctant to engage British battleships and the British battle line lacked the speed to force or sustain any engagement. In a gunnery duel between a modernized Queen Elizabeth-class battleship and a Vittorio Veneto-class battleship, the quality of the fire-control system would have been key,

The barrels of the main armament of nine 16in/45 Mk I guns mounted in triple turrets on *Rodney* are elevated while the battleship was serving as flagship of the 2nd Battle Squadron on 1 February 1939, somewhere in the Mediterranean. (FPG/Archive Photos/ Getty Images)

This is the No. 2 15in triple turret on *Roma* in spring 1942. The 15in/50 gun possessed an excellent range of over 46,000yd but suffered from an excessive salvo-dispersion problem which made it ineffective.
(M. Brescia Collection)

with the British holding the edge. Italian battleship gunnery was accurate, but actually hitting a target never occurred due to the salvo-dispersion issue.

It is difficult to defend the Regia Marina's decision to reconstruct the four older battleships given Italy's limited construction funds and shipyard resources. While the rationale to rebuild the two Conte di Cavour-class battleships was understandable as it provided some stop-gap capability until the arrival of the Vittorio Veneto class, the decision to expend similar resources to rebuild the two Caio Duilio-class battleships was nonsensical because it actually delayed the arrival of the new battleships. Even after the four old battleships were rebuilt, the result was four battleships with limited firepower and questionable protection. Against the modernized Queen Elizabeth class, their 12.6in/44 guns had limited penetrating power with their 1,155lb shells and they did not possess sufficient protection to defeat 15in shells at almost all battle ranges. The four battleships did have the speed to disengage from all the older British battleships, however. All factors being taken into account, the rebuilt Italian battleships were of very limited worth during the naval war in the Mediterranean.

On the other hand, the two Vittorio Veneto-class battleships possessed a good combination of firepower, speed and protection and generally performed well in service. However, they did have weaknesses. Protection remained an issue, particularly against underwater threats. The Pugliese system proved generally successful against torpedoes, but against non-contact explosions it failed. The biggest weakness in the Vittorio Veneto-class battleships was their horizontal protection, which proved to be a direct factor in the loss of *Roma*. The deck-armour layout was inefficient because it was composed of two primary armoured decks.

The protection problems were exacerbated by inadequate damage-control equipment. Flooding control was a problem because the two pump rooms were located outside the armoured citadel and thus were vulnerable. Combined with the lack of portable power-driven pumps, the ships were vulnerable to flooding. This was demonstrated at Cape Matapan when the single aerial torpedo which hit *Vittorio Veneto* almost led to the ship's loss due to progressive flooding.

AFTERMATH

The battle of Cape Matapan ended in disaster for the Regia Marina, but it had little impact on the struggle for control of the Mediterranean. Cunningham used the opportunity immediately following the battle to deploy three battleships to bombard Tripoli harbour on 21 April 1941. The next month, Force H and the Mediterranean Fleet joined to protect a convoy loaded with tanks for British forces in Egypt. *Queen Elizabeth* also joined Cunningham's fleet at this time.

The reinforced Mediterranean Fleet took a severe pummelling during the withdrawal of Commonwealth forces from Crete during 21 May–1 June 1941. Among other ships, *Warspite*, *Barham*, *Valiant* and *Formidable* were damaged and three light cruisers sunk by German battleships. The Italian battle fleet did not intervene.

In the summer and autumn of 1941, attention turned to the convoy war in the Central Mediterranean. With the help of better intelligence, and naval and air forces

The only appearance of a King George V-class battleship in the Mediterranean during 1941 was when *Prince of Wales* supported the movement of a convoy from Gibraltar to Malta in September. (M. Brescia Collection)

Following the damage inflicted upon the battleship by Italian manned torpedo craft at Alexandria on 19 December 1941, *Queen Elizabeth* did not return to service until June 1943. This photo shows the battleship leaving Norfolk, Virginia after repairs and modernization. *Queen Elizabeth* and *Valiant* were reconstructed to the same configuration, as is evident in this view. (80-G-411679 courtesy of the Naval History and Heritage Command)

based at Malta, the British took an increasing toll on Axis convoys. During July–December 1941, Axis shipments to North Africa dropped from 94 per cent of cargoes reaching their destination during the first half of the year to 73 per cent. Meanwhile, the Italian battle fleet gained a marked edge over the Mediterranean Fleet when *Vittorio Veneto* returned to full operational service by August 1941, joining *Littorio*, *Andrea Doria*, *Caio Duilio* and *Giulio Cesare*. Supermarina wanted to make the most of this advantage and decided to attack Force H.

Even as they took an increasing toll on Italian convoys headed to North Africa, the British also had to keep Malta supplied. A convoy from Gibraltar got through to Malta in July 1941, escorted by *Nelson*, *Renown* and the aircraft carrier *Ark Royal*. On 23 August, *Vittorio Veneto* and *Littorio*, four heavy cruisers and 19 destroyers sortied to intercept Force H on a mining mission off Livorno. The Italians waited south of Sardinia but failed to make contact. In September 1941, the Italian battle fleet got another chance to attack Force H and a convoy bound for Malta. The large nine-ship convoy left Gibraltar on 24 September under escort of *Nelson*, *Rodney* and *Prince of Wales*. The Italian battle fleet with *Vittorio Veneto* and *Littorio*, five heavy cruisers and 14 destroyers put to sea on 26 September under the same orders to avoid action unless an inferior enemy force was encountered. Despite getting to within 40 miles of the British force, confusing Italian aerial reconnaissance left Iachino with no option but to decide not to engage.

In December 1941, Italian battleships were committed to provide direct support for Axis convoys headed to Libya. After the recall of one convoy, *Vittorio Veneto* was torpedoed on 14 December by the British submarine *Urge* in the Strait of Messina. That one hit caused extensive flooding and repairs to *Vittorio Veneto* were not completed until June 1942. The next convoy was allocated *Caio Duilio* in direct support with *Littorio*, *Andrea Doria* and *Giulio Cesare* providing distant support. Concurrently, the British mounted a convoy operation from Alexandria to Malta. The British convoy was spotted by Italian aircraft and the Regia Marina's distant covering force was sent to engage it in what came to be known as the first battle of Sirte. After the usual confusion with air-reconnaissance reports, and wishing to avoid a night action, Iachino, the Italian commander, did not engage the British convoy's escort until the evening of 17 December when he opened fire from 35,000yd with *Littorio*'s 15in/50 guns. Darkness brought the action to a close with neither side having suffered major damage. The first battle of Sirte must be seen as an Italian victory because the Axis convoy reached its destinations safely.

The Mediterranean Fleet's battle line suffered heavily in late 1941. On 25 November *Barham* was torpedoed by *U-331* with the loss of 861 men. An even heavier blow was inflicted by Italian manned torpedo craft in the shallow waters of Alexandria harbour on 19 December. Both *Queen Elizabeth* and *Valiant* were placed out of action for a prolonged period by mines deployed by Italian frogmen operating the manned torpedo craft, leaving the Mediterranean Fleet with nothing larger than a light cruiser.

In March 1942 the British were forced to mount a major operation to relieve Malta. In the second battle of Sirte, fought on 21 March, *Littorio*, three heavy cruisers and eight destroyers were dispatched to intercept the convoy. In the resulting action, fought under storm conditions and in poor light, *Littorio* fired 181 rounds of 15in shells. The Italians aggressively attempted to engage the convoy which forced it to the south and eventually to scatter in an attempt to reach Malta singly. This exposed the ships of the convoy to air attack the next day. Ultimately, only a small fraction of the convoy's cargo was salvaged, making the second battle of Sirte a victory for the Regia Marina.

Vittorio Veneto returned to service in early 1942 and *Roma* began trials in the summer. The situation on Malta was increasingly desperate so in June the British mounted the largest operation to date to relieve the island. A six-ship convoy headed for Malta from Gibraltar while another convoy of 11 ships departed Alexandria. The Italians correctly assessed the Alexandria convoy as the main effort. On 14 June, *Vittorio Veneto*, *Littorio*, four heavy cruisers and 12 destroyers departed to attack. The two battleships came under heavy air attack the following day. *Littorio* took a bomb on its forward turret which caused no significant damage, but a Royal Air Force Beaufort torpedo bomber hit the battleship which caused it to return to port after severe flooding. Even against a single Italian battleship, the British convoy was forced

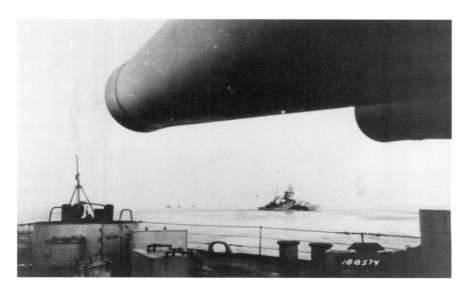

Valiant leads the Italian battle fleet into Malta on 10 September 1943 under the terms of the Italian Armistice. The scene is framed by the after 15in/42 Mk I guns of *Warspite*. (SC 188574 courtesy of the Naval History and Heritage Command)

Italia and Vittorio Veneto off Malta after the Italian armistice. After being surrendered in September 1943, Vittorio Veneto and Italia did not return to Italy until 1947 and were decommissioned in 1948. The Italians resisted scrapping them and they were not broken up until 1951–55. (NH 111459 courtesy of the Naval History and Heritage Command)

to return to Alexandria because the convoy escort was outgunned. The mere presence of an Italian battleship had gained a major victory for the Axis.

By mid-1942, the Regia Marina faced a severe fuel-oil shortage which sharply curtailed battleship operations. Accordingly, the climactic convoy battle in August 1942 prompted by a massive British relief of Malta faced only the threat of Regia Marina heavy cruisers. The fuel crisis left only the three modern Italian battleships operational. The three older battleships were placed in reserve.

The Regia Marina's battleships spent the rest of the war going from port to port to avoid air attack. *Littorio*, *Vittorio Veneto* and *Roma* were all hit but when Allied forces began to land on Sicily on 9–10 July 1943, *Vittorio Veneto* and *Littorio* were available, though they made no attempt to attack the landing force. Such an operation would have been suicidal against a British force of six battleships and two aircraft carriers.

On 25 July 1943, Mussolini's regime fell and the new Italian government concluded an armistice with the Allied powers on 3 September 1943. The Italian battle fleet was held in reserve as a bargaining chip during the armistice negotiations.

Following the announcement of the armistice, the Regia Marina was ordered to transfer its battle fleet to Allied-controlled ports. In the course of doing so, the battle fleet was attacked by Luftwaffe Do 217 bombers carrying Fritz X radio-controlled anti-shipping glide bombs off Sardinia on 9 September. *Roma*'s short career came to a tragic end. The first of two glide bombs hit the starboard side and penetrated the Pugliese system to explode under the hull. A second glide bomb probably entered the forward engine room and the resulting fires spread to the forward magazine which exploded. The ship capsized and broke in two, taking 1,253 men to their deaths. *Italia* (*Littorio*'s new name after the fall of Mussolini's regime) was also hit by a single glide bomb, but the damage was minor. *Italia* and *Vittorio Veneto* reached Malta and were escorted into port by a British force which included *Warspite* and *Valiant*. *Andrea Doria*, *Caio Duilio* and *Giulio Cesare* also reached Malta, meaning that five of the Regia Marina's seven battleships survived the war in an operational status.

BIBLIOGRAPHY

Bagnasco, Erminio & de Toro, Augusto (2011). *The Littorio Class: Italy's Last and Largest Battleships*. Annapolis, MD: Naval Institute Press.

Bragadin, Marc' Antonio (1957). *The Italian Navy in World War II*. Annapolis, MD: Naval Institute Press.

Brescia, Maurizio (2012). *Mussolini's Navy: A Reference Guide to the Regia Marina 1930–1945*. Annapolis, MD: Naval Institute Press.

Breyer, Siegfried (1973). *Battleships and Battle Cruisers 1905–1970*. New York, NY: Doubleday.

Burt, R.A. (2012). *British Battleships 1919–1945*. Annapolis, MD: Naval Institute Press.

Campbell, John (2002). *Naval Weapons of World War Two*. Annapolis, MD: Naval Institute Press.

Cernuschi, Enrico & O'Hara, Vincent P. (2010). 'Taranto: The Raid and the Aftermath', in Jordan, John, ed., *Warship 2010*. Annapolis, MD: Naval Institute Press, pp. 77–95.

Cunningham, Andrew (1951). *A Sailor's Odyssey*. New York, NY: Dutton.

Dulin, Robert & Garzke, William (1985). *Battleships: Axis and Neutral Battleships in World War II*. Annapolis, MD: Naval Institute Press.

Fraccaroli, Aldo (1977). 'The *Littorio* Class', in Preston, Antony, ed., *Warship*, Vol. I, Issue 3: 2–13.

Friedman, Norman (2008). *Naval Firepower: Battleship Guns and Gunnery on the Battleship Era*. Annapolis, MD: Naval Institute Press.

Giorgerini, Giorgio (1980). 'The *CAVOUR* and *DUILIO* Class Battleships', in Roberts, John, ed., *Warship*, Vol. IV, Issue 16: 267–279.

Greene, Jack & Massignani, Alessandro (2011). *The Naval War in the Mediterranean 1940–1943*. Barnsley: Frontline.

Greger, René (1997). *Battleships of the World*. Annapolis, MD: Naval Institute Press.

Lavery, Brian (2006). *Churchill's Navy: The Ships, Men and Organisation 1939–1945*. London: Conway.

Naval Staff (2002a). *The Royal Navy and the Mediterranean, Vol. I: September 1939–October 1940*. Abingdon: Routledge.

Naval Staff (2002b). *The Royal Navy and the Mediterranean, Vol. II: November 1940–December 1941*. Abingdon: Routledge.

O'Hara, Vincent P. (2008). 'The Action off Calabria and the Myth of Moral Ascendancy', in Jordan, John, ed., *Warship 2008*. Annapolis, MD: Naval Institute Press, pp. 26–39.

O'Hara, Vincent P. (2009). *Struggle for the Middle Sea: The Great Navies at War in the Mediterranean Theater, 1940–1945*. Annapolis, MD: Naval Institute Press.

O'Hara, Vincent P., Dickson, David P. & Worth, Richard (2010). *On Seas Contested: The Seven Great Navies of the Second World War*. Annapolis, MD: Naval Institute Press.

Raven, Alan & Roberts, John (1988). *British Battleships of World War Two*. Annapolis, MD: Naval Institute Press.

Sadkovich, James P. (1994). *The Italian Navy in World War II*. Westport, CT: Praeger.

Smith, Peter C. (1980). *Action Imminent*. London: Collins.

Whitley, M.J. (1998). *Battleships of World War Two: An International Encyclopedia*. Annapolis, MD: Naval Institute Press.

INDEX

References to illustrations are shown in **bold**.

Accademia Navale di Livorno 47, 51
aircraft carriers (Brit) 6, 7, 8, 9, 25, 26, 53, 54, 56, 57, 58, 60, **61**, 64, 65, 66, 68, 70, 78: *Argus* 60, **71**; *Ark Royal* 60, **61**, 64, 76; *Eagle* 25, 53, 54, 56, 57, **71**; *Formidable* 8, 66, 68, 75; *Illustrious* 58, 65
Alexandria 9, 25, 26, 46, 49, 53, 66, 76, 77: attack on harbour 9, 76, 77; convoys from 9, 51, 60, 64, 76–77, 77–78
anti-aircraft guns (Brit) 17, 30, 50: .50in 30, 31, 32, 33, 34; 2-pdr 30, 31, 32, 33, 34; 4in 31, 32, 34
anti-aircraft guns (Ita) 35, **35**, 36, 37, 38, **39**, 42, 50, **69**, **74**: 3.5in 23, 36, 38, **59**; 3.9in **5**, 35, 36, **37**; 20/37mm 35, 36, 38

battlecruisers (Brit) 6, 8, 9, 11, 26, 40, 53, 60, 64, **65**, **71**: *Renown* 8, 60, **61**, 64, 65, **65**, 76; *Repulse* 11

Cagliari, battle of 55
Caio Duilio-class battleships 18, **20**, 43, 72: armament 20, **20**, 36, 37, 38, **41**, 74; armour 20, 23, 36, 74; modernization 8, **9**, 19, 20, 23, 36–37, 38, **41**, 74; specifications 9, 20, 36, 41, 43, 74
  Andrea Doria 8, **9**, **9**, 20, 36–37, 38, 41, **41**, 43, **43**, 65, 74, 76, 78
  Caio Duilio 8, 20, 36–37, 38, 58, **60**, 74, 76, 78
Calabria, battle of 7, 8, 28, 31, 42, 49, 52–57, **53**, 54, **55**, **56**, 58, 70, 71, **72**, 73
Campioni, Amm di Squadra Inigo 28, 52, 54, 55, 56, 57, 58, 60, 64
Cape Matapan, battle of 9, 31, 42, 49, 51, 65–66, **67**, 68–69, 72, 74, 75
Cape Spartivento, battle of 8, 51, 60, **61**, **62–63**, 64–65, 71–72
Cavagnari, Amm d'Armata Domenico 27, 64
Conte di Cavour-class battleships 18, 20, 27, 37, 43, 72: armament **5**, **18**, 19, 34, 35, **35**, 36, 37, **37**, 38, **53**, **54**, 74; armour 19–20, 23, 34, 35, 36; modernization 1, **5**, 8, **9**, 19, 20, 23, 34–36, **35**, **37**, **37**, 38, 74; specifications 19, 20, 35, 36, 37, 74
  Conte di Cavour 1, **5**, 8, **18**, 19, 52, 53, 54, 55, **55**, 56, 58
  Giulio Cesare 8, 9, 19, **19**, 20, **35**, 37, **37**, 52, **53**, 54, **54**, 55, **55**, 56, **56**, 57, **57**, 60, **61**, 65, 71, **72**, 76, 78
  Leonardo da Vinci 19, 20
convoy operations: (Brit) 5, 9, 14, 17, 26, 49, 51, 52, 53, 58, 60, 64, 65, 70, 75, 76–78; (Ita) 5, 9, 26, 27, 48, 52, 53, 71, 75–77
Crete, operations off 48, 49, 65–66, 68, 75
Cunningham, Adm Sir Andrew 25, 49, **49**, 52, 53, 54, 55, 56, 57, 58, 64, 66, 68, 69, 70, 75

Dante Alighieri battleship 18, 19
destroyers (Brit) 6, 7, 9, 25, 26, 49, 53, 57, 60, 66, 69
destroyers (Ita) 6, 7, 9, 28, 52, 54, 56, 57, 58, 60, 65, 68, 69, 76, 77: *Giosué Carducci* 69; *Vittorio Alfieri* 69

fire-control systems: (Brit) 13, 32, 24, 42–43, 73–74; (Ita) 43, 73–74
Fleet Air Arm operations 6, 8, 24, 42, 50, 53, 54, 56, 58, **61**, 64, 66, **67**, 68, 77
French battleships 18, 21, 35

German battleships 10–11, 17, 18
Gibraltar **13**, 25, 26, 53, 58, 64: convoys from 9, 60, 70, 76, 77

heavy cruisers (Brit) **26**, 60: *Berwick* **61**, 64
heavy cruisers (Ita) 6, 7, 9, 28, 50, 53, 54–55, 56, 58, 60, 64, 65, 66, 68, 69, 76, 77, 78: *Bolzano* **55**, 56, **61**, **67**; *Fiume* **55**, **61**, 68, 69; *Gorizia* **55**, **61**; *Pola* **55**, **61**, 68, 69; *Trento* **55**, **61**, **67**; *Trieste* **61**, **67**; *Zara* **55**, 68, 69

Iachino, Amm di Squadra Angelo 51, **51**, 64, 65, 66, 68, 69, 76–77

King George V-class battleships 10, 11, 17: armament/armour/specifications 17
  King George V 8, 10, 42
  Prince of Wales 11, 17, **17**, **75**, 76
Kriegsmarine 4, 10–11, 14, 28, 47, 75

light cruisers (Brit) 2, 6–7, 9, **15**, 25, **26**, 53, 54, 56, 58, 60, 64, 65, 66, 68, 69, 72, 75, 77: *Ajax* **67**; *Gloucester* **67**, 68; *Liverpool* **55**; *Manchester* **61**; *Neptune* **55**, **55**; *Newcastle* **61**; *Orion* **55**, 66, **67**; *Perth* **67**; *Sheffield* **61**; *Southampton* **61**; *Sydney* **55**
light cruisers (Ita) 6–7, 28, 51, 52, 54, 58, 60, 65: *Duca d'Aosta* **55**; *Eugenio di Savoia* **55**; *Muzio Attendolo* **55**; *Raimondo Montecuccoli* **55**
Luftwaffe operations 5, 24, 49, 65, 66, 69, 78

main guns (Brit) 43: 12in 11; 13.5in 11; 14in 17, **17**; 15in 11, 12, 13, 24, 30, 31, **31**, 32, **33**, 34, 39–40, **40**, **41**, **41**, 43, **46**, **62–63**, 64, **65**, 73, 77; 16in 14, 15, 16, **16**, 17, **73**
main guns (Ita) 40–42: 12in **18**, 19, **20**, 24, 36; 12.6in 35, **35**, 36, 37, 40, 41, **41**, 42, **54**, 73; 15in 17, **18**, 21, 22, **22**, 24, **38**, **39**, 40, 41, 42, **59**, 68, **69**, **74**, 77; 16in 21
Malta **6**, 9, 25, 26, **26**, 46, 60: convoys to 5, 9, 14, 17, 26, 49, 51, 52, 53, 58, 60, 64, 65, 70, **75**, 76–77, 78; Regia Marina battleships to 9, **19**, 24, 49, 51, **77**, 78, **78**
manned torpedo craft (Ita) 9, 76, 77
Marine nationale (Fra) 4, 8, 18, 21, 22, 25, 26, 35, 41, 49, 58

naval treaty limitations 7, 10, 13, 14–15, 17, 18, 19, 21, 22
Nelson-class battleships 10, 11, 15, **16**, 70: armament 14, 15, 16, **16**, **73**; armour 15, 16; specifications 15, 16
  Nelson 8, 10, 14, 16, 76
  Rodney 8, 10, 14, 49, **73**, 76
North Africa, supply ops 52, 53, 71, 75–76
  Libya 5, 9, 26, 27, 52, 53, 71, 76, 77

Queen Elizabeth-class battleships 11, 13, 74: armament 12, 24, 30, 31, **31**, 32, 33, 40, **40**, 41, **45**, 72, 73, 77; armour 12, 24, 30, 31, 32, 72, 73; modernization 8, 9, 11, 12, 13, **13**, 24, **26**, 30–33, **31**, **32**, 40, **40**, 41, 42, 76, **76**; specifications 12, 30, 31, 32, 33, 40, 66, 73
  Barham 8, 9, 11, 12, 30, 32, 33, 66, 69, 72, 73, 75, 77
  Malaya 8, 11, 25, 30, 32, 40, **40**, **45**, 53, 54, 55, **55**, 56, 64, 65, 72, 73
  Queen Elizabeth 8, 9, 11, **26**, 30, 31, 32, 40, 72, 75, 76, **76**, 77
  Valiant 8, 9, 11, **13**, 30, 31, **31**, 32, 40, 58, 66, 68–69, 72, 75, 76, 77, 78
  Warspite **6**, 8, 11, **11**, 25, **26**, 30, 31, **31**, 32, **32**, 42, 50, 53, 54, 55, **55**, 56, **56**, 57, 65, 68–69, 71, 72, 75, 77, 78

Radar: (Brit) 24, 31, 33, 42, 68; (Ita) 39, 50, 71
Raeder, Großadmiral Erich 28
Rangefinders: (Brit) 42; (Ita) **5**, 22, 43, **69**
Regia Aeronautica operations 14, 49, 51, 53, 54, 57, 58, 60, 69
Regia Marina (battle fleet) 18
  aerial bombing of 24, 57, 71, 78

divisions 64: I/III/VII **55**, **61**
effectiveness/importance of 4, 27, 47, 48, 57, 58, 60, 65, 70, 71, 74
fleets 52, 53
fuel shortages 27, 78
operational use of 7, 26–27, 29–30, 50, 58, 60, 70: night fighting 30, 50, 71; rules of engagement 7, 24, 27, 51, 52, 54, 58, 60, 64, 70, 71, 72, 73, 76; salvo dispersion 2, 40, 41, 42, 43, 50, 68, 71, 74; ship strength (June 1940) 6
squadrons: 1ᵃ 28, 55; 2ᵃ 28, 51
surrender and internment of 9, **19**, 24, 49, 51, **77**, 78, **78**
Riccardi, Amm di Squadra Arturo 28, **28**, 64, 65
Royal Air Force ops 60, 65, 66, 68, **71**, 77
Royal Navy (Mediterranean Fleet) 49, 73
aerial bombardment of 53, 54, 57, 65
battle divisions: 1st **55**
cruiser squadrons: 7th **55**; 15th **67**
Forces A/B/C 54
Force H 9, 26, 53, 58, 60, **61**, 65, 70, **71**, 75, 76
main bases 9, 25, 26, **26**, 46, 49, 53, 58, 64, 66, 76, 77
night fighting 29, 30, 49
role of battle fleet/battleships 7, 26, 29
ship strength (June 1940) 6, 11, 25
strategy in Mediterranean 4–5
Royal Sovereign-class battleships 11, 13, 73: armament 13, **14**, **15**, **33**, 34, 40, 41, **46**, **62–63**, 64, 73; armour 13–14, 34, 58, 73; modernization 13, 33, 42; specifications 13, 14, 34, 64, 73
  Ramillies 8, 13, 14, **14**, 25, 33, **33**, 34, **46**, **60**, **61**, **62–63**, 64, 72
  Resolution 8, 13, 14, 34, 58
  Revenge 8, 13, 14, 34
  Royal Oak 8, 13, 14, 34
  Royal Sovereign 8, 13, 14, **15**, 25, **33**, 34, 53, 54, 55

Sardinia, actions off 53, 60, **61**, **62–63**, 64–65
Savoia, Amm d'Armata Ferdinando 48
secondary guns (Brit): 4in 30; 4.5in 31, **31**, 32, 40, **45**, 65; 4.7in 69; 5.25in 17; 6in 12, 13, 16, 30, 31, 32, 34, 40, **45**
secondary guns (Ita): 4.7in **5**, **18**, 19, 35, **37**, 42; 5.3in 36, 42; 6in 20, 23, 38, 42, **59**, **69**, **74**
Sirte, first/second battles of 9, 51, 76–77
Somigli, Amm di Squadra Odoardo 27–28
Sommerville, Vice-Adm Sir James 26, 60, 64
submarines (Brit) 6, 26: *Urge* 76
submarines (Fra): *Bévéziers* 58
submarines (Ger): *U-47* 34; *U-331* 9, 12, 77
submarines (Ita) 6, 27, 28
Supermarina 27–28, 51, 54, 58, 66, 76

Taranto harbour **6**, 53: attack on 8, 28, 58, **60**
torpedo bombers (Brit) 6, 8, 24, 42, 50, 53, **61**, 66, 77: Albacore 66, **67**, 68; Beaufort 77; Swordfish 54, 56, 58, 64, 68
torpedoes, use of/protection against 14, 16, 17, 30, 31, 32, 33, 50, 54, 57, 58, 60, 64, 68, 69, 72, 73, 74: Pugliese system 23, 35, 36, 74, 78

Vittorio Veneto-class battleships 19, **24**, 27, 35, 39, 43, 73, 74: armament **18**, 21, 22–23, **22**, 24, **24**, 26, **38**, **38**, 39, 41, 42, **59**, 64, **69**, 74, **74**, 77; armour 21, 22, 23, 24, 38, 74; modernization 21; specifications 7, 21, 23, 24, 38, 73, 74
  Impero 21
  Italia 78, **78**
  Littorio **7**, 8, 9, **18**, 21, **21**, 23, 39, 58, **59**, 76, 77, 78
  Roma 21, 24, **24**, 26, 39, 51, 74, **74**, 77, 78
  Vittorio Veneto 8, 9, 21, **22**, 23, **38**, 39, **39**, 41, 60, **61**, 64, 65, 66, **67**, 68, 69, **69**, 72, 74, 76, 77, 78, **78**

The T'alli Stone

Marjorie P. Dunn

The **Hallamshire** Press

1995

To Phillip Marshall and to Bob Dunn my husband,
for their help and encouragement.

Acknowledgements
To Sheffield Libraries and Information Services' Local Studies Library and
Sheffield Archives for allowing the use of research material.

Cover
'The Parish Church 1793', T. Harris.
Reproduced by permission of Sheffield Arts and Museums Department.

Published by The Hallamshire Press
The Hallamshire Press is an Imprint of
Interleaf Productions Limited
Exchange Works
Sidney Street
Sheffield S1 3QF
England

Typeset by Interleaf Productions Limited
Printed in Great Britain by The Cromwell Press, Wiltshire

British Library Cataloguing in Publication Data
   Dunn, Marjorie P.
     T'alli stone
     I. Title
     823.914 [F]

     ISBN 1-874718-16-4

Preface

*T*he *T'alli Stone* is set in South Yorkshire immediately after the Napoleonic Wars, at a time when the starving lower classes were ready to rise against oppression. Fanny Garnett, a respectable but rebellious girl, becomes infatuated with an idealistic reformer who is the victim of a vicious revenge plot.

This gentle but compelling love story particularly illustrates the lifestyle of the simple artisans of Sheffield, who, living in a backwater away from main coaching routes, developed strong enduring characteristics.

Fanny's strong will and determination is tempered only by the restrictions of her times and the devotion of the two men who love her; John, the radical, and Gervase, the shy, respectable business man.

Whilst this romantic triangle is played out against a backcloth of conflicting social restraints and radical fervour, it retains the simplicity of ordinary human life.

The T'alli Stone is a work of fiction, but many incidents have been drawn and adapted from local newspapers of the time. The names of some of the characters, their occupations and addresses have been borrowed from the author's family history, all else concerning them is fiction.

Sheffield Town 1797–1818

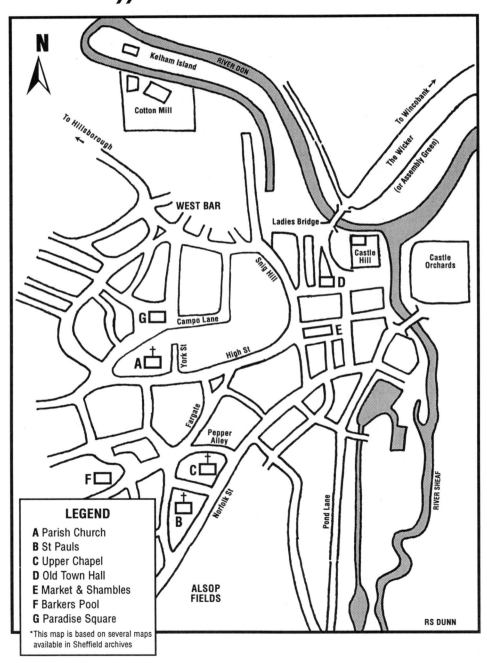

N

To Hillsborough

RIVER DON

Kelham Island

Cotton Mill

WEST BAR

Snig Hill

Ladies Bridge

To Wincobank

The Wicker (or Assembly Green)

Castle Hill

Castle Orchards

D

Campo Lane

G

York St

High St

A

E

Fargate

Pepper Alley

C

F

Norfolk St

B

Pond Lane

RIVER SHEAF

ALSOP FIELDS

RS DUNN

LEGEND

A Parish Church
B St Pauls
C Upper Chapel
D Old Town Hall
E Market & Shambles
F Barkers Pool
G Paradise Square

*This map is based on several maps available in Sheffield archives

Chapter 1

he grimy old town lay beneath a blanket of snow whilst its inhabitants slept, escaping from the toil of their labour and the cold of the spartan houses in which they lived. Icy blasts of wind swept down from the surrounding moorlands and whined as they whipped down the alleyways, beating against windows as they went.

Sheffield sprawled into the valleys, cut off from the outside world by the snow, and for once its cobbled streets appeared clean. The shuttered shops gave little comfort to any human being desperate or foolhardy enough to venture out into the January night, and within hours of its arrival the snow would be smeared by the soot of countless belching chimneys.

Had Bryce found the time to stand and observe this desolate scene he could not have failed to have been in awe of it, but there were more urgent matters occupying his thoughts as he forced himself down the street, against the gusting wind.

'God! What a night — why tonight of all nights?' he mumbled to himself as he stumbled along the uneven cobblestones. The wind moaned around him and flakes of snow settled on his brow; he drew his cloak closer to his small shivering body and pressed on. He hadn't gone very far when he almost fell over and cursed himself for his clumsiness, but he was very weary, weary of everything this winter, the shortage of work, the lack of money, and the ever increasing demands of his children. The children — how they squabbled, and outgrew their clothes, there were so many of them — five in all and three more in the churchyard round the corner.

Bryce loved his wife but he hated himself for his need of her. When the nights were cold and the wood gone, they would curl up together under the blankets for warmth, a warmth which in turn created another mouth to feed.

The wind whined and whistled down York Street reminding him of Sarah moaning in labour back at the house, and he thrust himself forward with renewed urgency. She didn't look right, he'd seen her like this before but never quite so spent and exhausted, he was afraid that he might lose her. Impatient with the midwife's efforts, he had decided to fetch Dr Hall whom he knew would be far from pleased at being roused so late, but then not much did please him these days. He owed Bryce a favour and now was the time to collect. The old misery didn't think twice when he wanted his chin shaved or wig curled in great haste, and sometimes it took him days to pay his bill.

As Bryce turned into the High Street the lantern swung and caught him a glancing blow but managed to remain alight. He reached the doctor's door and struck it so hard with the knocker that the noise echoed down the street. He waited impatiently, wondering to himself what kind of creature would want to enter this sad world on such a wicked night, and promptly struck the door again.

'Alright, alright — have a care there', called the gruff voice from within, 'who's a-dying this time?' As the Doctor opened the door the wind removed his night-cap and blew out his candle. He grunted and peered into the gloom of the lantern light until he recognised his caller.

'Please come quickly!' Bryce spoke agitatedly, 'Sarah's not well.'

'Eh! Oh well, I suppose I'd better come. You go ahead, I'll follow when I get my breeches on', grumbled the old man, 'and don't let those women interfere', he shouted after Bryce, 'especially that widow Platts, she's the bane of my life.'

Bryce retraced his steps quickly, trying to avoid the slush and thinking sadly that somehow he'd have to afford some new boots soon, as his were beyond repair. He reflected bitterly that business had been doing well until that dratted man Pitt had put a tax on wig powder in 1795; in the two years since then he and all the other hairdressers and wigmakers in the town, had experienced a sharp decline in trade. People weren't using wigs anymore, they refused to pay the tax and were fearful of the ten guinea fine if they were found doing so. Anyone still sporting a wig was crudely nicknamed 'guinea pig' and that insult speeded up the decline. He had been one of the best peruke makers in the town, trained by his father-in-law and he'd even had a shop in the High Street just below the doctor's house. Their removal to the York Street tenement and shop had been a backward step, the rooms were smaller and as well as being damp were gloomy, but he could still shave a chin closer than anyone else and curl a lady's hair to perfection. When the occasion arose, the more affluent ladies of the town still came to him to have their hair dressed, but these occasions were getting rarer these days. With the wigs, he had been able at least to earn extra money in the evenings when the shop was closed; then he had been able to make them in peace, dressing them and perfuming them. Now, however, it was shop hours only, when clients were there. He was going to need help in the shop now that Sarah was going to be busy with the baby; the thought of her lying there in pain made him quicken his gait and he forgot his other problems.

He reached the house and entered through the shop, which was quicker than going through the back yard. He paused to regain his breath and to compose himself. The house was strangely quiet, almost as though he had entered someone else's for his house was always noisy, but the children were fast asleep. His spirits fell — perhaps something was wrong? As he reached the foot of the stairs the air was rent by a sharp, piercing wail. The sound of the new-born child filled the air and he leapt forward up the stairs to be greeted, not by the worried faces which he had anticipated, but by the broad smile of his mother-in-law.

Sarah was exhausted but apparently safe and well. Widow Platts came up to him with a twinkle in her eye. 'Didn't trust us did you luv, haring off down the street like that? Mind you, no wonder, this one was so hard, I've never seen legs so long on a girl before. Bit red and crumpled but no harm done — going to be a pretty one that.' She paused in her excitement, 'Old Doctor Hall's too late again', she grinned mischievously as she spoke.

Bryce winced and wished that the snow would swallow him up when he thought of the old man climbing into his cold breeches for nothing. He peeped down at the bright pink countenance of his new daughter; a down of gold crowned the little face and he noted that she had the look of his grandmother Garnett, but thought it was to be hoped that she didn't inherit the stubbornness and fire of the old dragon. Grandmother was in the graveyard with his three dead children — Bryce didn't fear for them whilst they lay near her, she'd scare the Devil himself away.

He bent and gave his wife a hug, then left her to rest. He felt quite pleased with himself, and Sarah; he loved babies and even used to creep up the stairs whilst Sarah wasn't looking to see if they were still breathing. If only they didn't eat so much! There was a fire in the bedroom and Bryce decided that it would save fuel if he stayed there in the room with them both, while her mother saw to the other children, he gratefully took his place in the old armchair by the fire and watched the flame.

Pondering over the effect a new baby would have on the household, and the state of his business affairs, Bryce acknowledged that it wasn't just the wig powder tax that was the trouble — everyone was having a hard time after nearly four years of war with the French. The town was being over-run by an influx of poor wretches fleeing from an impoverished countryside; things were bad, Sheffield's housing and its amenities were being stretched beyond belief, turning houses into hovels of overcrowding. There just wasn't the money any more to feed the poor properly, or to provide homes for the increasing population.

The annual Cutler's Feast, that prestigious banquet and entertainment held by the town's cutlers was to cease and the two hundred pounds annually allowed for it would go to the Government to help the war effort — this time anyone who wanted to attend would have to pay for his own dinner! The money could have been better spent within the town, there was gloom everywhere with little light relief from the local newspaper; impending tax increases and threats of invasion seemed to be the only topics in print.

The militia was constantly on the alert to the threat of invasion and people were genuinely frightened, believing that they would awake one morning to see the French marching through the town. Why, only a little earlier in the month, an English sailor returning from Brest claimed that he had seen, at first hand, sixteen French men-o'-war, four hundred gunboats and thousands of men mustering on the coast, preparing to cross the Channel. The dratted French, they were even trying to build enormous craft, seven hundred yards by three hundred and fifty yards, to be driven by windmills and machines, in order to cross the sea! That neck of sea was a Godsend, Bryce concluded, at least it kept Napoleon occupied.

He had read of constant reports of there being fleets of air balloons and diving machines being built, but still they hadn't come. Madness! thought Bryce, madness that men should waste such energies to destroy each other when the money could help so many in need. Bryce remembered with pride the day he had joined the local Volunteers, and was pleased to think that he would be able to protect his country from the barbarians. Everything was getting out of hand now, all goods of British manufacture were to be declared contraband by the French, even when carried on neutral vessels. Who would order British goods if they could not guarantee receiving them? He admitted to himself that we had tried to starve out the French by seizing their grain supplies and other goods of substance, and we used neutral vessels to transport our goods, but lawful seizure of our goods by the French would hit us hard. He shook his head, nothing would ever be the same again.

A falling cinder from the fire roused Bryce from his reverie, and he realised he had passed the remainder of the night flitting in and out of sleep. Ah well, he thought, there's work to do, the children will be awake soon and I must take steps to find an apprentice to take Sarah's place.

There was no shortage of lads needing work and it wasn't long before a steady trickle of them came in answer to his advertisement. The first three lads he'd seen would have been better suited to stuffing horse hair into couches than handling the tresses of clients. One of these had appeared so filthy and dishevelled that even a chimney boy would have been preferable. Then there had been the awkward lumbering lad — he'd felt sorry for him as he stood there self-conscious and nervous, almost apologetic. He was almost ugly with huge hands, but he could read and write and seemed far too bright for the job that Bryce could offer him. He said that his mother was dead and that he worked for his father who managed a printing business; all he was allowed to do was sweep and carry but he wasn't allowed to do the interesting jobs. The father seemed to have little ambition for his son, but Bryce knew that he could never offer the lad anything better, nor more money, and let the lad go with a strange feeling of reluctance.

Within a couple of days Bryce had found himself a likeable lad, suitable for his needs, who was not over bright but clean and willing to learn. None of his assistants stayed long anyway, they soon got bored or found work which offered more money. It wouldn't be long before his own boys reached an age when they could join him in the business and then he wouldn't need to take strangers on any more.

He was quite surprised to find that, on several occasions, the awkward boy came back to play with his own boys, and felt that perhaps a little human kindness was what the lad really needed. Bryce was as soft-hearted as his wife, and he found himself doing exactly what she would have done. 'Come round to tea sometime mi lad', he offered. The look of gratitude on the boy's face as he nodded his thanks gave Bryce enormous satisfaction.

The boy's name was Gervase, and it wasn't long before he turned up regularly once a week to tea, usually on the evening when his father went to his Gentlemen's Club. The family accepted him as one of them and he began to look to Sarah as a mother, she took to any waif and stray; the more helpless they were the better was her devotion to them. Sarah was small and homely, with pretty fair hair which was slowly losing its lustre as she got older; she was easy to love and she listened to the lad for hours as he rambled on. He was far too philosophical for her, but she listened all the same. She felt a tug at her heart strings as she watched him play with the baby — they'd named her Fanny, and the first time he held her little hand it was like watching a huge bear they had once seen at a fair, with a sparrow perched fearlessly on its nose. He would play with her other children, taking them for walks and teaching them how to fish.

His name was a somewhat fancy one for such a lad, but then as his father was a pretentious man and felt more affection for his books than he did for his son, it was little wonder that he had given him such a name. Gervase, too, liked reading books and talking politics, but he still needed to play with children and because of his self-consciousness avoided his contemporaries. He seemed oddly ill at ease in the presence of a crowd of youths, never quite fitting in, always standing back on the fringes. Nevertheless he championed the Garnett lads whenever there was a clash with the boys from the Charity School in the churchyard. The verger never failed to report to Bryce on the latest skirmish as he sat, his chin soap-lathered, in the barber's chair.

Bryce listened with concealed amusement.

'They've been scrapping again', the verger complained wearliy one evening to Bryce, 'but that big youth keeps an eye on your boys, I'll say that. It's not right you know', he went on at length 'playing and fighting in the graveyard, but I suppose there's nowhere else for them to play. They're forever vaultin' o'er T'alli Stone — it's as smooth and shiny as their trouser seats.'

'You'll never stop them', Bryce returned sympathetically, 'it's a strange stone that one and an even stranger story behind it!'

'So I hear — did they never find out who the man was who lies there? I hear he had quite a lot of money on him when he fell to his death.'

'I've no idea, but they used the money to provide him with a marble tombstone, although most people hereabouts think it to be alabaster, and that's why they call it the T'alli Stone.'

Sarah was Gervase's confidante as he grew to manhood — he didn't ever want to marry because he didn't like girls, for they teased him about his size and ridiculed him constantly about his bookishness. He had never dared show his feelings before but slowly, as he learned to trust Sarah, he opened up his heart to her. He became very tall and was dark with determined intelligent features; although far from handsome, he had eyes which were soft and gentle to those who took the trouble to look beneath his reserve.

Gervase doted on little Fanny, precocious creature that she was, dangling her upon his knee and allowing her to pull the hairs on his hands and arms. In an evening, when the boys from the Charity School weren't about, Gervase would take Fanny into the churchyard and help her to leap-frog the 'Alabaster stone'. Only when she was tired and exhausted would she let him take her home without protest. The boys, as they grew, walked miles with him when he wasn't working or studying books borrowed without his father's consent from the printing office. He was slowly learning the background to the printing trade, after he had pleaded with his father to be given greater responsibility, and managed to afford the entrance fee to one of the town's subscription libraries. When Fanny was old enough to walk any distance he would take her and the boys on picnics, and for hours they would wander amongst the beautiful hills and valleys that surrounded Sheffield. They would fish in the rivers and streams which converged on the town, often bringing home the odd salmon for tea. It was different when Fanny fished with them; her dilly-dallying would delay them all and she would be constantly up to mischief until in the end they would return her to the house plastered in mud and armed with bunches of wild flowers.

Despite Fanny's curly golden hair and engaging smile, there lay beneath the surface a wild wilfulness that could be frustrating. Brothers Henry, Bryce and John would stand only just so much before they had had enough, for she would hide their things and pull off their caps, and very rarely would she own up when caught out. If they allowed her to fly their paper kites she would invariably let go of them or tangle them, and somehow she was always involved when a fish escaped their lines, due mainly to her chattering and badgering. In those idyllic rambles she learned the names of all the local birds, fish and flowers even before she was seven. She was by nature inquisitive, and questioned everything and everyone from an early age; by the time she was sixteen she was freely joining in adult conversations and political discussions in the Garnett household.

As time passed she grew leggy and beautiful, though headstrong and defiant, always challenging the boys, verbally and physically, until in the end they ceased to take her with them unless Gervase was there. He had a great influence on her way of thinking and was able to temper some of her overenthusiastic notions and ideas. He would never admit, even to himself, that she ran rings around him and that he tended to spoil her. The world around her, however, was changing.

The war with the French dragged on and on, causing many businesses to fail, and it wasn't just the poor who suffered from the downturn in trade; many middle-class families lost their firms and homes in the repeated slumps that the war period caused. Some would prosper for a while when the market was good or there were Government orders, but when these ceased, a downturn in trade would follow causing a general depression. Sheffield was a changing place. Whereas previously for generations employees had worked alongside their masters in harmony, now the trend was for the master to dominate them. At this time, as England stood alone facing a defeated and occupied continent, the inhabitants of Sheffield witnessed landlords seizing the possessions of the poor in lieu of rent, leaving families bereft of belongings and begging for food.

There were however, many townspeople who did prosper, and the more enlightened and benevolent of these contributed to Parish Relief, or organised charity concerts to provide an infirmary for the sick. New churches were built to accommodate the growing population, but non-conformity flourished as people questioned old beliefs and became disillusioned. Poverty, caused by the ravages of war and failed crops, brought the poor people almost to the point of insurrection; but as usual the fight for survival left them with little energy for rebellion.

The Garnett family survived, despite their trials and tribulations, and they found little need to change from the Unitarian beliefs which their ancestors had embraced years before. They had occupied the same pew for years, dutifully paying their rent, except when business had been so bad that Bryce fell into arrears. He was quietly reminded of his debt and accepted the suggestion that they take a cheaper pew in the gallery of the church, much to the delight of the children. Fanny was thrilled by the move as she was never very interested in the sermons and tolerated church whilst she whiled away the time in dreams. Now she could observe the congregation with their fashions and foibles from on high, she conjured up pictures in her mind's eye of the lives of the people below, of the goings on and the occasional scandal.

No one, apparently, discovered where the acorns and buttons came from which landed in old Doctor Hall's lap during prayers, but once one nearly landed on his bald head and Fanny vowed to be a little more careful in future. She was highly intrigued when, on her sixteenth birthday, a little package arrived at the house tied neatly with a beautiful blue ribbon; it had no card and the boy who brought it said that he didn't know the name of the man who had asked him to deliver it. It was a very simple but beautiful polished wooden box, and the contents were even more of a surprise. It was a collection of dried and wrinkled acorns mixed with a variety of buttons.

Flushed with surprise and some embarrassment Fanny realised that Doctor Hall had shared her secret all these years, and instead of seeing him as an old grump, she suddenly saw him in a new light and wondered what he had really been like as a young man. He had, in fact, quite missed her mischievous little game as she had grown older, for it had broken the monotony of many a sermon for him. He had emptied his pockets on returning from Church each Sunday and placed the missiles in the little box which stood on the hall table at home. The following Sunday, as she sat in the gallery looking down on the old man and all heads were bent in prayer, she gently let a final button land in his lap. As he looked up and caught her eye, he smiled, noting as he did that she was becoming a beautiful woman with fine grey eyes which twinkled even now with mischief. Once again she had charmed him. No words were ever exchanged for they weren't necessary, but a precious human bond had been formed.

When, eighteen months later the old man died and the flowers on his grave had withered and fallen into decay, one tribute remained. Bathed in beautiful autumn colours were several sprigs from an oak tree with the acorn caps still attached. The doctor's passing had saddened Fanny and when Gervase enquired the reason for her pensiveness, she trustingly told him the story, allowing him to share the secret and knowing that he would not make fun of her.

However, there lurked beneath Fanny's brightness, unsuspected by everyone, a dark, sad loneliness which reared its head when the precociousness did not have an audience. It may have been a need for love or security, or it may have been the need for her enquiring mind to be more deeply occupied, at a time when women were not expected to understand or take part in worldly matters. The female contemporaries in Fanny's life bored her with their trivial conversation and petty interests and she had an almost insatiable appetite for adult conversation, sitting for hours around the supper table when Bryce talked business, or reminisced.

The Garnett children from an early age had all helped in the family business and were quite adept at sweeping up hairs if nothing else. Sarah and Charlotte, the two older daughters, had both done their share but very quickly met available young men of moderate means and had married before they were twenty. Of the brothers, Henry had gone as an apprentice knife-blade forger, much to the consternation of his father, who feared the working conditions would ruin his health, although he admitted that the family hairdressing business, subject to the whims and fancies of the paying public, would not sustain the whole family. It was also an accepted fact that the boy had little patience in dealing with clients, neither had he any artistic flair. His brother John was nearing the end of his apprenticeship as a joiner and cabinet maker and would probably find sufficient work, even in these desperate days, to maintain himself and an eventual family. The oldest son Bryce, Bryce junior, had adapted very well. It did not go unnoticed that he had a certain way of charming the ladies and in spite of the fact that he had little head for book-keeping would take over the business when his father decided to retire.

There remained the problem of Fanny. She was not afraid of work and was quite competent in the dressing of hair but Bryce sensed a restlessness in his daughter which quite disturbed him, for whilst she got on remarkably well with his clients, it was almost like having a caged bird in his shop. Occasionally in quiet moments, he would observe her as she day-dreamed in a world of her own and then, when she realised where she was, would bustle about her work with renewed vigour, almost as though she felt guilty of her dreams.

Discussing Fanny's future with Sarah, Bryce decided that there was sufficient money available now and that perhaps she could go to Mrs Green's Boarding School for young girls on Western Bank. This would at least help keep the wildness at bay for a year or so and would finish off her education at the same time.

The family was prospering now, the vanity of the wealthy ensured this, but the wigs were almost a thing of the past except for small false hair pieces favoured by the ladies. The fashion for natural hair at the turn of the century demanded constant crimping and curling but whereas this increased the work of the artisan it did little to improve the condition of the hair. The result of such excessive treatment on the hair over a number of years necessitated hair being worn short and it was in need of constant professional attention. Bryce had no complaints at this situation and his family enjoyed the benefits of the upturn in trade. However, other trades were not doing so well and the sullen unrest within the town was beginning to worry Bryce; unemployment amongst the poor increased and they and the low paid workers were becoming almost militant in their outlook. After much consultation with clients, between the lathering of chins and the scrape of the razor, Bryce finally decided it would probably be a better and more sensible arrangement to send Fanny out of the town to board, and he had it on good authority that a school in Doncaster was extremely proficient at turning young girls into elegant and sensible young women.

Fanny received the news with mixed emotions. There was a large and possibly exciting world out there beyond the hills and valleys which she would miss, and she had heard many fascinating tales concerning the wealthy and elegant who travelled to York and London, on business and pleasure, through the coaching town of Doncaster. Many of these came to Doncaster, especially in September for the races, and Fanny had often envied clients who had returned from the races and filled her head with romantic dreams. Sheffield itself lay in a backwater, tucked away in the valleys off the major coaching routes, so it was never quite touched by the influence of London. Travellers only alighted in the town if they had good reason to do so, and others only left out of similar necessity. It was common gossip that in the towns on the Great North Road the fashions of London were proudly flaunted and promenaded, and that great ladies were to be seen alighting from coaches, helped down by elegant young dandies.

The school in Doncaster offered one subject in particular which shone like a beacon, beckoning Fanny on. This was geography, with it's use of globes and all the modern topographical aids now available, which offered an exciting vista of far off places. The fact that history, that dreary subject, the English language and something called 'Heathen Mythology' were also on the curriculum was completely masked by the offer of painting, drawing and dancing. She would go! In all Fanny's excitement it never occurred to her that she would miss her mother, and Sarah was in fact grateful that she did not have to despatch her daughter of eighteen years overcome with tears and tantrums, or perhaps she would have regretted agreeing to her going. Life would certainly be quieter without her and the house would be empty of her vitality. Sarah's heart sank a little at the thought of the long evenings ahead without her company, sad too that the last of her brood was leaving home.

The week before Fanny's departure was chaotic; her excitement disturbed the entire household, it was as if she was going to a far distant land, not just the twenty miles or so to Doncaster. Every item she possessed, which was small enough to carry, was being packed into her trunk and if it had not been for the prudence of her mother, they would have needed to borrow a couple more trunks to take with her. With the necessary sheets and towels which one needed to take, Fanny packed every item of clothing which she possessed, plus hats, ribbons, sewing items and books — the few that she had — and all her frills and knick-knacks, including her precious little box. Sarah feared that if Fanny continued in such high spirits she would make herself ill and be unable to travel.

The day of departure was cold and wet, as miserable as any January day could be at six o'clock in the morning, and the thought of leaving her dear mother and comfortable home for an unknown future sobered Fanny. She began to realise the full impact of what the separation would mean. Her mother insisted that she travelled dressed for comfort, rather than to be fashionable, in a heavy woollen dress and cape, a muff for her hands and new booties for her feet. Her father, who was to accompany her, carried two rugs for added protection. Having already kissed her mother farewell in the shop doorway, they hurried through the rain and muddy streets, past the Shambles and across town to the 'Tontine Inn' where, in spite of the weather, considerable activity was already taking place. Her luggage had been sent down the night before and the coach was already within the spacious courtyard when they arrived. An ostler led a team of horses across the cobbled yard to harness them ready for the journey. The popular red-bricked inn was not only the scene of countless comings and goings but also a place of auctions and exhibitions, as was evident from the number of posters littering the walls.

Fanny was thankful that her father had paid extra money for them to travel inside the coach, she pitied the poor folk riding on the top, who would be in a very wet and miserable plight by the time they reached their destination. Together they squeezed in next to a rather copious woman who was already half asleep. In the seats which faced Fanny and her father sat two men, both with stony faces, their breath steaming in the cold morning air, causing Fanny to shiver at the comfortless atmosphere in the carriage. Eventually after endless waiting, the coach set off, jolting the passengers violently against each other so that Fanny found herself pinned between her father and the large woman who had been awakened by the abrupt movement. The woman smelled and Fanny tried to draw away from her but there was such little space that movement was impossible. It wasn't long before the woman's jaw hung down, as if set or frozen, and sleep claimed her once more leaving Fanny free from unwanted conversation.

The journey was long and uncomfortable, broken only by the stopover in Rotherham where they were allowed to stretch their legs for five minutes whilst luggage was unloaded and more put in its place. Fanny had never been so uncomfortable before but thought the coach aptly named, for in her opinion 'The Defiant' held the road well in spite of the ruts, the mud and the steep hills; it was so heavily laden with luggage that Fanny had feared they would topple over on sharp bends. There was little wonder that one of the wheels worked loose, and only the quick thinking of the driver had saved them from what could have been an unpleasant incident. In spite of the constant lurching and bumping and the cold, the journey was a complete fascination to her and she snuggled down into the rug and observed her somewhat strange travelling companions. After a long slippery descent into one valley bottom, it was necessary to add extra horses to pull the coach up the steep hill at the other side, and as Fanny peered through the window she caught her breath in wonder.

'Where are we now?' she whispered in a low voice. In the valley lay the ruins of an ancient castle, perched as if frozen in time on the far hillside and surrounded by a swirling mist which added an eeriness to the gloomy morning. Within the coach Fanny felt held by some mystic power from the past.

'Conisborough Castle', one of the stony faced men informed her with an air of condescension. 'It's not difficult to imagine the battles and sieges which have taken place there over the centuries is it? They say that Hengist

16

sought refuge there and was beheaded in the castle. Certainly many famous people have passed through its gates but now it's just a beautiful ruin.'

Fanny thanked him for his explanation and hoped that he would not go on. Who Hengist was she neither knew nor cared at this precise moment, for the sight of the ruin gave her the shivers and she drew her cape closer to her body. She lapsed into one of her day-dreams, thinking of her mother back at home, for there would be no one to spoil her as Sarah had done. She recalled the day when her father had marched off to Doncaster in his lovely red tunic and white trousers. She had been only seven at the time, when half the town had gathered to see the Volunteers muster and march to fight the French — the children had considered it a huge game and were puzzled by the tears. Something had happened and the men soon returned; she learned later that some hoaxer had lit the warning beacon at Grenoside and it had all been a false alarm. One sensible fellow had even surmised it to be a hoax and had gone off quietly to do a spot of fishing.

She pondered on what life would have been like if the French had succeeded in crossing the Channel. The newspapers made them sound so barbaric, having killed off all their aristocracy during the worst days of the revolution. Perhaps they were all peasants now, so who was left to read to the children? In her childish way she imagined the French to be totally uncultured and fervently hoped that she would never have to meet any of them. Surely the war could not go on much longer, everyone was sick of it and the poverty it caused distressed her.

When eventually they arrived at Doncaster, Fanny was so cold and hungry that she could hardly stand and she had to be lifted down from the coach. Whoever was to have met them had not yet arrived, so they were at least given time to sit by the fire in the inn and to warm themselves with a hot drink. At last the fellow arrived to collect them, it was no great distance to the academy and a welcoming hot meal awaited them on their arrival. Bryce was reassured by this act of kindness and hoped such considerations were a reflection of the general running of the establishment. It seemed to Fanny that they had no sooner arrived than it was time for Bryce to leave again. The return coach left Doncaster at three in the afternoon, and she bravely hid her tears as she bade him a fond farewell.

The room into which she was shown, the one in which she was to spend the next fifteen months, was to be shared by two more young women and, although sparsely furnished, it was comfortable with a roaring fire in the grate. The three girls were to laugh, cry, fight and squabble together, until in the end they would emerge as three very elegant and independent young ladies. For the moment however, all were a little shy and reserved, but this gradually changed as all three unpacked their belongings and found that they had many items and tastes in common with each other, besides a sadness at leaving home.

During the first two months of her sojourn in Doncaster, Fanny found the icy-cold winds made her disinclined to go far from the house, the girls were content to huddle around a comfortable fire whilst endeavouring to adapt to their new routine and studies. Miss Greaves, the proprietress, insisted however that they all took a brisk daily walk within the vicinity of the academy, but apart from that, they were content to watch the world pass by the latticed windows, noting the differing mode of dress and giggling admiringly over the numerous dashing young men as they strode or rode by. The winds from the North Sea caused people to scurry, huddling beneath their warm capes, in order to ward off attacks of rheumatism, pleurisy and catarrh which were prevalent in the town in winter.

The occasional trip along French Gate and High Street, to peep into the shop windows, was as far as the girls were allowed to venture, but even so Fanny could appreciate the paved walkways which prevented their shoes from disappearing into a slurry of mud on the roads. Towards the end of March, with the lessening of the biting winds and the corresponding rise in temperature, the girls ventured further mingling with the townspeople and the increasing number of travellers. Miss Greaves felt that her charges were now familiar enough with the terrain and characteristics of this frivolous town, and just as the flowers and other plants sprang forth into the spring sunshine, so also did the elegance and delights of Doncaster reveal themselves to the delighted new boarders.

Fanny was amazed at the contrast between the two towns of Sheffield and Doncaster, which lay a mere eighteen miles apart, for the distance succeeded in creating two very differing cultures and life styles. She had heard much of the fashionable goings on in Doncaster, with its theatre, races, pleasurable shops and in particular the promenading by those people wealthy enough to have the time to spare. Then there were those notorious card games! These were the main topic of conversation when the races weren't on, and Fanny found it difficult to accept that anyone could risk such large sums of money on the mere throw of a dice or card, or even allow themselves the luxury of shopping all morning — if indeed they rose early enough to do so. For them to waste the quiet of the afternoon, which they did, in talking, shuffling cards, or rattling dice, even until midnight, whilst plying themselves with wine and choice morsels, appalled her. Not that Sheffield didn't have its own card tables, it did, but their usage was insufficient to be of note.

Doncaster had never sustained any great industry, relying instead on its general trades such as stocking knitting and the growing of choice asparagus, until, with the appearance of machinery, various small factories had emerged providing work for the less educated. The real wealth of the town came from the custom of the travellers who flocked through its gates. Most of these, and the people of fortune who came, seemed only to have pleasure on their minds as they strolled along, gazing in the windows of the shops which were full of finery such as Fanny had never seen before. The girls observed in some of the males a certain foppishness which was amusing, nevertheless the expensive dresses of the accompanying ladies were to be envied.

The girls flitted joyfully in and out of the twenty-four majestic colonnades which supported the slate roof of the meat market, and Fanny had to admit that its air of importance contrasted sharply with Sheffield's rather squalid market. The coffee houses intrigued them the most and they longed to join the many customers who seemed to spend the whole day gorging themselves on cake and gallons of liquid, whilst gossiping endlessly about goodness knows what. Some of the customers would, of course, be conducting business at the same time but to the girls, who were unfamiliar with coffee houses, it was not obvious.

Summer wore on, and the intense heat caused the girls to tire easily. Fanny longed for the smell of the heather, and yearned to return home, comforting herself by writing long letters to her mother. Sarah sensed her daughter's need for contact and wrote back more often than time really allowed, giving the coach driver an extra half penny each time if he would ensure that her letters were delivered. The more often the letters arrived with news, the more Fanny missed them all at home. She was, however, enjoying her life at the academy, and the discipline and grooming was having a marked effect on her appearance; the previous unsophisticated awkwardness had disappeared and she had achieved a slender poise that was most attractive. The sobering hard work and constant activity at the academy, did not however take away her loneliness, and she longed to talk to Gervase about her doubts and fears. There were days when she found life exhilarating, which encouraged her to believe herself capable of great achievement, and others when she felt lost and unloved by the world. Usually it did not take long for these periods of depression to pass and she was once again a lively creature, but she was disturbed by the extreme inconsistencies in her feelings.

July was a beautiful month and Fanny took to waking earlier than her companions who preferred to slumber and miss the magic of the dawn. She would uncurl slowly, with an almost sensual, cat like motion as the bright sunlight poured through the window onto her bed. The feel of the cool, thin cotton night-shift clinging to her body in the warmth of the sun's rays, made her vibrantly alive and conscious of a strange un-explainable desire to shed the night-shift and dance naked before the world. When she opened the leaded window, the scent of the garden flowers below wafted into the room, sweet and soothing. She leaned out, longing to be out there in the peace of the morning amongst the fragrances, and once called out involuntarily, 'I love you, sunshine!' Suddenly aware that she had spoken out loud, she spun round self-consciously, and was relieved to see that her two companions were still sleeping, oblivious of her outburst. She could not hide from herself the thrill which her body felt and she wished to be alone where no one could observe her, for then she would have allowed the sun's golden rays to dance on her soft naked skin.

Fanny flushed at her thoughts, feeling that her face must be as an open book to anyone seeing her now, and sure that they would be able to read her thoughts — innocent though they were. Hastily she com-posed herself and, deciding that she would go down into the garden, prepared herself for the day ahead.

As she bathed her face at the washstand and the cold water trickled from her hands down her neck to her breasts, she wondered how it would feel to have a man's hand touch her soft skin, she allowed these thoughts to linger. Then, feeling a little shocked and ashamed of her feelings, she dried herself and quickly dressed. The intensity of her emotions left Fanny in a mood which quite bewildered her; even her stroll in the garden left her restless and sad, quite blotting out the girl-ish dreams which had been born in the beauty of the morning. The young woman in her did not understand, and it took most of the morn-ing for her spirits to return. The chatter of her companions, over dinner, finally helped to relieve her of the brooding and she wished that she could be more like her friends, who seemed untouched by such deep affection for their natural surroundings. When she saw a bird, she want-ed to hold it, to spread its wings and discover its beauty, she needed to caress and smell the petals of the flowers, whilst the other girls sought only to adorn themselves.

With dinner over, she returned to her room to prepare for the after-noon session. A gentle knock on the open door lifted her from her thoughts, and Miss Greaves beckoned to her with a kindly smile. 'You have a visitor from Sheffield my dear, with a letter from your mother. I think it may be your uncle, but he asked if he might take you for a walk in the town. You may go providing that you catch up with your work later.' Thanking her, Fanny put her book down quickly and hurried after Miss Greaves onto the landing, eager to see if it was Gervase. Fanny descended the stairs with less than a ladylike bounce, hungry for news from home and delighted to see that it was indeed Gervase. He was her first visitor and she could impart all her news to her most trusted friend. This unexpected visit made a welcome break in the routine of the day. Her companions quickly followed her, peering with curiosity through the spindles of the stairs at the tall stranger below. They suppressed giggles when, totally out of character and on impulse, Gervase doffed his hat and with a mocking bow to them, addressed Fanny.

'May I beg the company of a beautiful young lady in a stroll around the town?'

With a gleeful bob Fanny replied, 'With pleasure, Sir'.

A ripple of amusement rang around the hall and even Miss Greaves smiled with pleasure. Collecting a hat from her room, Fanny paused before the looking-glass, placed the straw bonnet at a coquettish tilt on her head, then decided that it looked far too immodest, and placed it as it should be. She longed to talk to Gervase, unrestrained by the etiquette or embarrassment which was sometimes there with other young men to whom she was occasionally introduced.

Together they stepped out into the warmth of the afternoon sunshine and, in a very grown-up manner which Fanny had observed in elegant ladies, she placed her hand upon his arm, and thus they strolled through the town. Fanny was content. There was so much to tell, and to ask, that it wasn't long before she was quite out of breath.

'Would milady enjoy a cup of coffee in yonder coffee-house?' he enquired. Fanny nodded, no reply was really necessary, for the merry twinkle of excitement which flashed back at him from her eyes was answer enough. He glanced affectionately at her and, taking her elbow, passed her through the portal of the door, into an adult world.

With great effort Fanny suppressed her desire to skip to the nearest table and allowed herself to be led to a corner near the window and be lowered into a chair in a ladylike fashion. Gervase noted with interest how beautiful she was becoming, her fine hair so well groomed and her figure filling out the tight bodice of her dress. He felt quite proud to be an instrument in assisting this butterfly from its chrysalis, but could still detect signs of the old Fanny beneath the surface. She also was intrigued to see him in this light, so sure of himself and at ease, even graceful for all his bulk, and she felt that he was almost a stranger.

It did not take long however, for that old, more relaxed feeling to return as they exchanged more news. Her father had not been too well, but then she would read that in her mother's letter, which he gave her across the table. She intended reading it later and placed it in her reticule;

she would take pleasure in doing so when she returned to the academy; for now she was determined, as usual, to make the most of every minute of pleasure made available to her.

'Miss Greaves must have liked you', observed Fanny. 'We aren't usually allowed out with strangers. I wonder why she thought you were my uncle?'

A mischievous look came into his eyes, 'I had a feeling she might misunderstand my intentions if I told her the truth, and I also wanted to surprise you. Age has its advantages my beautiful Fanny, and I thought it far better to keep it simple'. A smile creased his face, 'I have to go to York on business and Sarah asked me to call upon you with her letter'. He watched as a flicker of disappointment flashed across her face. 'Don't fret, I would have called to see you anyway', he gently reassured her, and then endeavoured to answer her many questions about home. After all her excited enquiries were over, the conversation slowly became more serious and inevitably turned to the topic of the War which had just ended.

'Gervase, now that the War is over I do hope everything will get better, and that peace will bring back prosperity', she stated quite suddenly.

He was impressed by the seriousness in her voice and his face became pensive as he replied. 'It won't be that easy my dear, so many soldiers will find that there isn't any work to come home to and others will be too sick or injured to find employment. The long series of wars with France will take years to recover from. Waterloo may have been a victory for Wellington but this war has cost thousands of lives, and now is just the beginning of a long hard struggle to start all over again.'

Fanny broke in, 'Wellington's a very brave man, isn't he!'

'Yes, he is a brilliant and skilled military man but he's a hard taskmaster, with little fondness for his men. He treated them as fighting machines but they respected him in spite of his cold, aristocratic manner, and out of loyalty they earned him his victory. It cost many of them their lives to do so though. Without those men he couldn't have done it.'

She raised her eyes questioningly, 'If the soldiers return and can't find work, how will they manage?'

He shook his head. 'Sadly, the poor have little food and live in overcrowded hovels, so it will get worse. Even now, hungry children in rags wander the streets begging for food and few have shoes to keep out the cold. The people have had enough of hardship and want changes but there is neither money nor resources to help them. Groups of workers try to get together to bring reform but they are without good leaders and nothing comes of it.'

Much as Fanny enjoyed this longed-for visit to a coffee-house she couldn't stave off the feeling of guilt inside her, that she was fortunate whilst other young people went hungry. Gervase sensed her despondency and lightened the conversation by telling her about the victory celebrations that had taken place in Sheffield, and of the Chinese fireworks display which had been held on Sheffield Moor. A military band played popular pieces of music and the crowd had watched a magnificent exhibition of fireworks, some depicting scenes of recent battles. The pageantry, and the excitement it had caused on Hermitage Bowling Green, was not difficult for Fanny to imagine and she wistfully longed to have been there.

Gervase had only two hours to pass in Doncaster for he had to be in York by nightfall. The time passed all too quickly, there was just time left for Fanny to show him the Mansion House and market before he had to return her to the academy. He promised to endeavour to see her again when business called him that way, and it was just possible that he might get across for the races in late September.

Fanny watched him from the window as he disappeared into the distance, hoping that he would keep his promise and return to take her to the races.

Chapter 2

What was left of the summer months passed uneventfully, the girls improving greatly in basic skills as Miss Greaves and her assistants made sure that they were kept busy. Indeed Miss Greaves was so pleased with their progress that she promised to teach them a few dance steps, adding that the most promising of her pupils might be selected to attend the ball which was always held at the Mansion House during race week. The academy was much respected in the town, and as Miss Greaves' brother was a Town Councillor, she always managed to have four tickets allotted to her for this most important function of the season.

A great believer in encouraging her pupils to rise above themselves, Miss Greaves felt no shame in offering two of these tickets for this prestigious event each year, to her best pupils as an incentive. Fanny took to dancing with ease, her long legs adding to her natural grace. She often thought it such a shame that legs had to be concealed beneath skirts and pantaloons, for she felt with some justification that her legs were her best asset; nevertheless, hidden they must remain. Fanny was determined to go to the ball.

The weather had been particularly hot all summer. Even now in mid-September, the heat and lack of rain persisted and it was hoped that the good weather would continue until the week of the races was over. Dust however, lay everywhere and in everything due to lack of rain. It flew up into the air every time a carriage went by, and the girls seemed to spend most of their time brushing down clothes and cleaning shoes. Waste material attracted flies in abundance and smells of the most unpleasant kind were everywhere.

A malicious rumour spread across the country — intended to cut attendances at the races — that a contagious fever was at large in Doncaster, and although this was hotly denied by a statement in the newspapers, the rumour disturbed Sarah. Feeling a certain apprehension for her daughter's welfare, Sarah wrote with much advice on the subject.

Fanny was well enough, but she was in the grip of a fever of a different kind for, in addition to the hot weather, an air of expectancy and excitement was beginning to spread amongst the inhabitants. The town was preparing to enjoy its wealthiest time of the year, but unfortunately, also, with the influx of the rich, the gamblers and the showmen, came the rogues, all intent on returning home the richer by fair means or foul. Miss Greaves was rightfully protective of her girls at this time of the year and made them go out in pairs, she had seen and heard of many incidents in past years which did not please her and found the undignified level to which some humans would stoop in their quest for pleasure quite disgusting. Gangs of ruffians normally descended upon the town for race week, bent on committing heinous crimes, and a lady had to take great care in concealing her purse about her, or it could be gone in a flash.

There were many good aspects of the races, however, which Miss Greaves subscribed to, and one in particular gave her a great deal of pleasure. On Monday of race week a Fancy Works Fair was held in the Mansion House, for the benefit of the children in The School of Industry, and the young ladies of the academy worked hard for weeks prior to the event, making goods to sell. Fanny derived a great deal of satisfaction from the knowledge that her silk paintings would extract money from the wealthy to improve the lot of some poor children, and felt equally rewarded when informed that she had been selected to go to the ball.

With a little of the money which Fanny had left from her allowance, she indulged herself in the purchase of a length of fine apple green muslin, from which she could work herself a new gown. With the help of Miss Riley, the needlework instructress, she constructed a gown of the latest fashion. The delicate green colouring of the material highlighted her golden hair and fine grey eyes, and she concluded that it would be a great pity if her hair did not appear in the latest fashion too, for such an occasion. Fanny carefully counted what was left of her money in order to see if sufficient remained to allow her to indulge herself in her whim. Normally it was quite within her accomplishments to do her own hair, and that of her roommates, but this was her first ball. She intended to make the most of it, even if it meant being short of money for a while.

The other girl chosen to accompany the party to the ball was Hannah Gray, one of Fanny's closest friends, and on reading in the local *Gazette* that a certain Mr. Richard Simpson, hairdresser, would be arriving from London for race week, Fanny persuaded Hannah to go with her to his shop. As was usual for major seasonal events, artisans from London would arrive the week before and establish themselves in back rooms of other businesses in order to ply their trades.

Richard Simpson was a hairdresser and ornamental hair maker of great repute, as he let everyone know, but he was also a great charmer and flatterer, and of course, a great favourite with the ladies in Doncaster.

Full of confidence, due to her familiarity with the trade, Fanny almost dragged the slightly reluctant Hannah to Mr. Simpson's temporary establishment, chattering all the time about the style which she intended to ask for, and wondering also whether she would be able to pass on to her father any ideas from seeing Mr. Simpson at work.

On entering the back room of the shop which Richard Simpson had hired, Fanny held her breath, for standing before her was the most handsome fellow she had ever seen! He was a tall, slender man with dark curly hair, arranged in the most modern of styles. His dark, exquisitely formed features took Fanny's breath away, she quickly closed her mouth for she realised that it had been left open far longer than was politely acceptable, but she could not hide the pink flush on her cheeks. Giving no indication that he had seen her discomfort, he smiled directly at her, a smile extended to melt the heart of any member of the fairer sex. Fanny waited patiently while he arranged a lady's hair, observing the way his hands deftly and gently attended to every detail, until finally, having finished his task, he escorted the client to the door and closed it after her. All Fanny's lively chatter evaporated as she stood there in an uncomfortable silence, staring at the man. Richard Simpson turned to Hannah enquiringly.

'We, we . . . ' she stammered, wishing that Fanny would collect her thoughts and stop looking so strange. 'We . . . wondered if we could come next Wednesday to have our hair dressed for the ball?' She breathed in, glad to have got that out of the way and glanced sideways to find out what was ailing Fanny.

Richard Simpson beamed. 'The ball my dear? Why it would be a pleasure to dress the curls of two such charming young ladies', he answered, with an almost feminine gesture of the hand which quite irritated Hannah.

He turned momentarily to his perfumes, and Hannah took the opportunity to tug at Fanny's sleeve. The feel of a hand on her sleeve broke the spell and Fanny flushed again. She forced herself to speak.

'What time shall we come?' she asked lamely.

'Quite early, my dears, so many ladies have already been in — say eight o'clock, if it is not too early!' He raised an eyebrow for their approval as if he expected them to be horrified at such an early rising, and his dark sultry eyes seemed to Fanny to be the most devastating she had ever seen.

'Yes please, we'll come for eight o'clock, and thank you', she heard herself reply, and unable to think of anything further to say, left the shop.

'Good day', called out Mr. Simpson brightly as he looked up from the appointment ledger.

Outside the shop once more Fanny turned to her companion. 'Oh

Hannah! Isn't he just wonderful, and did you see his beautiful eyes!' Fanny regained her composure now and bubbled over with excitement. 'Aren't you glad we came?'

Well, thought Hannah, so that was what Fanny's strangeness had been all about. She did not like Mr. Simpson at all, he was too full of himself and quite effeminate, handsome he might be but what on earth Fanny saw in him was quite a mystery to her. 'He's alright I suppose, if you like men like that.' Hannah was kind hearted and saw no reason to destroy her friends dreams, for after all nothing could possibly come out of the infatuation.

The day seemed suddenly brighter to Fanny than it had been earlier and took on a new meaning for her. The shop windows seemed much more enticing now and she was completely oblivious to the hesitancy in her friend's approval of Mr. Simpson. She almost skipped back to the academy for she had never felt so alive and elated in her life before. Later, as she lay on her bed allowing her thoughts to enact romantic little adventures around the handsome hairdresser, she was convinced that there could never, ever, be another man in the world to interest her as much as he did.

The other girls found it impossible to comprehend her discourse, as she chattered on incessantly about Mr. Simpson, praising his good looks and charming manner. Tea was eaten in a complete whirl. The evening seemed to drag on painfully slowly and sleep was impossible; it was so long in coming that she feared her face would be ruined the next day by dark rings under her eyes, and all due to the handsome Richard Simpson.

Tuesday morning finally dawned. The excitement at the academy was difficult to suppress, for all the girls, by various means, were to attend the races, but Fanny was to be escorted there as a lady. Gervase was coming! He had sent her a message asking her to be ready by early afternoon. She was, of course, ready far too early and in a constant fidget over this and that about her attire, taking special care to look as elegant and poised as possible. Eventually Fanny could wait no longer and perched herself on a window seat, peering out into the street which bustled with activity, but he was nowhere to be seen. What would she do if he didn't come? She was just beginning to panic and wonder where Gervase might be in all that throng, when she was startled to see that a gig had drawn up before the house and was in fact being driven by Gervase. With a thrill of excitement she seized her bonnet and hurried out to meet him. 'Oh Gervase, a gig! You've bought a gig!' she cried.

He chuckled, entranced by her girlish delight. 'No, I'm afraid not, but it is quite a way to the race course, over a mile, and very busy, so I thought you would like to go in style with your dainty slippers. We must make a good impression, mustn't we?'

'Oh, thank you', Fanny responded. 'All the other girls have to walk there, except Phoebe whose father is coming, and Helen who has the spots.'

'I hope you don't get the spots, Fanny, at least until after the ball tomorrow night. Unfortunately I can't stay beyond morning as I have to be in York before nightfall tomorrow. One day I must take you there, we could take a boat on the river.'

'Oh, please, I would like that', she replied. 'It would have been a wonderful thing to do on a hot day like this. I thought you weren't coming, I sat in the window for ages looking for you.'

'What, and miss the races', he teased. 'You'd better tell Miss Greaves that we're off.'

Fanny giggled, 'Don't be such a tease'. She ran up the steps to tell everyone that she was leaving, and promised to keep a look out for them at the races.

Handing Fanny up into the gig, Gervase felt pleased that he'd thought of hiring it. The heat was increasing as the day wore on and he knew that the bustling crowd would have made the journey tiring; besides he had a surprise in store for Fanny and he needed the gig to make it possible. He had always been a prudent man, rarely spending a penny unnecessarily, but the cost would be worth it for the pleasure it would give them both. The roads were crowded and the pavements too were full of hustle and bustle, all heading in the same direction. Another reason for not walking was the ever present possibility of the attention of pickpockets.

As they reached the open spaces near the race course it wasn't long before Fanny spotted a huge rectangular building with a flat balustrade roof and first floor veranda teeming with people.

'What is that?' enquired Fanny, 'It is such a beautiful building.'

'The Grand Stand, quite elegant isn't it with the column supports, it offers splendid views of the races and surrounding countryside. We'll remain in the carriage and promenade round the perimeter. I'm afraid we're not grand enough for the stand.'

Fanny was amazed to see so many carriages and people crowded together, and thought that it would be nothing short of a miracle if the day passed without some form of accident taking place. Carriages of all shapes and sizes paraded up and down displaying their occupants, all adorned in their finest clothes. The ladies proudly showed off such elaborate decoration that Fanny felt quite a mouse even in her prettiest pale blue dress and ribbon-decorated straw bonnet. Gervase steered the horse with great expertise, which much impressed Fanny, and he himself was quite taken aback by the many admiring glances which Fanny drew from the passing young gentlemen. Fanny was pleased to be higher up in the gig as she could see much more than the people on the ground and she looked forward to taking a closer look at the stalls and booths in the distance.

A sudden roar caused them to spin round in the direction of a large circle of people craning their necks towards the centre of a ring. Being able to see above the crowd to the centre she saw two men engaged in fighting each other.

'The crowd love a prize fight', Gervase remarked. 'It sounds as if someone is getting the upper hand', he added. 'Not the place for a lady I'm afraid.' Thundering hooves momentarily drowned his voice and was followed by a sound mixed with cheering and moaning as the race, which had been taking place, ended. 'In a minute I will get one of the lads to watch the horse so that we can walk. Many families meet at the races, even the gypsies have a gathering spot.' He looked round. 'He looks a likely lad, he'll make more money this week than he normally would in two or three months.' He got down and handed the reins to the youth, 'Now then my lad, take good care of this outfit and there will be an extra shilling in it for you'. He took Fanny's arm and they strolled along, taking in the sights and peering into the gaily coloured booths full of foodstuffs and entertainment. Fanny had never seen a 'peep-show' before. Gervase gently pulled her away and led her to a stall upon which ginger bread was displayed in countless different shapes, making her mouth water in anticipation. During the course of the afternoon they alternated their activities by watching the races and visiting side shows. Fanny loved the horses, with their powerful muscles and long sturdy legs, pounding down the track. Making her promise not to tell anyone of his act, he put a small bet on a horse for her, warning her that it would probably lose anyway. She stood nervously waiting for the race to begin, her heart beating as the horses left the starting point heading in their direction, but the horse came in last, she was glad it wasn't her money that they had put on the horse.

The lively sound of a fiddler caused Fanny to feel extremely light-hearted and on an impulse she insisted, despite his protest, on purchasing a bag of Pontefract liquorice as a present for him, in return for such a wonderful outing. She also bought another bag to send home to her mother with a note, already written, in appreciation for the little parcel of goodies which Sarah had sent.

Having exhausted the many activities in a frantic three hours Gervase led Fanny back to the gig.

'Oh, do we have to go back now, it's not late at all?' pleaded Fanny.

'Come, I have a nice surprise, we'll take the gig where it is more peaceful', he said, refusing to enlighten her.

Fanny did not have to be dragged; she loved surprises and on reaching the gig skipped aboard without waiting for help. Gervase paid the lad, guided the horse between the stationary carriages and climbed aboard himself.

'You shall be my woodland nymph, Fanny, we're going on a ride. I have another surprise but you must wait for that.'

Fanny found it difficult to contain herself. It would be like old times again and she wished the day would never end. Gervase smiled at her eagerness and said, 'You're still wild beneath all that schooling'. Then gently and almost fatherly added, 'Don't be too proud to let a man hand you into a carriage, a man enjoys that privilege, besides, ladies don't rush, not well bred ones'.

'I know, but I can't always wait for other people, it wastes too much time', defended Fanny, knowing that he meant well.

'Don't be too independent, not everyone knows you as I do.'

They drove some distance along rugged tracks and eventually pulled in by a bridge, allowed the horse to drink at the river's edge and then tethered him to a post in the adjacent field.

Fanny could contain herself no longer. 'Oh, Gervase, what is the surprise?'

He laughed and pointed under the seat to a basket. 'Lift the lid.' He watched as she gingerly lifted the lid to be confronted by four or five small muslin parcels and a flagon.

'A picnic.' Fanny could hardly believe her eyes and suddenly realised that they had hardly eaten anything except liquorice and an apple since lunch time. 'I didn't realise how hungry I was.' She helped lift the basket from the gig and together they carried it to the river bank where Gervase stood the flagon in the river to cool. Quickly unwrapping the muslin bundles, he revealed a delicious array of morsels, two pieces of chicken, cold ham and eggs, tomatoes and bread, all to be washed down with a flagon of cider. 'Where on earth did you get all this?' she asked.

'Do you like it is more to the point? Come, let us eat it before the flies get it.' The country air had sharpened their appetites and soon all that remained were the muslin pieces.

The intense heat of the sun mellowed in the early evening, casting long shadows from the trees onto the grass, and time stood still as they rested in the peaceful meadow by the river. Fanny told Gervase of her life at the academy, of her hopes and desires but he could not help but note the wistful sigh in her voice as she spoke of her longing for home. Gervase was saddened by this and realised how much he too had missed their outings. He reassured her that Christmas was not so very far distant and promised to take her dancing on her return, if Bryce offered no objection. At the mention of dancing Fanny remembered the ball and described the gown she had made in such detail that it wasn't difficult for him to imagine how lovely she would look.

Suddenly, tired of talking, Fanny removed her slippers and waded up to her calves in the river, splashing at him as he sat on the sweet-smelling turf. He took a stone and playfully tossed it so that droplets of water wet her face. Beneath the surface nothing had changed and he envied her youthfulness, his own adolescence had been so grim that he wanted hers to last forever. Together they watched a kingfisher as it flew by, resplendent in its colourful plumage. She gasped at its grace. 'It wouldn't stay long enough for me to draw, even if I had my pencil, would it?' she lamented.

They lay on the grass looking up into the clear blue sky and the peace and stillness seemed to engulf them. Fanny stretched out her long limbs and rolled to face him. He inclined his head towards her not really knowing why and his heart tugged as he saw the beauty of her eyes. Fanny laughingly leapt to her feet and ran after a bird which flew over them. Was he going to kiss me then, she mused, or was it her imagination? A rabbit darted across the field, distracting her thoughts. 'Come on, let's try and catch him', she called, and promptly ran after it.

With a sigh for the sudden loss of a special moment, Gervase got to his feet and called to her. 'Come, my dear, we must return soon or they will start to worry, even think that I have absconded with you. Help me put the basket back and give the horse a final drink.' The world seemed to stand still and the peace of the evening was broken only by the creaking and rumbling of the carriage. Gervase held the reins firmly in his large capable hands, his bronzed face enhanced by the evening sun looking almost Romany in appearance. Fanny glanced frequently towards him. The smell of the moorlands on his jacket and the smell of leather always reminded her of home. She'd never thought of it before but in a rugged way he was not unattractive.

'Why aren't you married?' she asked shyly. He considered her question for a long moment and then replied.

'I suppose I have never loved anyone enough, or trusted them sufficiently to ask them to share their life with me. What I did see of my own parents' marriage did not endear me to the idea of matrimony, but then the ladies don't flock for my attention so I suppose I shall remain a bachelor, it suits me well enough. Why do you ask?'

'I just wondered', she proffered. How sad, she thought, he is so very kind and interesting, I suppose he wouldn't have so much time for us if he had a family of his own. She glanced once more at him secretly from behind her lashes, noting his strong face and broad shoulders.

Taken aback by her feelings Fanny suddenly found herself hoping that he might after all kiss her, and the more she thought about it the more she found herself longing to nestle her head into the shoulder of his jacket and feel his face on her cheek. With a sudden movement he pulled firmly on the reins, trying to slow the horse down before it reached a deep rut in the surface of the track — and the spell was broken. Fanny came out of her reverie with a reluctant start. He saw her as a child, she knew, but then she didn't love him anyway for wasn't she in love with Mr. Simpson whom she would see tomorrow? Suddenly the track joined the wider main road approaching the town and as the buildings began to become more numerous Fanny returned completely to reality.

'Ooh Look! It's Mr. Simpson.' That was all she said, staring at a fine looking fellow walking along the pavement. With a sideways glance Gervase saw the tinge of pink rise in her cheeks and wondered just what Mr. Simpson had done to cause such a stir in the child. Not that she was a child anymore, why, only today he had observed in her a change that heralded the onset of womanhood. It would not be long before her eyes would be open to the world, and he would be sorry when she no longer needed him, but he supposed it was inevitable.

Excitement rose in Fanny as she thought of Mr. Simpson and the morrow; they had now come to a halt outside the academy and, on helping her down, Gervase was then sprung upon by Fanny who threw her arms round him, knocking his hat to the ground. 'Thank you for such a heavenly day', she exuberated. 'I will always remember it.'

Retrieving his hat before the horse could trample it into the ground, Gervase turned round, only to find that she had already slipped away from him and into the house.

Fanny burst open the door of the bedroom with such a commotion that the girls were not quite sure what to expect and, breathless after running up the stairs, she gave them all an enthusiastic account of her outing. The day had been a happy one for all of them but they quite envied Fanny in that she had been escorted by a man, whereas they had been carefully chaperoned by a vigilant Miss Greaves. However, there was still tomorrow to look forward to for Hannah and Fanny, and Miss Greaves insisted that they retire to bed early.

The warmth in the house caused Fanny's face to burn and she was horrified on catching a glimpse of herself in the mirror to find that her face had been burnt by the sun; instead of the usual flush of pink, her cheeks were crimson. 'What ever will it look like tomorrow for the ball?' she lamented to herself and almost wept with disappointment. No amount of washing would remove the glow, and Fanny finally retired, dreading the thought of what she would look like in the morning. It was not long before the effects of the day's exercise and fresh air took its toll and drowsiness soon overtook her, engulfing her in a deep sleep. Once, Fanny woke with a start from a wretched dream in which she believed she had overslept and that it had been too late to go to Mr. Simpson's shop, leaving her hair in a dreadful mess for the ball. However, there had been no need to worry, Miss Greaves did not fail to wake them in time and even the night had, after all, taken away the redness from Fanny's cheeks, leaving in its place a delicate bloom.

As she stood with Hannah, once more before the doorway to Mr. Simpson's shop, panic welled up inside Fanny at the thought of meeting him in the flesh, causing her knees to tremble so that she almost fell through the door. Richard Simpson gave them a short bow and led Hannah first to a chair whilst Fanny watched his deft fingers in fascination until it was her turn. Conversation with such a charmer was not easy. She had imagined all manner of dialogue with him but now she was tongue-tied. If this had an adverse effect on the man she was unable to tell, he smiled constantly and behaved as though she was the only person of importance to him. He was good at his work; her father would have approved of the fashionable style he was creating and she would try to make a drawing of it for Bryce to copy. Mr. Simpson's practised art with women drew Fanny out of her embarrassment and it wasn't long before she regained her confidence and chatted excitedly about all manner of things. He raised the soft golden curls which framed her face up onto the top of her head, and tied them with the dark green ribbon which she had purchased earlier in the week. The result was quite charming.

It transpired that he also intended going to the ball and hoped to be able to renew her acquaintance there. This, Fanny felt, must surely mean that he was attracted to her and she did not know how on earth she was going to be able to wait all day before seeing him again.

Miss Greaves abandoned any hopes she had of getting the two girls to concentrate that day. They were, as she put it 'In a sea of dreams', and dismissed them from her sight. For hours the two companions practised their dance steps, each taking a turn in the gentleman's part until it was time to prepare themselves for the ball.

The reflection in the mirror pleased Fanny. She had worked hard at the dress and she saw that it fitted perfectly. A tingle of nervousness ran down her spine and she tugged at the bodice in order to reassure herself. Sarah would have been proud of the vision in the mirror, tall, slender and alluring in the high-waisted gown. Nature too, played no small part in this creation. The adding of dark green velvet ribbons to the underside of the bodice, and green slippers, made an exquisite contrast to the soft green muslin, but Fanny still pulled self-consciously at the low cut front, convinced that too much was revealed. She need not have worried, however, as Miss Riley insisted that an edging of delicate lace be added to the low frontage to maintain the modesty becoming in a young woman.

'Oh, Fanny, you look simply beautiful!' cried Hannah when she saw her friend. 'I wish my hair was that colour.'

Fanny laughed at the expression on her friend's face, for she had been thinking that perhaps Hannah herself, might be a rival for Mr. Simpson's affections. 'I was just going to say the same thing about you', she laughed. The two dresses were not unlike, both were exceedingly pretty, but Fanny had the advantage of height and of course the addition of her golden hair. Miss Greaves would be proud of them both.

The carriage came to a halt some distance form the Mansion House, for there were many carriages already waiting in line to deliver their splendidly attired occupants at its doors. As each empty carriage moved away the nerves of the party from the academy worsened, until Miss Greaves' brother, who was accompanying the party, endeavoured to raise a smile or two by telling amusing stories. In past years the ball had been slow to liven up and they had been guided by Miss Greaves' experience in the matter arriving at nine-thirty, instead of nine o'clock, when dancing was in full swing. Strains of music drifted from the open windows into the warm evening air, giving a magical atmosphere to the Mansion House which was bathed in the light of the street lamps.

Gracefully, helped by a flunkey, the party from the academy left their carriage and ascended the four steps into the glitter of the foyer. Once inside the sumptuous building with its rich furnishings, the sound of music and laughter drew them quickly towards the ballroom.

In the rich glittering light of the chandeliers some of the dancers were already engaged in a Gavotte, and Miss Greaves carefully steered her girls towards the only obviously vacant group of chairs in the far corner of the room, and proceeded to advise them on yet another point of etiquette.

'Remember dears', she glanced round, taking stock of all she saw. 'Remember, don't appear too eager to accept a man's invitation to dance, reluctance is the best ploy, and . . . ' she stopped, leaned across and tapped Fanny on the back of her hand with her fan, 'don't ogle either — it is not polite.'

'No, Ma'am', responded both girls gravely, but Fanny had spotted Mr.

Simpson and was having difficulty in stopping her gaze from wandering in his direction.

Fanny whispered from behind her fan, 'Hannah, he's here, over there by the door, doesn't he look dashing! Do you think he will come over?' she asked hopefully.   Miss Greaves coughed gently, her eyes catching those of the girls with great suspicion, and announced, 'Now, my brother will take each one of you onto the floor in turn, don't forget — heads up — and don't scamper'. Mr. Greaves rose. 'Fanny first, if you please Thomas.' Miss Greaves had it in mind to keep the fidgeting Fanny occupied.

Thomas Greaves was a small dapper man in his fifties, unmarried like his sister, but light on his feet, with a perfect sense of timing and a good sense of humour to match. Often when he came to the academy to tea and rehearsed the girls in their dancing, he had them in stitches with laughter at his little stories. He was much smaller than Fanny and it was easy for her to see over and beyond his head, enabling her to observe Mr. Simpson as he stood across the room, resplendent in his close-fitting trousers and velvet jacket, beneath which his high-collared shirt flaunted an enormous fashionable cravat. Simpson was engaged in earnest conversation with another fellow and seemed totally unaware that there was a dance in progress at all. Mr. Greaves led Fanny back to the ladies, announcing that his sister could count herself proud of her tutorship. When Hannah had completed her turn about the dance-floor, Mr. Simpson invited his sister to partner him and it was during this period that two young men in military uniform appeared before the girls, who shyly accepted their invitation to dance.

The music was enjoyable, but it was with great difficulty that Fanny contained herself; the dance-steps seemed far too slow for the tempo and she would have enjoyed herself much better doing a jig. Mr. Simpson remained with his friend and seemed not even to notice her presence. Fanny was quite put out for she had made a great effort to look her best for him. Escorting the young ladies back to their seats, the soldiers bowed to Miss Greaves who had just returned with her brother. She gave them a stern look, for they had not approached her about dancing with her charges and she did not approve.

A mood of despondency and disappointment then descended on Fanny. Would Mr. Simpson never look her way? He had said how much he would enjoy seeing her at the ball and yet so far he had ignored her. Fanny toyed with her fan because she felt unable to meet Miss Greaves' eyes which she knew were studying her, and fought back a tear. So engrossed was she with her thoughts, she barely heard a voice address Miss Greaves. It was Mr. Simpson asking if he could dance with Miss

Garnett. The suddenness of the request put Fanny off guard and she could barely bring herself to do more than nod in acceptance, much to her own annoyance, and in her fluster she almost trod on his toes. Unable to relax, Fanny once more found herself tongue-tied and each time the music brought them together she froze. For days she had longed for this moment but her feet were as lead. His breath smelt strongly of liquor and she found the familiarity with which he held her rather frightening. Bending over, he whispered into her ear. 'You look lovely tonight.' She had the feeling that he was mocking her and felt rather embarrassed. Did he think her a hussy? She was rather relieved when the dance came to an end and she hoped that he would not ask her again, for if she refused him Miss Greaves would suspect some impropriety.

In despair she asked to be excused for a few moments and retreated to a less crowded side room. The pots of beautiful gaillardias and fuchsias in the room did nothing to lighten her spirits as slowly she regained her composure and started to walk towards the entrance into the ballroom, but before she could do so, she saw Richard Simpson nearby with his friend who was chatting rather loudly. She drew back for fear of being seen.

'Methinks the young lady in green has a fancy for you Richard, a pretty little thing but a little naive for you I would have thought — not really interested, are you?'

'Me? Not a bit!' replied Simpson, 'The pretty young piece came into the shop. When she's not tongue-tied she chatters incessantly. No — she's not for me — I like 'em with a bit more flesh on 'em, come on let us get another drink.'

Fanny drew back even further behind the door lest they should see her and add humiliation to the discomfort and hurt which she felt. How could they talk about her like that. She had heard of such men before but had expected there to be more obvious signs of weakness in their character. Richard Simpson had looked flawless.

Returning to her seat she found Thomas Greaves ready to dance with her again, and fighting back the tears she found herself hating men. Throughout the evening Miss Greaves noted with satisfaction that the girls had behaved well. It had occurred to her that Fanny, who was headstrong, might have been a problem, but she had been demure, even a little subdued. Miss Greaves was totally unaware that Fanny was not only nursing hurt pride but was feeling rejected by the whole world.

The rest of the week proved to be rather miserable; a promised visit to the theatre had to be cancelled because Helen's spots turned out to be a serious bout of food poisoning caused by an infected piece of meat. The heat and flies had been particularly bad and although the kitchen staff had taken great care with the food, somehow the meat had become contaminated. Strangely, not all the girls had been affected at the same time, but Helen was not a strong girl and seemed to pick up infections more quickly than the others. She had apparently eaten meat on the Monday whilst they were at the Fancy Works Fair, which she didn't attend, but by Thursday morning all the girls of the academy were affected.

Fanny was not disappointed by the cancellation, as she found Shakespeare rather tedious, and having read 'As You Like It', in preparation for the visit to the theatre, was quite relieved not to have to see it performed on the stage. The only part of the tale which she thought had merit was the clever way in which Rosalind had disguised herself as a boy. In preference she would continue to read 'Pride and Prejudice' by Miss Austen which one of the girls had smuggled into the academy, in fear of it being found by Miss Greaves or one of the assistants who strongly disapproved of such romantic nonsense.

The infection kept the girls marooned in the house for some time, whilst the careful cosseting of Miss Greaves and her ladies protected them from a situation which often caused great tragedy in poorer sections of the community. While Fanny was suffering from stomach pains and nausea she cared for nothing, not even the unpleasant incident with Mr. Simpson, she wanted to go home. Gradually, as she returned to her old self, she thought of the poor, who suffered similar sicknesses with such regularity due to the insanitary conditions, and she felt guilty at her own good life. In this light the arrogant Mr. Simpson seemed of little consequence, and she hoped that he would get whatever fate he deserved.

Christmas was approaching rapidly now and providing that the roads were passable she would be going home, nothing else mattered.

Chapter 3

*Y*ork *was at its best* now that the gentry had chosen to go to Doncaster for the races, and Gervase preferred the quieter atmosphere of the town in which to do business. He loved this old place, with its ancient and modern buildings, especially the new ones with their elegant lines and colourful walls, which stood in sharp contrast to those of Sheffield where everything had developed in a jumbled fashion, and where most of the buildings were in a crumbling, dilapidated state. He realised, of course, that but for the war, they would have been pulled down years ago.

He strode purposefully along the cobblestones of Lendal Street in the direction of the river, where he would be able to relax and gather his thoughts ready for his business appointments which had been arranged for the following morning. He stood watching the water as it flowed swiftly by, leaving him in a world of his own. There was no one who knew him there to interrupt his thoughts, and day-dreaming was a luxury which he seldom allowed himself, for he had always worked hard with one purpose in mind, to achieve moderate success. Life for him had changed for the better the day he had become acquainted with Bryce Garnett and his family, and this contact with his new found friends had given him a sense of belonging and a determination to succeed. He reflected on the long hours of drudgery which he had worked for his unbending father and realised now that his father had not hated him, but in his own unhappiness had kept him at arms length to avoid emotional involvement. Gervase had toiled with purpose in mind, being determined to learn all he could in the printing trade, and he had set out to master each stage of the work, from typesetting and bookbinding to the intricacies of business methods. His father had died quite suddenly, leaving him only halfway towards his goal and Mr. Wells, the replacement chief clerk, was not only ungrateful for Gervase's efforts, but did all he could to obstruct his further progress, fearing his competition. It was fortunate that at this time James Montgomery, journalist and publisher of the local *Iris*, in Hartshead, required a bookbinder with some willingness to travel abroad and Mr. Wells had been more than willing to recommend Gervase for the position, thus resolving any possible conflict in the future.

War-ravaged Europe had not been the safest of places for a young man of twenty-four to venture in, but his travels coincided with the short-lived period of peace in 1805, and these journeys gave him the self-assurance which he had previously lacked. As an artisan he was generally allowed access to cultural European centres and, providing that no evidence or suspicion of spying arose, his journeys were unhindered. Initially he had travelled with an older man who was glad of his assistance and company, but Gervase learned quickly and was soon able to work on his own. His experiences in travelling broadened his outlook considerably and for that he would always be grateful, since it resulted in him being able to see beyond the narrow-minded constraint of the town Burgesses and business men. Religion also fascinated him, not so much the need for it but the application people in other cultures made of it, for these encompassed many interesting and new ideals. No one belief embraced all these points, each in its own way offered comfort and extracted devotion, but religion sometimes was the cause of war and much suffering, and often raised in men the feeling of superiority over others. He wanted none of it. His admiration for Montgomery was strong but he had little stomach for his hymns, though he realised that their publication was of financial benefit to the firm. Years of good steady work with Montgomery had enabled Gervase to accumulate a fair amount of possessions one way and another, until now at the age of thirty-four he was financially secure.

Now the war was over, Gervase could see a bright future for the printing trade. The public were demanding a greater freedom of the press and desired literature of a humbler kind, causing the growth in the number of circulating libraries to increase.

The opportunity had now arisen for him to buy a business of his own in the High Street, and he was in York to ensure that his contacts would be able to supply him with raw materials and goods, if his bid at the auction next week was successful. He had also come to sell a few pieces of jewellery left to him by his grandmother, which he had kept for just such a need as this. Had he a wife then he might have kept the items, but as yet he had never felt a strong desire to share his life with another. He had decided to keep one item, however, a beautiful dress brooch with a garnet stone mounted in gold, which he loved too much to part with.

The premises on offer in the High Street were leasehold, but it was the contents which attracted Gervase most, consisting of shop fittings, some of which were quite worn, toys, which were not really in his line of business, and presses. These presses were nearly new, as were the founts of type and other printing accessories, and the order books were full. Gervase had chosen to have an agent bid on his behalf, because he feared that if Montgomery found out about his ambitions, and the bid failed, he would end up out of work. James Shaw, the late proprietor, had a good reputation for quality work in the town and, providing Gervase could get started quickly, there was no reason why the business shouldn't continue to prosper. The shop had the added advantage of having living accommodation upstairs. He could rent it out to bring in extra money, or house an apprentice there as part of his wages. Gervase didn't fancy leaving his own comfortable house, with its spacious rooms and large garden; he wasn't that short of money. The garden reminded him of his mother, who had died when he was young. She had pottered around there raising a couple of chickens in a corner, and growing flowers amongst the vegetables. These were the only times when he could recall her being truly happy.

After deliberating for some considerable time, Gervase, feeling quite pleased and confident about his plans, left the river to continue on its journey and retraced his steps back through the town to his lodging house. The route took him past a bookshop and printers of high repute. It was not with idle curiosity that he decided to enter these premises, for he was quite keen to make note of the layout of its merchandise, the positioning of counters and the like. He knew that it would be some time before his own shop became as organised or attractive as this one. Whilst browsing through a pile of old books he spotted one containing bird illustrations, it was bound in beautiful Morocco leather; the fine detail of each etching was such that Gervase could not resist buying it for Fanny. He would give it to her on one condition, that in return she would reproduce the kingfisher in the book onto one of her silk paintings, just for him.

The following day, business concluded to his satisfaction, Gervase caught the coach for the long tedious journey home, preferring to sit up-top in spite of the dust, rather than suffer the sweltering heat inside the crowded coach. There would not be time to call in on Fanny on the way back but he would at least change seats when he got to Doncaster for one inside the coach, for the evening air could be quite cold in September.

The coach pulled in at Selby on the way and Gervase chatted amiably with the driver as they drank at the post inn whilst patiently waiting for the horses to be changed.

The driver, sensing Gervase to have a sympathetic ear, remarked, 'Disgraceful it is, time more was done about 'ooligans what apprehend us drivers'.

'More trouble?' enquired Gervase, who was quite used to hearing drivers complain.

The man grumbled heatedly, 'Only that some idiot removed the aft pin from the wheel of a coach near Doncaster, could have bin really nasty that could.'

Gervase quickly agreed with him, thinking to himself however, that the childish behaviour of some of the coach drivers themselves was nothing short of vandalism. Then he asked, 'Not racing today are we?'

'Given it up Guv, some of these old coaches ain't safe to race with anymore. 'Sides you never know these days if company spies are out to catch you. I can't afford no 'efty fine on my wages. I ain't as young as I used ter be, I don't need to keep up with the lads no more, I keep my job 'cus I'm reliable.' He lowered his glass and rose to his feet. 'Time ter go, best get this lot back on board and away.'

Gervase decided to take the longest route home after alighting from the coach, in order to stretch his legs. There was a distinct chill in the autumn air and when he reached the house it felt cold after being un-lived in for several days. He set about lighting the fire which he had left ready prepared in the grate before relaxing into a comfortable arm-chair. He was used to the house being quiet, but tonight the stillness disturbed him, leaving him restless and even the soft light from the lamp and the friendly glow of the fire could not dispel the sense of loneliness which he felt. He knew that the feeling would pass but even so it unnerved him, and he compelled himself to tackle some of his outstanding paperwork, before retiring to bed.

The ensuing week passed quickly enough and the day of the auction arrived causing butterflies in the pit of Gervase's stomach each time he thought of the bidding ahead.

The sale-room above the 'Tontine Inn' was crowded with people, many of them just curious bystanders enjoying the atmosphere, and he began to wish that he hadn't arrived quite so early; in fact there was no real need for him to be there at all for he had given his agent instructions as to how high the bid could go. He had often attended booksales on behalf of his employer, but possibly in future, he would attend them on his own behalf, as there was a growing market for second-hand books and he would need a constant supply for the shop. He wondered how Montgomery would take the news of his leaving. Montgomery himself had started off his career as a runaway who had applied for a job as a newspaper clerk and finally ended up owning the paper. These days, however, he was becoming too interested in publishing his hymns and poems and Gervase could see the day coming, not too far ahead, when he would retire. Gervase was no newsman and would have no desire to take over when the day came. If his bid today was a success then his future would be secure enough. There was little point in hanging around the salesroom in a state of nervousness, so in a sudden about-turn Gervase left the inn and returned to Hartshead where he worked, aiming to return at seven o'clock to hear the outcome of the auction.

He had succeeded! The business was his. He had hardly hoped for such an answer but as he had managed to obtain all that he wanted for far less money than he had anticipated, he was well satisfied.

The tension that had gripped him during the past week disappeared leaving him feeling elated and satisfied with his success. Now he could plan ahead. It was a relief to him to know that there was a small amount of capital spare, for there were many items which he still required; not only did he need paper and other necessities, but he wanted a horse. A horse would speed up the collection and delivery of orders and he had seen an advertisement in the *Iris* that morning which aroused his interest, a sale of horses and gigs which was to take place at the Corn Market in a few days time. As Gervase wasn't interested in obtaining a grand outfit, just one to suit his basic needs and pocket, he would bid for this himself. Whether, from now on, there would be sufficient hours in the day to fulfil all that would require doing, was another matter. He would work for himself and be his own master; and with no family ties to hold him back, he could put his heart into the venture. Now to face Montgomery.

There was no antagonism shown by Montgomery when he received Gervase's news. Yes, he was more than sorry and very disappointed to lose him after all these years, but as the situation stood now there was nothing to be done, Gervase had completed the deal over the High Street shop and all that he hoped was that they would be friendly rivals, and good friends.

Immediately after Gervase had signed all the necessary documents relating to his new acquisition he headed for the shop and proudly unlocked the door. The smell that greeted him was that of old paper, linseed oil and stale bodies and he immediately threw open the windows. Indeed the machinery was fairly new but not well maintained and the stock and counters were in a complete shambles. A formidable amount of rubbish had been allowed to accumulate, mainly because James Shaw had been loath to part with any item which might have a use in the future. Clearing this was going to be Gervase's first priority. Even as a boy the risk of fire in printing shops had been impressed upon him, and discarded rubbish and carelessness invited fire.

In spite of all Gervase's hard work and good intentions on taking over the shop he still encountered problems, mainly concerning the two boys who had been previously employed by the late Mr. Shaw. Both boys had been used to a lax form of discipline which Gervase set

out to change, and this resulted in Edwin, who had served a full apprenticeship, promptly applying for a position with a rival printer in Snig
Hill and refusing any offered incentive whatsoever to stay. Tom, on the
other hand, had no option in the matter, he had to stay because as odd
job boy and manual worker he was totally unqualified to find other employment. He had been connected in some way with the previous proprietor's wife and the man had been obliged to keep Tom on for fear
of displeasing her. Gervase had no choice either; Tom knew where
everything was and how to operate the machinery, and until a better replacement could be found, the boy had a job. He resented Gervase's
interference but was wise enough to conceal it most of the time. A notice in the local newspaper asking for a suitably qualified apprentice to
replace Edwin brought no response, consequently Gervase was forced
to place further advertisements in newspapers as far away as Nottingham. The response was much slower than expected, and both Gervase
and Tom were forced to work up to eighteen hours a day in order to
complete the work already on the order book. There was little time
spare for contemplating the coming social whirl of Christmas but then
it had always been a lonely time for Gervase and he preferred to be
busy.

Fanny could dream of nothing else but Christmas. The weather was
mild for the time of year and the roads were in a good state for travelling, thus enabling her to return home in the week preceding the festivities. Sarah was clearly over the moon with joy to see her daughter return after being away so long, and she proudly observed in Fanny a new
confidence that pleased her, for she was turning into an elegant and
beautiful young woman. Now that Fanny was home again the house
would become alive and the visitors would call in more often, bringing
their laughter with them. Sarah's other children had homes of their
own, oh yes, they called in, and young Bryce still worked in the shop,
but she felt that they called on them more out of duty than desire.
Fanny's illness in October had caused her to lose weight but her spirits
were high and because she had longed so much for Christmas she was
determined to enjoy it. When she was not helping in the house or
shop, Fanny took to taking long walks in the crisp, bright afternoons
and sought out the familiar haunts which she had missed so much.
    The buildings looked pokier than she remembered, sootier and
more impoverished, and she felt as though she had been away much
longer than eleven months. There was also a look of discontentment
on the sullen faces of some of the workers as they passed her by in
their shabby clothes. Previously Fanny had wandered freely, unaware of

any tension, but the truth dawned on her as she looked down on her own attire, that she was obviously well-dressed and well-fed, her bearing was that of a gentlewoman, but they were ragged and half-starved. She was moved by the plight of children running barefoot in the cold, some begging and others just staring back vacantly. Doncaster was far away in life-style as well as in miles, and she looked now searching for the truth and hating what she saw.

A leering drunk lunged at her from a doorway, causing her to freeze in fear — perhaps the impression given by her frozen pose held the man back, for he turned and shuffled away, pathetically perhaps, but the incident was significant enough to warn Fanny against wandering the back streets as she had previously done.

It was a very shaken Fanny who emerged from the back alleys into the busier part of the town, and as she crossed the empty graveyard to reach High Street, she paused to calm herself. The world which she had known as a child was disappearing fast, the scales of innocence were being torn from her eyes, leaving her sadder and wiser, and needing to talk to Gervase.

Where was he? He had bought a shop, that she knew, but she was puzzled by the fact that he had not called at the house during the three days since her return. Surely he must know that she was back — curiosity burned within her and she decided there and then to visit him at the shop. All that Fanny could remember of Mr. Shaw's shop was its dreariness, owing to the premises being set back from the other frontages and therefore in shadow. Today, however, the tiny panes of glass in the bow windows were illuminated by hanging lamps which beckoned to the passers-by.

Fanny entered the shop, which smelled dingy, looked dingy and felt dingy, and the only welcoming thing she could see in the place, apart from the lamps in the window, was the glow from the stove in the corner. The surly face of the youth who came from the back room in answer to the doorbell was much less friendly than either of these.

'Can a get yer owt, missis?' he grunted, in anything but a pleasant tone of voice.

'I don't think so', replied Fanny, horrified as the lad wiped his nose across his sleeve. 'Would you be good enough to tell Mr. Webster that Miss Garnett is here?'

'Ees gon art, an sez if it's important yu'll afta cum back.'

'Just remember to tell him I called', insisted Fanny.

'Suit thi sen', was the rude reply she got. Fanny cringed at his crudeness and wondered where on earth Gervase had got the boy from; it hardly seemed good for business.

Turning to leave the shop she almost knocked the pile of books from Gervase's arms as he came through the door. The look of pleasure on his face when he realised who it was brightened the room up considerably.

'Well, well, Fanny, so you've found out about my little venture then!' He spoke whilst stacking the pile of books on the counter before they fell from his arms, and placed his hat on top of them. 'I've just purchased these at an auction — come and see.'

'You didn't tell me about all this. You are a dark horse, you must have been planning this that day when you came through Doncaster', she chided playfully, 'I tell you all my secrets'.

He watched Fanny's slender fingers as they toyed with the new books. 'I didn't dare hope that all would go as planned, or even if I would have the courage to go through with it. It's going to take time to sort things out, the shop's in a terrible mess and I need an apprentice, but there is plenty of work so far. I'm my own boss, Fanny, even if the work is hard.' He looked up, as Fanny bent her head close to his and whispered in his ear.

'Who is that dreadful boy who came in just now?' she lamented.

Gervase whispered back as if sharing a secret. 'Unfortunately the best I have at the moment.' He straightened up and added on a more serious note, 'It's Tom, he's had a rough time but works hard enough doing all the heavy, dirty jobs while I compose type and bind books. I've got an older fellow coming in a few days time, from Nottingham. He's just finished his apprenticeship and wants to make a fresh start with another company. He trained with a company I dealt with over there so I know he should be fairly good. I'm going to allow him to stay in the two upstairs rooms so that he can guard the premises'. He turned to her enquiringly, 'Come, what tales have you to tell?' He watched as the sparkle in her eyes dimmed and noted how much thinner she had become.

'Not much really happened. After the ball the whole academy went down with food poisoning, and we were all too sick to go very far.' She paused for a moment, 'That's all'.

'You've lost a little weight — I can tell.' He looked at her slim figure. 'God, but she's going to be beautiful', he thought to himself.

Fanny refrained from telling him about the incident which had just taken place in the back street. She would just have to be more careful in future. Besides she was curious about the shop and began poking around amongst the shelves and drawers. He left her there, feeling quite unneeded, and returned to the work which he had begun earlier in the day.

She could see it all now, rows of shelving neatly stocked with books, all the brass inkstands polished and arrayed, along with the quills and globes, in a display in the window. She rather liked the idea of working amongst all these beautiful works of literature and decided to sound Gervase out on the idea.

Gervase did not hear her approach above the thud of the press and only became aware of her presence as traces of her perfume filled the air. 'You Madam, have been raiding one of your father's perfume bottles again. Doesn't he wonder why they go down when you are around?' he teased, while at the same time pushing a curl of hair from her face back under the bonnet, from which it had escaped. How lovely she looked standing there almost flirting with him. 'What is it now?' he asked suspiciously.

'Well, I was wondering' she paused deliberately, 'when I'm finished at the academy, could I come and work for you? I've learned book-keeping and I could organise the stock, and serve the customers.' The last sentence came out in a rush, leaving her quite breathless.

'If, when you've finished your schooling, I'm still in business after all these interruptions, I may just consider taking on a decorative assistant.'

'Men!' she retorted.

Gervase chuckled. 'I have a small gift for you when I call tomorrow night, so be good or you won't get it.'

'What is it?' she pleaded.

'Wait until tomorrow night.' He watched her as she turned and flounced good-heartedly from the room and out of the shop. He admired her lively spirit and good humour, for it took the dullness out of everyday toil, and he was quite pleased now that he had bought the book for her.

Each Christmas the Garnett family followed a strict set of rituals but, whereas each member was expected to join in the fun, none ever felt compelled to do so. On the evening before Christmas Eve Bryce usually provided his own little treat, taking the whole family, grandchildren and all, to an equestrian circus which annually arrived in the town for the festivities. This year the travelling company were to perform 'Wallric the Lion'. No one ever complained of the cold as they all trotted excitedly down Spring Street to the circus, for the children were such a handful that rounding them up kept everyone warm. The children sat snuggled under their capes and blankets, enthralled by the funny antics of the animals, and tears of laughter ran down their little cheeks. Even old Bryce couldn't prevent his eyes from misting up as he laughed at the animals prancing around.

Fanny loved the atmosphere of these visits and she sat next to her father, happy to be home amongst them again. Somehow her father looked older than she remembered him; his face was drawn and tired, but then he too had not been well during her time away and he had been left with an irritating cough which worried them all. She thought that if only he could give himself a break from the hard work it would give him time to recover.

The following morning Fanny woke to the delicious smell of baking gingerbread. Sarah had already been up for hours, as she usually was each Christmas Eve morning, making the bread for the children. Every Christmas Sarah also made each grandchild a rag doll or animal and this year was no exception. With all the scraps of cloth which she had collected during the year she made lions, hopefully to look like Wallric, though her efforts in this respect led to some amusing results. She looked forward to the early evening when, after tea, all the children would be brought to the house for this special treat.

By early evening the weather had changed completely. The dry crisp afternoon gave way to torrential rain which lashed at the window panes, turning passers-by into sodden miserable wretches. The wild outside elements excited Fanny as she listened to the drumming beat of the rain, grateful that she was inside where everything was cosy and warm.

One by one the families arrived, soaked to the skin. The house was soon festooned with countless dripping coats and completely overrun by scampering children, whilst their parents clustered together in the tiny living kitchen. For two hours the house was in turmoil; parents sipped their spiced wine and ate the cold supper which Sarah and Fanny had spent all afternoon preparing, whilst the children were banished into the shop to play. Bryce had removed all the razors long before they arrived in case they hurt each other, then he left them to play with the contents of an ancient wooden chest in the corner of the shop. The children loved emptying the chest of its old wigs and with Fanny's help they tried them on. Some were so large that they covered their faces as well as their heads. Fanny found the beautiful chestnut one that had been her favourite as a child and rescued it from their clutches.

'Ooh, Aunty Fanny, please try it on', one of the children pleaded, until one by one they all chanted gleefully at her, 'Don't be a spoilsport, try it on' they chorused. 'Please.'

Fanny obliged, to keep them quiet and to see the look on their happy faces.

'It doesn't look like you at all. It makes you look pretty!' whooped one of the boys. Fanny wasn't sure whether to box his ears or not at this remark and playfully tweaked his nose.

It was almost time for them to go home and Fanny made them tidy away all the wigs. She lovingly ran her hand over the one she had worn and took it up to her room until they had gone so that the children would not play with it anymore. Before the children left they formed a little queue in front of Sarah's chair to receive their ginger bread and Wallrics, then off they went, leaving the house peaceful once more.

With the invasion over, Sarah, Bryce and Fanny sat exhausted amongst the debris of dirty dishes and left over crumbs, enjoying the peace but Fanny listened for the sound of footsteps, knowing that Gervase would be here soon, and wondering what his little gift would be. The sudden knock at the door took her by surprise, for the heavy rain outside had deadened all other sounds, and she hastened to let him in.

'My, it's good to come in out of all that rain.' He removed his tall hat which dripped water from its brim and passed it to Fanny to hang over the sink. 'It looks as though the French have invaded after all', he remarked as he looked around the room.

Sarah returned his smile, 'It does look rather like it — come and sit down. Fanny, get Gervase a glass of wine and a piece of gingerbread'.

Fanny brought the wine and joined the two men who were sitting at the table deep in conversation with each other. Sarah nodded contentedly in the big armchair by the fire, oblivious to them all, and free from the toils of the day.

'How's the shop getting on?' Bryce asked of Gervase.

'It's hard work but I'm optimistic. I was expecting a fellow from Nottingham to arrive any day now but I received a letter from him today to say that he won't be arriving for another week, he's too sick to travel.' He sipped from his glass, 'I could do with him as soon as possible but I suppose another week won't hurt'.

'Let's hope he's good at his job. There's a shortage of trained apprentices at the moment.' Bryce turned and looked at Sarah. 'Fanny, just prop your mother up will you before she falls out of that chair.'

She gently eased her mother back into the chair, it had been quite a day for poor Sarah and she was no longer interested in the cares of the world. Fanny turned to Gervase enquiringly. 'What have you done with my surprise?'

'She doesn't change, does she Gervase!' Bryce leaned across and filled his pipe. 'Keep her waiting, lad, I would.'

'Actually I do have a little problem. I ought really to have cleaned out the two upstairs rooms for this fellow when he arrives. I looked up there today and it really is a disgrace. I was wondering if Sarah knows some woman or other willing to do it for me. I'll pay, of course, but I just haven't the time to spare to clean the darn place out myself.'

'I'll do it for you if I can have my surprise', Fanny spoke up quickly, then added, 'Really, I'd like to help you and I do have a little spare time on my hands.' The more she thought about the offer the more pleased she was that she had volunteered; it was one way in which she could repay him for visiting her in Doncaster.

'I would be grateful', he replied, concluding that he had kept her waiting long enough in his little guessing game, and handed her the package. He was extremely grateful for her offer of help and considered himself fortunate to have such good friends. Gervase watched her face as she unwrapped the surprise, and saw the joy in her eyes as she turned some of the pages. 'Look at page seventeen' he instructed.

'I can't believe it, it's a Kingfisher — Oh Gervase, I'll always treasure it.' Their eyes met. His were kind and invoking, and Fanny blushed at their intimacy for she knew he was also remembering that day by the river, and she smiled back at him, enjoying their little secret.

'I would like to ask you a favour in return. Would you paint the kingfisher onto silk for me?' He wanted the intimacy to go on.

'I shall take great pleasure in painting one for you', she replied shyly, 'but first I will come and help you. Will the day after tomorrow be convenient?'

It was agreed that she would go to the shop at ten o'clock on the appropriate day and Gervase would ensure that Tom gathered together all the necessary tools for her to work with.

Gervase had many rare and precious books himself and he was pleased to observe the care and gentleness with which Fanny turned the pages of her new acquisition before placing it in the old Chippendale bookcase for safe keeping. The bookcase was Bryce's pride and joy, and was the only decent piece of furniture which the family had managed to retain out of a number of pieces left to him by his father. The rest had been sold off in leaner times to pay the rent. Bryce's father had been a learned man who had gone to great lengths to ensure that his children could read and write, and this was one ideal which Bryce had endeavoured to repeat with his own children. Fanny carefully folded the wrapping tissue and placed it in the map drawer beneath the bookcase, for further use.

Christmas day came and went, offering Bryce, Sarah and Fanny a welcome break from the humdrum routine of work; it was set aside for quiet enjoyment and, apart from a visit to church in the evening, they did little else but relax. The cough which had distressed Bryce over the past months seemed a little easier and Fanny was relieved of some of her anxiety over him.

The two rooms to be cleaned above the shop in High Street were sparsely furnished and looked almost exactly as the previous owner had left them. There was even a depression in the mattress which gave the impression that James Shaw had only just got out of bed. It was more than obvious that Mr Shaw had been as lax in his housekeeping as he had been in his discipline of the boys, for dust lay everywhere and there were even mouse droppings on the mattress.

Fanny threw the poky windows open wide in disgust, hoping that the cold wind which whistled in would dispel the awful smell from the room. The sweeping, dusting and tidying took her most of the day and she stopped only in order to eat the bread and cheese which Sarah had brought to her. She stood back to appraise her work, satisfied that little more could be done in the fading light and she resolved to return early the following morning to finish off.

It was with some surprise, that, on returning the next day, she found a further depression in the bed and also that the candle snuffer had been taken off the candle. Perhaps she had been mistaken! Gervase confirmed that no one had even been upstairs since she had asked them not to, until she had completed her work. Fanny had quite enjoyed the challenge of creating a pleasant home from the veritable tip which she had found there, and she decided to fetch a few items from home to make the place more homely. She replaced the moth-eaten curtains with an old but presentable pair which Sarah could manage without, filled a chipped jug with dried flowers and returned yet again the next morning with a few bits and pieces which she managed to talk Sarah into parting with. This time the snuffer was exactly where she had left it, but there was another depression in the bed. Had she forgotten to straighten it out after her previous discovery? Fanny shook her head and gave up!

In response to her call, Gervase climbed the stairs, closely followed by Tom, who, after hearing Gervase's exclamation of delight, could only respond grudgingly, 'Awl reet a suppoas'. She didn't like Tom, but managed not to let her feelings show, Tom, on the other hand, made it quite plain that he wasn't fond of her either, and a look of resentment flashed across his face when Gervase praised Fanny.

The days which followed Christmas brought with them the usual lull in the season's social calendar, and there was always a flat spell after all the excitement was over. The probability of there being extremely bad weather for the next two months made spring seem so very far away. Bryce was not his usual cheerful self. The break had only arrested his cough a little, and Sarah was becoming increasingly anxious about him, even to the point of persuading him to give up his pipe. Fanny, too, was worried and was reluctant to return to Doncaster. Even the memory of the academy was fading into the past and she wanted to remain at home.

Suddenly, as often is the case, a small event filled the gap and created great excitement. Gervase, in his gratitude to Fanny for all her hard work, sent Tom round with a special invitation, requesting her to accompany him to a dance the following evening, at the Assembly Hall in Norfolk Street. Fanny, of course, was delighted. Gervase had spent a considerable amount of time printing this special invitation, just for Fanny, and she was touched by the gesture and rather proud to see her name in print. She had brought with her the green dress and accessories which she had worn for the ball, hoping that she would be given such an opportunity as this and also to show her mother her handiwork.

The following evening Fanny stood once more in her precious gown, waiting this time for Gervase to collect her.

'Do I look alright — will he like it?' Fanny implored of her mother, yet again.

'You will do — now stop wittering on or else I shall refuse to answer you next time you ask', Sarah chided her daughter. She had to admit it, she had never seen Fanny as radiant as she was tonight; of all her children Fanny had been the one whom she had spoilt the most. Warm memories stirred within Sarah as she remembered the first night that she had waited excitedly for Bryce to collect her. Now they were old and grey but the warmth was still there. However, she and Bryce had been in love and Fanny and Gervase were not.

'He's here, mother', whispered Fanny, suddenly struck by a bout of nervousness, as she glanced into the mirror for reassurance. This time her hair was different, Bryce had softened the style in her sketch, bringing the curls around her face in order to maintain the sweet innocence of youth. Had he been working in London, Fanny believed that he would have been one of the best hairdressers in the capital. She stood where Gervase would see her the moment he entered the room, and waited for his reaction. She was not to be disappointed, for the look of admiration on his face was plain enough to see.

'Sarah, is she real, or am I dreaming?' he teased. 'I really came for Fanny but as she's not here perhaps I could take this delightful creature instead. You can have the truffles I bought for Fanny.'

At the mention of truffles Fanny sprang to life. 'You enjoy teasing me — don't you? Perhaps I will stay at home and eat the truffles instead of going to the dance.' Seizing her cloak and slippers she waited impatiently while he talked to Sarah and it seemed that they would never leave.

Gervase, in spite of his size, was extremely light on his feet and well practised in his dance steps, and Fanny felt that many looks of admiration were being directed their way. However, she could not help but wonder where the expertise had been obtained from as she had never seen him in such social circumstances before. He was obviously well known, for he nodded and chatted with many of the couples, and she was quite shocked to note how young and attractive some of the single young ladies were. She was suddenly struck by the realisation that there was a part of Gervase's life about which she knew nothing, and she felt strangely excluded. Gervase, however, was perfectly charming and attentive, escorting her as though she were a china doll, and she loved every minute of it, refusing to think further than the present, for tomorrow she would have to pack, ready to return to Doncaster the following day.

Chapter 4

ohn Andrews sat dejectedly staring out through the coach windows. He felt miserable. The shocking cold which had laid him low for the last two weeks had left him with a hacking cough and little desire to do anything energetic at all. He reflected bitterly on the happenings of the past six months, believing that their pressures and viciousness had contributed to the breakdown of his health. He had been hounded, compelled to hide in his uncle's damp and dingy cellar, and now he was being driven away from his beloved Nottingham to this godforsaken town.

He had always been a robust young man, an optimist and perhaps a dreamer, but all he had ever really wanted to do was to help his fellow men. He was no modern day Robin Hood, but he did have high ideals for which he was sadly misunderstood. If it had not been for his uncle's friendship with the Mayor of Nottingham he would now be rotting in some gaol or prison hulk. The damp of the cellar had seeped into his bones, and the isolation into his soul, until he had become so ill with cold that his uncle had feared for his life, and sought to find him a position out of town. Of all the places to choose, Sheffield, with its smoke and grime, appealed to him the least, but there was no other choice, for if he had remained any longer in such conditions he would probably have died.

The circumstances surrounding his downfall were only an extension of the feelings of the majority of the working population, as a civil war of words raged from one end of the kingdom to the other, in a fight against the Government's proposed renewal of the property and income tax. The tax was originally imposed only to raise funds for the war, but the war was over and the poor could not afford the tax, and of course the rich didn't want it either. Now the Government not only wished to keep the tax but to increase it by a proposed five percent. The population needed to organise on a united front if they were to stand any chance of successfully opposing the Government. However, half the population were afraid to speak out for fear of losing what little they had, and the remainder, through deprivation and misery, no longer had the will to fight. Nevertheless, petitions were being organised in many areas of the country and many thousands of signatures collected, to be sent to the House of Commons before the original Act expired in April.

As a fervent supporter of the abolition of the original bill, as well as the proposed increase, John Andrews had made his views known all too publicly in the ale houses of Nottingham. With the help of his flute, he had encouraged his fellow drinkers to sing subversive songs against the bill, an act which had not been appreciated by the local magistrates. Many times he had been compelled to retreat via the back entrance of an inn after a warning from a lookout. His employer, Charles Sutton of the *Review*, had been sentenced in July to eighteen months imprisonment for alleged contempt of the Government, insulting the army and encouraging Luddites; a punishment for printing a satirical letter, allegedly from a British soldier in America. The soldier claimed that he had done worse things there as a war hero than he had ever done when frame-breaking back home as a criminal. Sutton was not the only publisher to suffer from the lack of press freedom; even Montgomery in Sheffield had been placed twice in York Castle for similar offences.

John Andrews' last escape had been a narrow one. He fled from an inn to seek refuge at his uncle's house, and arrived only seconds before the Mayor's warning was delivered. His uncle had immediately concealed him in his dank cellar to await an opportunity of getting his nephew away. There he had been compelled to remain, due to lack of opportunity of escape, for six weeks, only emerging late at night when the servants had gone home. It had been only by chance that his uncle had spotted Gervase's advertisement in the Sheffield *Iris*. The newspaper had been left behind by a traveller, staying in a Nottingham inn which was frequented by Mr Bailey, John's uncle, and he had immediately made contact with Gervase on behalf of his nephew, and as a result, travelled to Sheffield to meet him. Mr Bailey was a well respected figure in Nottingham business circles, and as the power of his influence was not unknown to Gervase, it had been something of a surprise when the letter requesting an interview arrived at the shop.

Mr Bailey explained that his nephew had been a little indiscreet in publicly expressing his opinions on the current political situation, and needed to make a fresh start away from Nottingham. Gervase was far from happy about the political situation himself, and having inspected the young fellows indenture and samples of his work, agreed to take him on trial, providing that he kept himself away from controversy. In truth, however, there had been no other applicant for the position and Gervase was getting desperate for experienced assistance, so he had no alternative but to set him on.

John Andrews' dreams were shattered, his efforts all spurned. He was near to abandoning all hopes of ever working alongside men who could lead deputations to London, and if the people were afraid to be rallied then he'd be best served leaving them to their fate. Gradually during his incarceration he had formulated a plan. His future now lay across the ocean in the New World, where men were free to publish and practise what they believed. His new dreams were exciting and lay in the American Territories, where independent minded artisans were welcomed. He had a second cousin who had left the cotton mills of Belper, turning his back on his wealthy family and stealing away into the night, armed with his knowledge, to sail for America. His lack of faith in the future of England's over extended cotton industry, and a great deal of faith in his own abilities, had compelled him to try his luck elsewhere. It had been illegal to export technical knowledge but he had memorised all the plans and techniques in his head ready for the flight. He had done amazingly well, eventually owning cotton mills of his own. This too was where John felt his future must lie, in a country where there was freedom to print without hindrance, and ideas could be formulated into reality alongside people of vision — but first he must earn sufficient money to give himself a good start. He must also avoid conflict with the authorities and keep his opinions to himself.

The coach from Nottingham was late in arriving, and Tom stood in the cold rubbing his hands together vigorously in an attempt to warm them before thrusting them, once more, into the depths of his grubby pockets. Gervase had given Tom instructions to meet the coach and to stay put until it arrived. The man on the coach posed a threat to Tom's very existence, and he secretly hoped that the coach would never arrive, or that some disaster would befall it. Tom was simple-minded, not with the innocence of a child, but with cunning and deviousness caused by the need to survive. Now his survival was threatened again and no matter who the fellow was, Tom hated him!

James Shaw had not, in fact, been Tom's uncle; he was not a relative either, but the responsibility of the lad had been forced upon him. Mrs Shaw had formerly been married, to one Albert Linley, a widower with a young son. Less than two years after that marriage she had become a widow herself, left with the responsibility of young Tom. She had been a strong capable woman when James Shaw met her, and he for his part had security to offer the pair of them. The marriage was a strange one and it wasn't long before it became obvious that there was little love lost between any members of the party; Shaw's wife was domineering and the boy surly, with the result that conflict was forever present in the household. Mr Shaw's easy-going methods of working did not endear him to his scolding wife and it wasn't long before he bitterly regretted the liaison altogether. Much to his relief his wife died after a few years, but he was lumbered with Tom. He provided a bed for the boy, under the bench in the printing room out of his way, fed him, clothed him in his own cast-offs and felt no compulsion to provide anything more. The lad had been able to fathom out only the simplest of jobs in the shop, mainly because he couldn't read, and in consequence all the dirty and heavy labouring jobs fell to him.

Tom did not tell Gervase of his background, nor did he inform him that he lived at the shop. It had never occurred to him that the upstairs rooms would be cleared, so he had simply moved into his uncle's bed and used the spare key, which his uncle had given him, to come and go when Gervase went home. Fanny's suspicions that something odd was going on upstairs had not been without foundation. Tom had taken great care to cover his tracks but had never been used to making a bed before and didn't know how to plump up a mattress. He bitterly resented Fanny's interference and was both pleased and relieved to see her return to Doncaster. Now he had the newcomer to contend with and nowhere to sleep.

Blowing onto his hands for warmth and peering intensely at each disembarking passenger, Tom looked a pathetic figure in his uncle's ill-fitting cast-offs. He disregarded female passengers and men over forty until finally the last passenger climbed down, clutching his bag. He was a well-dressed young fellow and in spite of his sickly pallor nothing could disguise the fact that he was well-bred, good-looking and had clean blond hair. Tom was far from happy at what he saw, for it made him feel obliged to carry the fellow's bag. He informed him that Mr Webster would send the gig down later in the evening to fetch his trunk, then the odd pair walked the quarter-of-a-mile or so to the shop in silence. Tom felt disinclined to talk and John stared at his new surroundings with dismay and wondered how long he would be able to stand the place, nor was he overly impressed by the exterior appearance of the shop.

'Come in, young man. I'm Gervase Webster — you must be John Andrews. Welcome to Sheffield.' Gervase held out a hand to greet him and was pleased to find the other's hand firm and cordial.

'Thank you. I am John Andrews.' John glanced round, dismayed at the drabness of the shop, but, in spite of the conditions he felt cheered by the genuine friendliness of his new employer.

'You've met Tom. I suppose he pointed a few things out to you!'

'Not exactly.' John was surprised, for the large man standing before him was a complete contrast to the sulky boy who had met him and he was puzzled by the fact that the two should be connected in any way at all.

'I'll fetch your luggage later, I presume you have some to be collected?'

said Gervase, observing the small portmanteau which Tom had almost thrown on the floor. He liked the fellow's pleasant, open face, it was obvious that he had been ill, but he seemed sturdy enough. 'We've prepared the upstairs rooms for you and as long as you keep them clean no one will bother you. Tom, take him up and show him round. There's a brew of tea on the stove when you're ready to come down for it.' It was one of Gervase's little luxuries — the ancient iron kettle simmered constantly on the stove ready to make countless cups of tea in order to break the monotony of routine.

Tom grudgingly carried the portmanteau up the stairs and dumped it on the bed. 'That's it' he muttered, pointing to the second room, 'yer'll not bi wantin' me nah', and scuttled back down the stairs.

In spite of the feelings of apprehension which had accompanied John on the journey from Nottingham, right up until the time he had opened the door to the shop, the welcome which he had received from Mr Webster did much to boost his spirits and he felt much more inclined now to make an effort than he had done for weeks. His room was rather pleasant, if somewhat sparse, but it was obvious that some trouble had been taken to make the place clean and comfortable and even a low fire burned warmly in the grate. However, it was not America. He was thirsty and the offer of tea was too tempting to keep him upstairs for long. He quickly removed his coat and followed Tom.

'Tea's on the stove, John. Tom, here I want you!' summonsed Gervase. 'Now I want to make it clear from the beginning that each man is expected to pull his weight. I expect honesty and loyalty and will stand no nonsense. In order to get this business on its feet we're all going to have to work long and hard, and without being constantly supervised. I'm a fair man, and in return I can offer you both permanent employment and a reasonable wage. There are going to be problems, I know that, but if we work together I don't think you will regret it.'

'Sounds fair enough to me. When do I start work?' asked John.

'I'm going now to fetch your trunk.' He turned to Tom, 'I want you to show John where everything is, then when you've done that, give him the key and you can go home'. This time he addressed John, 'Never go upstairs leaving the door unlocked, and always put the shutters up at night, we've got a few light-fingered scoundrels in this town. I'll be back later, perhaps we can have a chat then'.

Tom closed the shop door and stared into the inky blackness of the night. His thoughts were no less black, and directed towards the man who had taken over his bed. There was nowhere for him to go. During the summer months he could have slept in a barn or under a hedge, but the Arctic weather of mid-January could bring death to the lonely occupant of a barn. There was however, one place, if he dared to use it. The first time he had used it was also the first time he had tasted gin; when he had been with two older boys hanging around the old well in Barker's Pool, they had become so intoxicated that it had been impossible to walk home. The fear of being found in such a state prompted them to climb into the loft over the archway of the 'George and Dragon' in Bank Street, where they had slept until being evicted by the irate innkeeper at six o'clock next morning.

It was far too early to go to the 'George and Dragon' now, and what little money there was left must last him all week, but he had to go somewhere. It was unsafe to hang around the Market Square like a vagrant, even if that's just what he had become. There was a place, down by the river, just under the arch of the bridge, which he'd used in summer when he had nothing better to do. He'd spent hours there peering at the couples kissing and cuddling and doing things which intrigued him, but they wouldn't be there now that it was winter.

The path down to the arch was darker than he'd imagined it would be, and the light from the lamp on the bridge cast weird shadows onto the water. It was cold and he was miserable, he vowed to bring the old curtains, which Fanny had discarded, next time. He would also bring some candle stubs; although he would be careful for he had never stolen anything before.

Sitting hunched, with his arms embracing his knees, Tom was frightened by a sudden movement from behind, and if it had not been for a stone stoop standing between himself and the water he would have fallen in. The smell of the thing reached his nostrils even before he had time to turn to see what was behind him and he knew that it was a dog. He could feel its breath on the back of his neck and was petrified. He knew it was coming closer and it caused the hairs on the back of his neck to stand out. What if it bit him? He had heard of people going mad after being bitten by dogs and wanted to run away. A low whimper came from the dog and he wasn't sure what to do. The whimper turned to a pitiful whine, and Tom felt the animal creep closer and snuggle up against his thigh. It didn't move anymore but whimpered again and put its nose onto his foot. He no longer cared if it bit him, or that it was covered in fleas, it was warm and soft, and pitiful just as he was, and he put his arm around its body for warmth. Much later, when his feet had gone numb with the cold and his belly rumbled with hunger, he set off for the 'George and Dragon', but the dog followed in the distance. It was there again when Tom left the inn and it climbed the stone staircase into the loft after him. By the time he had piled the old sacks into a makeshift mattress in a corner, the dog was ready to jump into bed with him. 'Cum on den' he called gruffly, with a soft catch in his throat.

After a week of sleeping rough in the corn loft, Tom began to smell. Gervase was a fairly patient man but one thing he detested was the smell of unwashed bodies. He had accepted Tom with all his short-comings, but the odour from the lad was becoming slowly worse, until one day he arrived soaked to the skin from a heavy downpour of rain. As he sat before the old iron stove, sodden and forlorn, the stench from his dirty steaming clothes began to fill the shop until it was too much for Gervase to stand anymore.

'Good God, lad, when did you last have a wash? You are stinking out the shop!' He found himself shouting at the boy.

'It's nowt to do wi nobdi else' snapped Tom resentfully.

Gervase felt his patience being stretched to the limit. 'Oh yes it is! I don't want the smell of you turning my customers away' and added, 'and I have told you before to speak correctly in the shop.' Gervase wasn't quite sure what it was that the indignant boy uttered under his breath but he'd had quite enough. 'Right Tom, you and I are going to come to an agreement. You take a bath and get your clothes washed, and keep doing so, or you lose your job.' Tom recognised the look of determination on Gervase's face and knew he wasn't going to be able to get out of it. 'Now get that old hip bath from the outhouse and put some containers of water onto the two stoves.'

'It's not reight whot tha's mekin mi do' Tom replied with a sulky voice, but half-accepted the inevitable.

'It's one thing or the other, understand?' Gervase wondered why he was bothering with the lad at all when there were probably hundreds of boys out there who would be grateful for a job. Oh God, he thought to himself, they probably all smell as bad as each other.

'Ahm not mucky, 'sides it keeps mi warm. It's this owd stove that stinks', returned the offended ragamuffin.

'Now!'

Muttering profane words under his breath, Tom reluctantly left the stove and went out into the back yard, slamming the door to as he went. The mis-shapen hip bath lay in a corner of the outhouse, half full of rubbish; neither Tom nor his uncle had used the bath since the death of Mrs Shaw. When Tom tipped out the rubbish a mouse scamp-ered out from amongst the pile of debris. He leapt forward trying to crush it with his foot but the creature quickly darted into a hole in the corner for safety, Tom noisily dragged the bath indoors, looking at Gervase in defiance.

'Wash the bath out first with water. Get it from the rain barrel and fill the containers from there too. John can stay in the room to make sure you get washed properly.'

'Ee's not standin' thear, an ahve nowt else to wear, tha'll kill mi off mekin mi use watter', protested the lad.

'Well at least you'll be a clean corpse' responded John.

Tom's eyes bulged with rage. 'Shut yer gob or I'll thump thi.'

Gervase mused at the scene before him, not daring to laugh out loud, then stated in a very serious manner. 'There are some old clothes of mine in the cupboard under the stairs. When you've bathed you can use those and then wash your own. Dry them round the stove. Now get on, you're costing me money while we're wasting time.' Gervase left the room and went back into the shop. 'John, you stay with him', he shouted over his shoulder as he went.

Tom sprang at John, 'If tha watches mi, ahm not gerrin in that watter'. He spat the words out with such uncontrolled venom that John felt discomforted. It was obvious that the lad didn't like him but John was surprised at the strength of his feelings so undisguised in his voice.

There was almost a foot of water in the bath by the time the cold water had been added and Tom just stood gazing at it in horror.

'Ah've nor'ad a bath fer years an ah waint like it. Ah'm onli doin it fer 'im' he spluttered, pointing to the shop. Gervase returned with a bottle which he had just fetched from Sarah. 'Wots that chuffin' rubbish?' He stared in disbelief as Gervase emptied the perfume into the bath. 'Ees tryin t' turn mi into a bloody dandy.' John busied himself with some compositing for a charity concert poster and suppressed his amusement while Tom gingerly put one foot into the water. 'Its too bloody 'ot!' he yelled.

'Shut up and get on with it, you scruffy devil, and wash your hair too, its crawling filthy.' The thought of lice made John shudder.

'That does it, one o' these days Ah'm gonna get thi fer this.'

An unspeakable amount of scum had accumulated on the surface of the water, not to mention live vermin, when Tom had done, for sleeping in the loft with the dog had added to the grime that had built up over the years. He let the water trickle through his fingers and made waves on what small surface of water there was, like a child with a new toy.

Gervase returned with a pan of clean tepid water. 'Get up lad and stand still.' Tom remained seated. 'Now!' Gervase demanded.

'Tha'l' burn mi wi' that.' His protest was more to do with not wanting to leave the warmth of the water than anything else. Nevertheless he did stand up.

'Shut up — it's not hot.' Gervase poured the water over the boy's head and fetched another container full. The transformation was amazing as the water flushed the dirt, first from his head, down his face and over his chest, until he stood in a pool of thick filthy water. 'Here use this old towel.' Gervase threw the towel and wondered if it would ever come clean again.

Tom rubbed himself until he glowed. His body no longer felt hard and crusty, he wasn't even sure what he felt like but it wasn't an unpleasant feeling at all.

The act of the compulsory bathing had a strange effect upon Tom, who took to following Gervase about and hanging onto his every word, anxious to do his bidding, until in the end Gervase came near to tripping over the lad's feet and was left with no option but to tell him. 'In heaven's name lad, stop following me everywhere — I'll tell you when I need you!' However, the tone in Gervase's voice was neither angry nor unkind and he felt rather moved by the boy's devotion.

The truth came out sooner than expected. By the middle of February, when the weather was damp and miserable and there was hardly anything else to do other than work, Tom and John toiled as many hours for Gervase as he could offer them. Gervase was more than satisfied not only with their work but with business in general, and he was especially pleased and surprised with Tom. He was hard-working and dependable, usually arriving at the shop early in the morning long before Gervase but it had taken patience and persistence on Gervase's part to draw the lad along. He had avoided questioning him about his family or past, because the boy seemed to clam up when he did, and Gervase thought it better no to pry.

This morning however, Tom was over two hours late and Gervase could not push from his mind the nagging fear that something was wrong. He was angry with himself for not pressing the boy for details, as now he had no means of contacting him and there had been no messages as to his whereabouts. Gervase pondered on all the possibilities which could have effected Tom and felt foolish about his deep concern.

The arrival of the Town Constable half an hour later only increased his regrets and fears. 'Are you Mr Webster?' enquired the man in a doubting tone.

'I am, constable. What's the matter?'

'We've had some trouble in Bank Street and arrested a lad on a vagrancy charge. Says he works here — a Tom Lindley. I don't suppose there's a grain of truth in it is there?' He paused, expecting a negative reply, then carried on, 'They're all over the place these lads, running wild and sleeping rough'.

'Yes, he does work here and he's late — where is he now?'

'He's had an accident and is pretty shook up, nothing serious you understand, but he's badly bruised. The innkeeper's wife at the 'George and Dragon' is taking care of him. She says he's always hanging around there late at night.'

Gervase was becoming concerned and wished the constable would get on with the matter. 'What on earth happened?'

'He says he was sleeping off the ale in the old corn loft above the archway at the George when the lot caved in, stonework, floor, contents, the lot. He and his dog went with it. Landed on a horse which had to be destroyed because its leg got smashed. Apparently the archway's been needing attention for some time now but the weight of the pair of them must have finished it off. Where does he live? It's not the first time he has slept there apparently.' The constable paused again but his lengthy dialogue had given Gervase time to gather his thoughts, and although he was stunned, he realised that unless he could give a sensible account for Tom, the lad could very well end up in serious trouble.

'He belongs here alright, but we've had a few words lately and he's stayed away in a fit of temper. Don't worry he'll not do it again. I'll fetch him back if you think he's fit to move.'

'I'd give him half an hour, then he should be alright but he's going to ache for a good while. You'd better keep an eye on him. If we catch him roaming around again he'll go to the house of correction at Wakefield — mark my words, we've no time for the likes of him, before you know where you are they're out thieving.'

Gervase saw the constable off the premises and assured him that there would be no recurrence of the incident, but could not for the life of him work out why Tom was sleeping rough. It certainly would account for his dirty unkempt appearance — and the arrival of the dog on the back doorstep.

The 'George and Dragon' was one of the older hostelries in the town and this was probably the reason for its unsoundness. It was not a place usually frequented by Gervase, for he found the taste of its ale had little to recommend it. Pulling up before the inn, where men were attempting to remove an enormous pile of rubble, Gervase was astounded by the fact that Tom had survived at all. He entered the dreary place to find a despondent Tom seated by the fire.

He had been sitting now for over two hours, nursing his bruises and considering his plight. He knew that if Gervase didn't help then he was almost sure to end up serving a month of hard labour in Wakefield House of Correction for vagrancy. As each new set of footsteps approached Tom prepared himself for the worst. He had a grudging admiration for Gervase whom he had to admit was a fair boss, even helpful when he was in difficulty, but Tom doubted if he would be willing to get him out of this mess. Never before in his life had he found anyone in whom he could put his trust and there had been no reason for him to suppose that Gervase would be any different from the rest. Perhaps, had he taken the risk and told Gervase, he would have been in less of a sticky position now.

Tom looked sheepishly up at Gervase as he entered the inn and was just about to open his mouth to speak when Gervase cut him short. 'Shut up, lad. I'll talk to you when we get back to the shop.' At least the lad had the sense to keep his mouth closed and Gervase breathed a sigh of relief. One look at the lad's sad condition was evidence enough that unless something was done to help him he would end up amongst the criminal classes.

Tom didn't know which part of his body hurt the most, but he felt sure that the ensuing confrontation with Gervase would probably be just as painful as the physical bruises. He limped feebly from the building and climbed into the gig; no words left his lips as he postponed the dreaded moment when he would be compelled to give an account of himself and the incident.

Having practically stood surety for the boy, Gervase had little choice but to endeavour to resolve the matter. There was enough work to do without playing nursemaid to a foolish boy and immediately the pair closed the door behind themselves Gervase questioned him. 'Right my lad, I want to know the truth. The full truth — or I shall wash my hands of you completely. No job. Nothing. Why in heaven's name did you sleep in the loft, it isn't the first time either. Doesn't your mother know what you're up to?'

'She's dead. Mi father's dead and mi uncle's dead, an' ah've not got nobdi. I allus slept 'ere til ee cum, an ah've got no place to sleep nah.' He pointed scornfully to John who was working in the back room.

Gervase sighed. He had tried, with some success, to improve the boy's speech but each time he became upset he reverted to his natural way of speaking. 'Take your time. What's John got to do with this, anyway?'

Fighting back the tears, Tom slowly and hesitatingly blurted out the whole story, until, unable to control himself any longer, he burst into tears. The story was an incredible one and Gervase was shocked by the fact that he had not suspected any of it at all.

'Wot's tha' gonna do wi mi nah?' The boy's eyes pleadingly sought his, and he realised that Tom had become his moral responsibility.

'What am I going to do with you now!' repeated Gervase, trying to correct him, but not unkindly. 'I'll tell you what, you can have another bath to start with'.

'I 'ate yer. Mi bodi aches all o'er an all tha can think on is 'avin another laugh at mi.' The tears evaporated and sparks of anger filled his young eyes.

'A good soak in a bath of soda water will stop you aching, blockhead!' Gervase pointed out.

Tom thought for a moment and then quite suddenly he turned to Gervase and mumbled, 'Thanks,' then added, 'Can tha larn mi t' read them books, like what 'e can?'

'It's not very easy Tom, and some of those books are very boring.' He found it difficult to dismiss the hope in his eyes, 'Perhaps we could start with a few easy ones first'. He cursed to himself for his foolishness and wondered where on earth it would all end up. It certainly would be a challenge; nevertheless the boy had a determination about him which Gervase admired and it did seem to be a ridiculous situation employing someone who could neither read nor write. What on earth James Shaw had been thinking of, Gervase could not imagine. 'I'll teach you, if you promise me that you will go to Sunday School to learn there as well.'

'Oh, not Sundi School! Cissis is wot gus thear', protested a horrified Tom, 'Aww no.'

'A deal's a deal' insisted Gervase adamantly, 'and you can sleep in the place you slept in when your uncle was alive, but the dog stays outside in the outhouse, if you clean it out for him.'

The deal had its good points, Tom could see that, besides there seemed to be no alternative. 'Awreet then, but . . .' and just to prove that he had some say in the matter added, 'not too many baths.'

Gervase smiled. 'No, not too many. And give that scruffy dog of yours a bath as well.' The dog might not be such a bad idea after all. He had already spent a small fortune having shutters fitted to the downstairs windows to keep out thieves, but one shopkeeper in the town had even had the iron bars on his shutters prised off. The dog would raise the alarm. He was going to have to feed the animal as well as pay the dog tax. 'Ye Gods, they'll be taxing the air we breathe next' he muttered to himself.

Chapter 5

The month of March brought with it brighter days after the hard winter, and Gervase found himself longing to escape once more onto the surrounding hills and moors. He had found in John a man to whom he could relate both socially and in his political beliefs and, in spite of being master and employee, the pair got on well together. The younger man had been well trained during his apprenticeship and was capable of assuming a considerable amount of responsibility, much to Gervase's relief and satisfaction, with the result that there developed between them a relaxed relationship in which neither took advantage of the other's position. When time permitted, Gervase invited John to join him on his walks up the steep rugged slopes and into the winding valleys.

Few men could resist the magic of walking in the Peaks, where whispering winds blow down from the heather-clad heights into the green fertile meadows below, and yet only a privileged few were given this opportunity, or indeed had the time to spare for such luxuries. Gervase knew this and never ceased to be grateful for his own good fortune in being allowed these precious moments. The gift of wandering for pleasure was denied to the hungry and over-worked, whose sole concern was to survive from day to day, living from hand to mouth, and pleasure itself was only a dream. Gervase acknowledged that, in spite of the little affection which his father had shown him, he had at least provided him with the necessities of life, teaching him to read and write, and stimulating his appreciation for finer things. He could have been born as Tom had been, or one of the country's countless half-starved children. At least his father had spared him that.

The two men, after walking many miles, would stop and perch themselves on some craggy outcrop of stone, or pause by some playful stream in order to consume their lunch and converse upon the problems of the world. John confessed his longing to travel to America and his ambition to start a new life there. Gervase listened with great interest, for he found the younger man's enthusiasm rather refreshing, but believed the man's disposition to dream to be a flaw in his character which, if allowed to run free, could lead to trouble. John would take out the flute, which he always carried in the inside pocket of his coat, and play a melody that would echo out and bounce back from amongst the rocks and trees. The tempo of the music would mirror his mood; when he was in a buoyant frame of mind he would play an Irish jig, when he was troubled it would be a haunting composition.

'What a beautiful instrument' said Gervase admiringly, the first time he saw John take it from his pocket.

'It belonged to my father. It's a long story, but he won it playing cards when I was a boy.' John fingered the flute, caressing the highly polished wood and picking out the elaborate silver filigree ornamentation with his index finger. 'I always keep it hidden in my coat pocket when I'm not in the house. My father ran off you know, it sent my mother quite mad. Some days she would stay in bed, then the next she would wander off, sometimes to the canal. One day she didn't come back and they found her floating in the murky water, they were never sure if she had done it deliberately or not. Her brother, my uncle — you met him, brought me up. He's a good chap really, I think he found me to be a bit of a handful, him being a bachelor and all that.' He raised the flute to his lips but didn't play it. His eyes looked unseeing across the moors. 'They say my mother was pretty. I hardly remember now.'

'Life seems to be full of tragedies and entanglements. Have you any idea where your father is now?' enquired Gervase.

'No. I don't really care. The only thing I have left of him is this flute. I love it for its beauty and its music rather than because it was his.' He fell silent again. 'Like a magic wand it draws people, a musician is welcome anywhere.'

Gervase glanced at him knowingly. 'According to your uncle it didn't do you any good in Nottingham, did it?'

'The people need rousing from their lethargy. It's a dangerous game — fighting for survival. If enough people were to muster under the same banner they could achieve freedom from poverty. I just sought to bring them to a realisation of that fact.'

'Those same people have seen a long war. Many have returned from fighting too sick to work. They find bread too dear for them to buy for their families and those that can work often can't find any to do. All they want is peace, they don't want to march and risk going to prison or transportation. That wouldn't help their families.' Gervase fell silent. He was only too aware that the country needed changes, including relief from crippling taxes, but it would have to be done within the law.

John considered his answer, for Gervase was his employer. 'You are a fair minded employer, but many are greedy at the expense of their workers, particularly the children. This property tax should be taken from the poor and be paid by the rich.' He hesitated — had he spoken too freely?

'Not all employers are rich, my lad. I agree that the avaricious ones need curbing, but many are struggling for survival themselves. At least they are providing work.' Gervase felt the need to issue a word of caution. 'Take my advice, keep your mouth tightly shut unless you know that you can trust someone, and you can't be sure of that these days.'

They strode on in silence, each deep in his own thoughts but troubled by the same root causes. Gervase had his own thoughts as he viewed the town below. He knew what conditions were concealed behind the stinking, smoking chimneys; the hills merely formed a golden frame for a canvas of misery and poverty.

There were March winds of a different kind blowing over the town in 1816. The British Government had until April 1st to consider whether to renew the crippling Property Tax, or to amend it to a proposed modification of a five percent increase.

For those who could not read the newspapers, or had insufficient money to buy them, the barber's chair was the next best way to hear the current events, providing of course that one was willing to listen to a twisted and embellished version. Certainly the literate barber held a privileged position in the community, for not only did he have on hand the printed version but also the opinions of both eminent citizens and the less informed of his clients. Rumours were always circulating in the town, and a clever orator could easily sway a gullible crowd to a fervent fever pitch with his version of happenings.

On the 1st of March a meeting was held in Sheffield Town Hall, to consider the proposed modification to the tax, and Samuel Shore Esquire, of Meersbrook, took the chair, declaring 'I never would have thought to declare it possible, for such to happen, for an assessor to enter a merchant's house to demand an examination of his ledgers and accounts . . .' and so it went on — until in the end a petition was sent to the House of Commons from the meeting, against the tax.

In this same week, the House of Commons received six other petitions from across the land, two of these being presented by a Mr Dundas representing Edinburgh and Leith. Although he presented the petitions he felt that he must dissent altogether from the petition which he had brought, as he did not himself want to oppose the tax because he saw it as a necessity. Mr P. Grant returned that he was glad to see that so many had signed it, but would have appreciated it more if the petition had been handed in by a representative who concurred in the same sentiment. No wonder the poor cared little for the connivance's of politicians, with their empty promises and lack of real understanding of poverty, for they rarely saw their own representative.

On the evening of March 18th, the ale houses of Sheffield were aglow with jubilation at the reports of rebellion at the Town Hall. A foundling petition in favour of the Property Tax had been placed there anonymously awaiting signatures, and a bellman had been sent through the town during the day displaying the following notice:

'A petition now lays at the Town Hall to compel the *rich* to pay the Taxes and *not* the poor. You are all invited to go and sign immediately.'

That night a jovial jig and an extra jar of ale was called for to toast the unknown hero, and many a man turned out for work next morning with a sore head but with the feeling that it had all been worthwhile. There was further merriment the following day when those who could read, did so to those couldn't, and read out Montgomery's caustic editorial in the *Iris*. James Montgomery stated, with regret, that such a circulation had been passed around by someone unknown, and felt that to make comment on such proceedings would be to tread upon a worm — 'but let it crawl back in peace to the obscurity from which it came'. They greeted it with raucous laughter and jeers, for the people loved nothing better than a bit of mischievous intrigue and once again the men in the ale-houses lifted their jars in a toast to the unknown stirrer.

Gervase, on the other hand, winced when he read Montgomery's editorial and was pleased that he no longer worked for the sanctimonious old fool, not that he, or anyone else, wanted a tax but the event had certainly proved that there were still many inhabitants who had retained their sense of humour. Someone in the town had printed the petition, but no one was ready to admit to being the culprit.

He took a sideways glance at John who was rolling about with mirth at the whole carry on, and did secretly wonder if the blame lay closer at hand than he cared to admit. As little harm was done, Gervase decided not to pry any further and let the matter drop.

Before the month was out and amid much speculation, the Government reached its decision. Gervase was hoping that there would be at least no increase but so far there had been no indication as to which way they would vote.

'They threw it out. The House of Commons rejected the Property Tax', John rushed in bubbling over with the news.

'What! All of it?' Gervase could hardly believe his ears. 'That won't be the end, you mark my words. The Government is in a plight and it's going to have to raise the money from somewhere, you bet your sweet life it won't be from the rich. At least now we've got a breathing space.'

John rubbed his hands together triumphantly. 'It's a start. We can achieve more if we try hard enough.'

'Look, there is an auction tonight at the Sale Room in Fargate, why don't you come along?' Gervase was feeling quite relieved at the news. 'I was hoping to pick up some of the small items but now I think I could risk getting some of the books from that house clearance I told you about, they should sell well.'

On the Sunday following the abolition of the Property Tax the people of Sheffield thought that retribution had come to them in no uncertain manner. The walls of buildings moved and the ground shook beneath their feet. The earth tremor came and went without causing any damage but had been sufficiently terrifying to sober up the population.

Chapter 6

It would seem that when one problem is solved, then another is quickly sent, as if to ensure that the human body and soul is kept at its busiest. Gervase had spent the last five months tackling problems both large and small but the one which beset him now left him with a heavy heart, in the knowledge that this was one of which he could not change the outcome. He had neglected his friends the Garnetts while he sorted out his own affairs, but each time he had called at their home it had been with the knowledge that Bryce's cough was getting worse. His hair was becoming white and Gervase was struck by his loss of weight. The worry had taken the cheeriness out of Sarah's disposition and it was now obvious to everyone that Bryce was succumbing to the hairdresser's disease.

He was not sure that Sarah had been wise to withhold the truth from Fanny for so long, and he felt saddened that not only must she leave the academy for ever, but that she must return home to the shock of seeing her father as a changed and dying man. It was already too late to soften the blow, and he, Gervase, felt powerless to help her. Henry, her brother, had already left for Doncaster with instructions to bring Fanny and her belongings back home.

Gervase was sorry too that she must return to become engulfed by the day to day routine of housework, which would confine her lively enquiring mind. He had always been disappointed that the intelligent mind of a woman should be constrained by the social order of things, for he had so much enjoyed the times when Fanny had spoken her mind, and he had encouraged her to think for herself.

Returning to the academy had been difficult enough for Fanny; the Christmas break had renewed her attachment not only to her family but to the whole town and its people. She hated the flatness of Doncaster, and she found after being back for a while that she was unwittingly packing all her unneeded belongings neatly at the bottom of her trunk, ready to go home.

She had in no way been fooled by her mother's deception about her father's health, seeing it more as wishful thinking on her mother's part that all was well, for she had seen the signs so often before. Fanny's association with other hairdressing families had made her familiar with the deadly chest complaint, for it had already claimed the lives of many local wigmakers and Fanny blamed the finely ground starch and wheat flour, used for powdering wigs. When the Government placed the tax on powder they probably saved future generations of hairdressers from untold misery. However, the older wigmakers still complained at their loss of earnings and were still hankering to have the tax removed, but the damage to their health had already been done.

Sarah still wrote loving letters to her daughter, but they were shorter, less cheerful than they had previously been, and Fanny sensed that her mother was avoiding writing to tell her the truth about her father's health.

On the day when Miss Greaves called Fanny from the sewing room into the sitting room with an air of softness about her expression which was not often seen and called out, 'Fanny my dear, would you come this way'. Fanny knew instinctively that something was wrong.

Miss Greaves motioned to Fanny to take a seat. 'Sit down please.' A strange feeling came over Fanny as she sat down and she dared to ask, 'Miss Greaves what is wrong?' She knew the news would not be good.

'I'm afraid that your father is very ill, my dear, and your mother needs you to help at home. Your brother is here in the dining room having a bite to eat after the long journey, but you must both leave on the next coach.' She paused for a moment to allow Fanny to compose herself. 'I am most sorry my dear.'

Fanny hung her head. She was shocked but not surprised by the news. 'Thank you. I had suspected as much, but as mother didn't write to say he was worsening, I presumed that he was getting better.'

'It's still a shock, I know. We shall miss you. I fear that you may not be able to return to us and it is a great pity, for I don't like to lose my girls before they have completed their studies, but I'm sure you will do well.' Miss Greaves allowed her voice to fall and she said softly, as though allowing herself an indulgence, 'You are one of my most gifted pupils — even if you are a handful sometimes — it will be the academy's loss. However, you are called to serve your family at this time and I am sure you will be of great comfort to them'. Miss Greaves seemed suddenly human beneath the formidable exterior and Fanny wondered why she had never noticed this before. 'I'll come with you and help you pack your things.'

'May I see my brother first?' whispered Fanny, not even sure which brother it was, but she hoped it was Bryce.

'Of course, dear, just give a knock on the door when you are ready for me.'

Whilst Henry waited impatiently for Fanny he looked around the large oak-lined dining room with envy. What wouldn't he have given to have been sent away to school. He had always resented being the youngest in the family and that there had been very little money to go round, however by the time Fanny had come along business had picked up, but it had been too late for him. He stared down at his hands, calloused and permanently ingrained with grit dust from forging. Yes, Fanny had been the lucky one — born at the right time and with talents that had eluded him. Once, as children, they had been very close, until his working life-style and then his marriage had drawn them apart, so that now he often felt both awkward and unrefined in her presence.

Slowly Fanny crossed the hall to the dining room. She was deep in thought and her heart was full of sorrow, but she could not allow herself to shed her tears in public. She was disappointed not to find Bryce waiting for her, for she longed to run into his arms to be comforted. Henry stood before her, sad and drawn, and Fanny felt herself experiencing a sense of wretchedness at being incapable of comforting him.

'I'm sorry Fan, but father's dying — you have to come home with me to help mother take care of him.' He had the same bushy eyebrows as his father, ones which met in the middle when he frowned, and although he did not have the same twinkle in the eyes, he kindled in Fanny the memory of her father, sufficiently to bring a lump to her throat.

'I don't mind going home, I just wish he wasn't going to die.' She didn't quite know how to express her feelings to Henry. 'How is mother?' Her voice sounded distant and unfamiliar to herself.

'She's broken hearted naturally. Father struggled on in the shop until the pain became too bad and now he spends most of the day in bed.'

'Why didn't you fetch me home before this? I would have been quite content to go.' Fanny bit back a tear but could not stifle the sob in her voice. 'It might be too late already.'

'Father didn't want to spoil your chances Fan, he's proud of you being here.' He found himself becoming embarrassed by her agitation and said roughly, 'Get your things together, we'd best be off as soon as we can'.

The other girls were still with their tutors while Miss Greaves helped Fanny to pack her belongings, and when finally they stood together before the heavy wooden front door of the house Fanny murmured, 'You have been good to me. Please say my good-byes to everyone here — I can't bear to say it to their faces. Thank you for all that you have done for me. If ever I come to Doncaster I will endeavour to call and pay my respects to you'. She was almost sure that Miss Greaves also had a tear in her eye.

'Go now dear, your brother is anxious not to miss the coach.' She quickly hugged Fanny in a brief farewell and bustled her into the carriage.

Having placed Fanny into the carriage, Miss Greaves stood back and waved from the doorway before going into the house and pulling the door to behind her. She leaned back against the closed door and thought how strangely empty the house would seem without Fanny's high spirits, and she chided herself for becoming so attached to one of her pupils.

The coach bumped tediously back along the Sheffield Road, but for all the interest Fanny took in her surroundings she might as well have been asleep. Suddenly before her stood Conisborough Castle. Was it really only fifteen months ago when she and her father had first seen the castle peering out through the mist? Now she knew who Hengist the bandit was, and a smile appeared on her lips as she recalled her father's dear face and his kindness.

The smile irritated Henry. Why, he asked himself, must she damn well smile? She smiled at everything and he could see nothing to smile about. The only time she didn't smile was when she was angry. He didn't really understand her. When she was not being skittish she was too darned serious. Henry wanted to shake her, shout at her and say, 'Stop smiling, Father's dying. Cry! Damn you!' Fanny's smile, however, hid her from the prying eyes of people, and from the hurt which they stupidly cause one another with their loose, thoughtless words and silly deeds. Idle chatter was like idle hands, contributing nothing constructive to the world. There was nothing to say which would help her, and the effort of thinking her thoughts out loud was too painful and tedious.

For two months they cared for their father, Fanny watched as day by day his precious face became more sallow and emaciated, until weak and in pain, and through lack of medical understanding, he gave up and waited for death. There was no cure, nor anything other than laudanum to kill the pain, it made her think of wars, of men who died in pain, and of amputations which must have taken place with little to stop the pain, and wondered where mankind got its courage from. From God? She wasn't sure any more, when there was so much hunger, sickness and dying — what was the point of it all?

Fanny constantly encouraged her father by telling him that he would get better, and chattered on about all manner of things in the hope that he would not see how hopeless it was, but she could do nothing for the pain. There were few occupations that were free from disease, terrible working conditions and low wages. At least the Garnett business was clean and provided a reasonable living, and when she considered the children grinders, their lungs filled with dust which made them cough blood until they died prematurely, then she could consider her family fortunate.

When the end finally came, Sarah was broken and lost, and Fanny was left with an emptiness that was hard to fill. He had been her champion and ally as well as her father, never minding her whims and fancies, and in spite of their differing opinions he had always given her every encouragement.

The coffin was placed in the shop because there was no space for it anywhere else, but there he was at least amongst his own things. The separation would be made even harder by the fact that he could not be placed in the family burial plot in the old church yard round the corner, that grave being full, so they would have to take him across the town to the new yard. His departure brought to an end one chapter of Fanny's life.

Everything about her was in a state of change. There were changes in the town which had completely escaped her during her preoccupation in caring for the family, and changes nearer at hand. Soon the smell of flowers and grass which came from the large garden adjacent to the shop would vanish, only to be replaced by the noise, and smells, of builders. Then would come the sound of hooves and carts on the cobbled yard they had built, until the house would be swallowed up, like the rest of the town, by a sea of stone and brick.

Work slowly filled the gap in Fanny's life. Although young Bryce was a good artisan he had little or no head for book-keeping, but, as a result of the training which Fanny had received at the academy, she was competent to take on the task herself. Fanny was good at handling money, and could not abide waste of any kind. She deplored the way her father had conducted some of his business, for in his gentle way he had been reluctant to press some of his clients for payment of the money which they owed him. Fanny would have none of this. In a very feminine but forceful way she left them under no illusion about her thoughts on the matter, and contrary to family expectations, succeeded in gathering in the outstanding debts. Only the most hardened of customers attempted to delay their payments and Fanny decided that they would be better off without them, yet they still came. She cleared out all sentimental rubbish in order to make more space in the shop but she kept the wigs, which the children loved to play with, in the chest.

Brother and sister worked well together. She readily acknowledged that it was his skill which brought clients into the shop, and he admired her for her business skills. Sometimes a clash would occur when Fanny was overly fussy about tidiness, but he forgave her, and carried on just as he had always done.

Gervase had done all in his power to assist Sarah and Bryce through their troubles but he was relieved at the arrival of Fanny to ease their situation. The responsibility placed upon Fanny's shoulders had a most remarkable effect on her, and although she was still only nineteen years of age her reactions and capabilities were those of a fully mature woman. The admiration which Gervase had for her multiplied with each passing day as he watched her knuckle down, first in caring for Sarah and Bryce, and then in taking charge of the shop. He had seen her face grow weary and tired with caring, then become wrought with grief, until now the challenge of taking charge of the shop was bringing the light back into her eyes.

The turmoil and upheaval of the winter and spring had not allowed either Fanny or Gervase the time to spare for socialising, but the anticipation of approaching summertime provided an uplift for their spirits. For the rest of England, however, the longed-for glorious summer weather of 1816 did not appear and the persistent dampness and lack of sunshine made the farmers complain constantly of ruined and failed crops, until England was once again in the grip of food shortages, low wages and discontent.

Gervase had spent the spring developing a profitable sideline, and at every opportunity he attended auctions and house clearances, sometimes travelling many miles, in order to obtain rare or popular books for re-sale, or to increase the stock of the circulating library which he had established. There were many clients as far away as London, Nottingham and York who subscribed to his list of 'wanted books' and his judgement and keen prices were gaining him a considerable reputation in the trade. With the passing months John talked less and less about America, and as his flair and proficiency in laying out display posters brought in more and more orders, Gervase became even more dependent upon his skills, until he began to dread the possibility that the man would eventually leave his employment. When opportunities presented themselves, and the weather permitted, Gervase and John continued to spend their Sundays out walking, much to the envy of Fanny who felt compelled to escort Sarah to Church.

A sort of truce developed between John and Tom, making life much easier, but neither John nor Fanny could conceive how Gervase found the patience in keeping his promise of teaching Tom to read. Fanny thought that it would have been much easier to use a hammer than patience on the boy's brains, and would probably have given the task up. Tom, however, took great pains to make sure that Fanny saw the results of his efforts when she came to visit the shop, and she was forced to admit that the boy had tenacity, yet she wondered whether it was a love for letters that caused the dedication, or simply his desire to please Gervase.

Such was Sarah's recovery now, that Fanny was able occasionally to spend a little time away from the shop in York Street for her own pleasure, and when she was not visiting an old girlfriend or one of her sisters, she called to see Gervase. Today, however, she had a special reason for calling because she proudly carried a small package wrapped in tissue paper in her hand. Fanny entered the shop, only to find that there was no one there. She rang the little bell which sat on the wooden counter and tapped impatiently with her fingers as she waited for someone to make an appearance. Fanny was pleased that it was Gervase who came in answer to the bell, for he was the one person whom she had come especially to see.

'Come through Fanny, we were just discussing our proposed walk for Sunday, that's if the weather improves. What can we do for you?' Gervase asked warmly. 'You're a welcome break from the monotony of the day.' He opened the door of the back room and let her pass through.

'I came to bring you a little something' Fanny responded with excitement. 'Guess what it is?'

John raised his head hopefully. 'What is it — ginger cake? Has Sarah made something to eat?'

'No — mother's busy!' Fanny shook her head. 'All you can think about is your stomach.' Sarah, who was always full of love for everyone, often baked little tit-bits for Fanny to bring across, but today she had a grandchild to attend to.

'Come on then, what is it?' John repeated. Fanny had gradually come to enjoy John's good sense of humour and quite enjoyed teasing him back.

Gervase intervened. 'Fanny Garnett! Stop teasing and tell us what it is!' His strong mature face looked almost childlike with curiosity and Fanny had a sudden feeling of regret that she had not given him the painting when they were alone.

She passed the parcel shyly to Gervase. 'I've finished the painting for you — really it's not all that good, but I hope you will like it.'

He observed the earnest look on her face and took the small package from her outstretched hand. She had lovingly wrapped the painting in the tissue paper in which he had brought her the gift at Christmas, and he was strangely affected by the look of trust on her face as she watched him open it. Hidden within the tissue lay a small oval-shaped painting of a kingfisher in a gilded frame, Gervase was struck by the quality of the brushwork which added such fine detail to the colourful bird. He was well aware that Fanny had been fully occupied since her return, and yet she had obviously taken great care and worked long and hard to achieve such perfection on his behalf, he was deeply moved by her efforts.

The painting had taken Fanny many hours to complete but she did not regret the course which she had taken, for she was proud of the results and happy to repay Gervase for the help he had given them all over the past year.

John peered over Gervase's shoulder. He had in the past done a considerable amount of painting himself, but he too was surprised at the quality of her work and said admiringly. 'I think it is a remarkable likeness of the bird, the colours are well blended — congratulations Fanny.'

Tom grudgingly admitted that the painting was 'awreet', and eager to share in the praises, fetched a slip of paper on which he had been practising his letters. 'What do you think of this?' He almost begged of Fanny, who looked at the spider-like writing. He was indeed improving, and realising just how important her answer would be to him, she took the paper from him and carefully scrutinised it.

'Why Tom, you certainly are improving, keep it up and you'll be as good as John before you've done' she proclaimed kindly. Tom beamed from ear to ear with self-satisfaction. Praise from Miss Fanny was praise indeed.

Fanny turned to Gervase and said coyly, 'Where are you going on Sunday?' She had been taking Sarah to church for months now and was tired of the pious preachings of the Minister; besides, if the two men preferred walking her beloved hills to attending church, then there was no reason why she shouldn't go also.

Gervase knew exactly where the conversation was leading. He could read her mind like a book, and was one step ahead of Fanny. 'Just down the river and over Wincobank Hill' he stated, as though that was the end of the matter and turned to John and said, 'Right, back to work'.

Fanny did not see the twinkle in his eyes but had no intention of letting the matter drop. 'Mother doesn't need me on Sunday.' There was no reply from either of the two men. 'Can I come along too?'

Gervase stopped, laid down his quill and spoke directly to John. 'We don't want a chattering woman along with us, do we?' Fanny also knew more about Gervase than he realised and she knew that he was teasing her. 'Maybe we'd be better off listening to the Minister, don't you think so, John?' quipped Gervase.

'I think I'll stay in bed', rejoined John. 'Besides, no woman can walk quickly enough for us in silly little shoes and I don't think I could stand the chatter.'

'I've got longer legs than you — you miserable little printer' she shouted, throwing a lump of sealing wax from the bench at John. The wax completely missed John and hit Gervase.

'Right that's it. John, get some of that soot while I catch her.' Gervase strode quickly forward, reached out his long sturdy arm, caught her by the wrist and playfully pulled her towards himself, his fingers entwining with hers as he protectively held their soft coolness in his own. Suddenly he felt himself to be like a foolish young boy and tenderly released them. He looked into her lovely young face and realised how precious she had become to him. 'On second thoughts we will allow you along — providing you make some gingerbread for us.'

'On condition that you don't torment me all day' she quipped back, as she left the room.

'She's a good sport' added John who watched the flurry of her skirts as she flounced out, but neither man had failed to notice the look of happiness on her face. A look which had been sadly missing over the past few months.

The three walkers began their Sunday morning trek through deserted streets, and on reaching Lady's Bridge, they crossed onto Assembly Green heading for Brightside. The early dew still clung to the grass and foliage, and although the sky was overcast the air was warm as they followed the course of the River Don. The river wound its self through the widening valley on towards Rotherham, but the recent heavy falls of rain had caused the banks to be muddy, and Fanny was grateful that Sarah had not discarded Bryce's old pair of boots. Although Bryce had been smaller than Fanny, their feet had been almost the same size and by wearing an old pair of his socks, they now fitted her perfectly. Fanny had often borrowed her father's boots in bad weather and now found them very comfortable beneath the dark muslin dress which she wore. The small wicker basket which contained the bread, cheese, hard boiled eggs and gingerbread was carried in strict rotation by the three companions on the outward journey of three miles.

Gervase had planned the route carefully from an old map in the shop, endeavouring to cover at least one new path on each of his outings. He planned to leave the river where it turned sharply and was joined by Blackburn Brook, near where the old paper mill stood. This was one of Fanny's favourite places. Here the stone-built mill faced a weir which roared noisily on its way downstream, and where salmon and trout played in the still head of water in front of the weir. Dragonflies darted over the rippling trails of weed in the water and ferns bowed in the wind, the noise of the weir drowned out their voices. Gervase did not usually buy paper from this mill but seeing it reminded him that he was running short of certain types which he should re-order immediately.

The silence which followed, as they left the Don and walked up Blackburn Brook, was luxurious in contrast, for now they could hear the birds singing, and their own voices again. The variety of wild and beautiful flowers added a quality to the day, a day that was far removed from the hustle and bustle of town life, and the trio were in a light hearted mood as they climbed upwards to Wincobank Hill. In spite of the clouds which often shut out the sun, the day was warm and dry, but the long uphill climb tired Fanny; nevertheless she was determined to keep up with the men who had said that she wouldn't be able to make it.

The men took turns now to carry the basket and although they had already halted at an isolated farmhouse to purchase milk, the fresh air had given them all a great appetite. They chose to sit on the rich mossy grass in a clearing of the wood in order to eat, and it wasn't long before the little basket was empty. John hooked the empty basket onto his stick and carried it jauntily over his shoulder as they renewed their journey. Emerging from the woods, they wandered along the ridge of Grimesthorpe to Hall Carr and then descended to the town below. In the distance the towers of the two town churches were visible in the clearer Sunday air, and beyond that a faint purple hue of the oncoming heather could just be seen.

Fanny's feet were tired from the weight of the boots, for she had not walked this far for two years, but she bravely plodded on. Deny her fatigue she might, but Gervase knew from the droop of her shoulders that she was tired; he recalled the familiar drag of her feet at the end of those long childhood walks, and he hoped that they hadn't walked her too far. Reluctantly the companions reached the town and went their separate ways. The lovely fresh clean air and the exercise brought a rosy glow to Fanny's cheeks and it wasn't long after she had climbed into bed that a deep, peaceful sleep claimed her.

Every bone in Fanny's beautiful body ached, when she arose the following morning, making work very hard to bear. She longed to be back in the woods and found herself unable to concentrate on any of the tasks before her. The mantle of responsibility was a challenge which she enjoyed, but the Sunday outing had released the tension and brought the spring back into her steps.

It did not, however, take long for Gervase's life to return to normal, for the growing shortage of paper began to create problems. The delivery which he had been expecting did not arrive, and unless he was able to obtain a supply very soon, then he would not be able to complete two very important outstanding orders. Someone would have to go out in the gig and bring sufficient paper back with which to do the job. He could not send Tom who had never handled the gig, and he could not spare the time to go himself as there was more important work to do. It would have to be John. In any case, whilst the orders stood uncompleted, it was impossible for John to change the type in the galleys, but if he could persuade Fanny to show John the way out to Hoult's Mill at Wadsley, then the pair could be there and back very quickly. Fanny knew the way from the walks which they had taken in the past, and Gervase was confident that she would be only too pleased to escape from her chores.

Fanny found the offer of a ride in the gig too good an opportunity to refuse, and after making a few quick adjustments to her attire nimbly climbed up and sat beside John.

The track by the river was firm from the wheels of many carts, but the wet weather had softened the surface and formed a film of churned mud, which splattered up from the wheels. The air was cool, but as the sun broke through the clouds it caught the raindrops, which were still on the leaves and blades of grass, creating a dazzling shimmer of silver, and the smell of hay hung heavy in the air. Slowly this beautiful riverside area was being swallowed up by the spread of industry, and each year the number of mills increased until they were now beginning to fill in the meadows. So much had changed, even in the short number of years while Fanny had been growing up, and she wondered just how much further the sprawl would go before it stopped.

John controlled the horse skilfully as they followed the track out beyond the buildings, and the further they went the more the tentacles of industry loosened their grip on the land. The speed of the gig caused a wind to blow in their faces and Fanny removed her hat to prevent it from being blown off, thus allowing her hair to flow back freely in the wind. John was struck by the beauty of it. The pair chatted amiably about work, families and common ordinary things.

A powerful feeling of exhilaration gripped Fanny as John drove faster and faster along the track, until it seemed as if the gig would overturn, but she did not complain for it made her feel wild and free once more. The dream however did not last, for the dark imposing stone mill came into view and it wasn't long before John drew the gig to a halt before its door.

Fanny wandered along the mill race, picking the odd flower here and there, whilst John went about the business which had brought them there. His easy going company had relaxed her and Fanny sat on the bank peering into the water looking for fish. She was totally unaware of his presence until he sat down on the bank beside her and Fanny was pleased to see his smiling face again. He had been watching her for several minutes as she ran her fingers through the water, oblivious to anything other than the feel of it on her skin and the warmth of the sun on her head. John felt disinclined to disturb her solitude and stood for a moment or two before joining her. They sat together then, on the stones instead of the grass which was far too wet, and cast tiny pebbles into the water, watching as the rings rippled outwards, until they merged with the smoother surrounding surface water.

'I missed all this when I was away', Fanny spoke half to herself and half to John. 'You almost believe that you will never see it again, and yet when you come back it is still here. It is hard to believe that for hundreds of years people have been walking this way, doing the same things and having the same thoughts.' She fell silent, listening to the plop of the stones as they hit the water.

'I didn't want to come to Sheffield, with its reputation for dirt and grime, but it grows on you. The hills and valleys are so endless and varied, but as a town I prefer Nottingham. Have you been there Fanny?'

'No, only to Doncaster.' He looked at her in surprise. 'It's not so easy to get out of the valleys onto the Great North Road — have you been to London?' Fanny asked inquisitively.

John took the flute from his pocket as he spoke. 'My uncle took me once. It was so busy and noisy that it frightened me, but then I was only eight. There was plenty to see, I suppose.' He placed the flute to his lips and softly played a sentimental ballad which Fanny had never heard before.

'May I have a go?' she begged, when the music had finally died away. He passed the flute to Fanny, who had no idea how to hold it, and then he leant across placing his hands gently on hers to guide her. She was suddenly conscious of the closeness of his head next to hers and she trembled as his hands covered hers.

'Purse your lips and blow into the hole', he whispered softly into her ear, and she found herself flushing with confusion. A piercing squeak rent the air as Fanny blew into the hole and she almost dropped the flute in surprise.

'I'm not very good am I?' she mused, and returned the instrument. She had suddenly lost interest in music for she found the touch of his skin had made her own tingle. 'Perhaps we had better get the paper back to Gervase. Did you manage to get it for him?' she heard her own voice ask, as if it were a stranger speaking, and not really wanting to leave at all.

'Apparently the rags for making the paper haven't been sent up from town yet, also one of the sieves for the pulp needs repairing, but they've given me enough to finish the two jobs. He'll deliver the rest the day after tomorrow.' He stood up, towering over her, and she suddenly realised how handsome he was. He offered her his hand to help her up from the stone upon which she had been sitting; his grip was firm and warm, and as he pulled her up she found herself looking into his unmistakably admiring eyes. His grip tightened possessively on her hands before he let them loose, and he took her head tenderly between his own hands and kissed her gently on the lips. His mouth was soft and sweet. Fanny found herself closing her eyes, lest he see the depth of her passion, and returned his kiss with abandonment.

Slowly he withdrew his lips from hers and as he did so forced her head backwards to allow his eyes to meet hers, and kissed the tip of her nose. 'Come — it's late, we'd better start back', he said huskily, and taking her hand in his, he led her reluctantly back to the gig.

Slowly the town reappeared, and as it did so a strange sound disturbed the air. It was an unusual, eerie, drumming noise, monotonously intermingled with the incessant clicking of machinery.

'What on earth is that, it sounds almost human?' Fanny asked, a little frightened by it. 'Like children and yet not like children, dead and lifeless', she paused, 'What is it?'

'They're factory children! Did you not realise that they were here?' The noise became louder as they approached a large ugly building.

'How awful!' exclaimed Fanny.

Driving past the mill, John pulled in behind a clump of trees and bushes which separated the track from the mill. He climbed down and tied the horse to one of the tree trunks. 'Get down, Fanny. If there is no one about I'll show you, but you may not like what you see. It grieves me sorely to witness such inhumanity.' The chanting ended as they approached. 'They probably got tired and were not working fast enough for the overseer; he makes them sing in order to keep them awake. They don't have a desire to sing but he does it to save having to whip them, then he can't work them at all.'

'Whip them — how could he! What kind of a mill is it?'

'A cotton mill.'

'How can you tell?' persisted Fanny, an edge of doubt creeping into her voice. 'Not in Sheffield, how do you know?'

'The clicking of the machinery, it's everywhere in Nottingham, Yorkshire and particularly in Lancashire towns, and full of these poor wretches. You think that the children in Sheffield grinding shops have a rough time of it, but they at least have homes. These poor little mites are brought here as apprentices from other poor parishes who don't want the responsibility of supporting them. Most of them are orphans or illegitimate. Nobody really cares as long as they don't have to feed and clothe them, so they send them to the factories where they get food and clothing in exchange for work. Let's find a window low enough to see through.'

He led her to the top of the goyt that fed the undershot mill wheel, and she climbed precariously onto a ledge. 'Can you crane your neck?' Careful you don't let anyone see you.'

It took a while for Fanny's eyes to focus through the dirty glass into the dimmer light within the building. There were rows of machinery, with rows of children, bent and dirty, working in front of them, and she gasped in horror, 'But they're only babies, some of them'. As her eyes grew accustomed to the darkness within, the reality was sickening, for some of the children were little older than six years of age, lifeless little machines themselves. 'That boy has only got one arm', she cried in disbelief.

John raised his voice angrily. 'It gets me so mad when I see them. They get so tired after working twelve hours that they fall into the machinery, one by one they get maimed, or die. See there, under the benches, that's where some of them sleep.'

'You mean they don't go out of the mill at all?' Where are their parents?' She shook her head in amazement.

'Probably dead or too sick to care for them.' John managed to position himself in such a manner that he too could see through a broken pane of glass. 'That's the overseer now.' He indicated a squat, burly figure who had just entered the room. 'Don't move or he may see you', he warned.

The overseer suddenly challenged a young boy of about ten years of age, who was operating a shuttle, and Fanny sensed that something was wrong when the boy cowered back from the man who was speaking to him. Suddenly the boy was struck by a glancing blow across the cheek, which sent him reeling onto the frame of his machine. The stunned boy rose, and although Fanny could not hear the words which were being exchanged it was obvious that he was attempting to defend himself. The man's face turned crimson with anger and he raged like a mad bull. The other children seemed to stiffen and yet no one turned to watch. Suddenly the boy darted away, only to be snatched back by the bottom of his jacket, until his face was held only inches away from the revoltingly vile face of the overseer. The man reached for a leather strap from beneath his belt and proceeded to set about the boy with such viciousness that Fanny screamed.

'For God's sake, keep your voice down!' John urged.

She trembled with nausea caused by the awful sight and could hardly raise more than a sob now. 'But he can't do that.'

The sickening lashes continued as the frenzied man struck the boy again and again, first on the neck, then his breast, back, sides and anywhere the strap could reach, even about his head. At first the boy ducked and weaved like an animal in a hunter's grasp, until he weakened and his resistance dissolved. In the end he fell in a crumpled heap to the floor, a blood-soaked bundle of rags. Neither John nor Fanny moved. They were stunned by the sickening sight which they had just witnessed, and unable to come to terms with such cruelty, they stood rooted to the ledge on which they were standing.

A sudden movement further along the path prised John back to reality. 'Look out!' he yelled at Fanny.

'What the bloody hell do you think you're doing up there — bugger off, and mind yer own business', hollered a rough looking character, brandishing a stick in their direction.

'He means what he says, Fanny. Quick, let's get back to the gig before he lets into me — he won't touch you dressed like that, but he'd as leave give me a beating as look at me.' It wasn't easy to get down from the ledge in a long skirt but Fanny managed it, tearing the hem of her dress. Breathless from running, they reached the gig still hidden behind the bushes and Fanny flung herself up into it whilst John grabbed the rein. As he jumped in after her he knocked her to the floor.

As she fell, Fanny's hand dashed against the rusty hinge of an old box which lay on the carriage floor with such force that a nasty gash appeared, causing her to yell out in pain. John ignored her and whipped the horse into a gallop. 'Hold on until we get past the next mill. I daren't stop before then. If he gets a close look at my face he'll have me done over one dark night.' They rounded the bend and John brought the horse to a halt. 'He'll not follow now, he's more interested in getting the machines working — don't ever go back there again, it isn't safe. If he recognises that hair of yours you'll know about it.' Fanny's face was ashen and he wasn't sure whether it was from shock or pain. 'Let me look at that hand.' He was worried by the size of the gash and the quantity of blood that was oozing out. 'We'll have to tie it up with my cravat and get home right away.'

Fanny didn't answer, for she felt far from well. A sickness welled up from her stomach as she thought back on the ghastly incident which had just occurred, and the sight of the blood flowing freely from her hand made her feel dizzy. John took the cloth and tied it tightly to stem the flow of blood, then kissed the fingers of the wounded hand. 'I'm sorry' he spoke softly, 'it's my fault, I shouldn't have stopped there at all, and I'm afraid this may leave a scar. We'd better hurry back.'

Gervase was surprised to see them return so quickly. He knew Fanny's inclination to linger when out, but he had made allowances for that when he despatched them. John burst into the shop, his cheeks flushed.

'What the devil's all the commotion about?' he questioned John with sudden alarm.

'Quick! The horse reared up and Fanny's gashed her hand on a rusty hinge' he replied, and turned to go back outside.

'You must have been going at a devil of a pace — or messing about. I thought you said you could handle a horse! Where is Fanny now?'

'I can handle a horse, but something frightened it and I lost my grip' John retorted, though Gervase suspected a certain sheepishness in John's eyes. 'I'll fetch her now.'

'No you won't, I'll fetch Fanny. You go and get the kettle of boiling water, and find some cloth, clean cloth mind you — and some salve.' Gervase surpressed a feeling of irritation being far from convinced by the explanation, but now was not the time for an enquiry. He would probably be lucky to get the truth anyway, but at this moment he was more concerned about Fanny. When he saw her ashen face he was even more convinced that he was right to be suspicious.

He washed the wound thoroughly, taking care to remove even the slightest sign of dirt. Fanny winced with pain and gritted her teeth but she was grateful for his lack of questioning, for she had no desire to lie to Gervase. His gentleness and concern comforted her and it made her realise how much she missed her father. 'I'm going to have to bind it tight when I've cleaned it thoroughly, it is deep and will never heal up unless I do.' Gervase knew that it would indeed leave a scar, but hesitated in telling her for fear of upsetting her further. He realised that it was probably more John's fault than hers anyway.

'I suppose you did get the paper I sent you for?' he asked John, half expecting the answer to be no.

'That's outside. I'll go and get it in.'

'Yes, and when you've done that you can take Fanny home — without the gig.'

The tasks of tending to Fanny's hand being over, John took Fanny home, but the affair was far from over as far as she was concerned. 'What are we going to do now — do you think the man will look after the boy? I think he enjoyed hurting him, isn't there anything we can do? We can't just leave him!' Fanny pleaded, completely forgetting the pain in her hand.

John had been considering the situation ever since leaving the mill. However, now that Fanny's hand had been attended to he could put his mind back into the matter. 'He'll probably clean him up and tell outsiders that there had been an accident. If the lad dies then the evidence will die with him. There are some unscrupulous doctors about who will close their eyes to anything for a fee. If he lives, and he's got any sense, he'll keep his mouth shut out of fear. They have to be tough to survive the mills. The overseer has got it in for him now anyway, I bet he has another go before long.'

'Why doesn't someone stop it all?' she demanded.

'It's all to do with money; the children are cheap labour, they're frightened and unable to protest. No one will listen to them and no one wants homeless children, except the factories.'

Fanny found speech difficult because of the anger which welled up inside her. What was the point of it all? The beautiful dresses, elegant furniture, the balls; when death, cruelty and filth were commonplace. 'Can't we do anything, anything at all?' she saw John hesitate. 'Please do something.'

'I'll go and report it to the Town Constable. With proper care the lad may live, and at least the overseer may be prevented from repeating his act.' He realised that he was taking a risk by drawing attention to himself but how on earth could he ignore that which he had witnessed. If the boy died through lack of attention then he would be as guilty as the overseer, and he might as well give up every principle he had ever held.

With Fanny safely back at home, John did not return immediately to the shop, instead he went in search of the Town Constable.

Thomas Smith was victualler of the 'Royal Oak' as well as being constable, and he sat at one of his tables, away from the troubles of the weekend which had just ended. The streets were reasonably orderly now, and everyone who had wasted their well-earned wages from Friday night until Sunday morning on ale, had returned to work. No doubt to earn enough money to repeat the ritual the following Friday night. The robberies had been committed and the felons had either been caught or had gone their own way. The grinders were a rough lot and best left to fight amongst themselves. If anyone was foolhardy enough to interfere with them, then they too were looking for trouble. He looked up from the papers arrayed in front of him, as John entered the inn.

'Are you Thomas Smith, Town Constable?'

'That's me. Now then, what can I do for you?'

John cleared his throat. He knew full well that if he failed to put a good case forward then the constable might not even go out to the mill with him. 'I've come to make a complaint of assault on a young boy who I think may die as a result.'

The constable got up without asking questions. 'Right, lad, lead the way. We'd better get a doctor as well. Where's the lad now?'

John replied cautiously, 'I'm not sure of the name of the place as it's some distance out of town, but I'll take you there'.

There were many doctors living in the area around Paradise Square, through which they had to pass, and it didn't take long for them to find one who was both available and willing to accompany them. John vaguely outlined the problem to the doctor and advised him to make use of his horse. 'It's quite a walk. If you want to follow on your horse then we'll lead the way.'

'No need, my friend. Got my chaise in the yard and we can all squeeze in. Where did you say it was?'

'He doesn't know the name of the place — come on let's get going.' The constable spoke up before John had time to answer, and cut short any need for further explanations.

They rounded the bend and approached the mill when John announced, 'He's in there, badly beaten up by an overseer, I think that's who it was but I'd know him if I saw him again'.

'Damn! You didn't say that it was at the old mill. It's best not to interfere in their business and those kids are varmints. The overseers will see to him.'

'I tell you he's in a bad way. I want to make a formal complaint against the man myself — I saw him do it.' John turned to the doctor. 'You're involved now, so you've got to find out what's happened to the boy.'

'He's right, you know, I just can't ignore the fact that he might need attention.'

The constable shook his head. Damn it, he'd been a fool caught off guard. He should have found out the details first instead of presuming it was some well-off child in trouble. What was an educated fellow doing messing about with the mill anyway? Now there was no choice, he had to look into the matter. The chaise stopped before the mill, and standing on the steps stood the vulgar man who had chased Fanny and John away with the stick.

'What do you lot want 'ere, ain't nobody needin you' he growled.

Thomas Smith took control, 'We've brought the doctor to see an injured boy who we understand works here'. So far so good. John felt pleased with himself, for by being evasive he had secured the attention of both the constable and the doctor. He had also placed them in a position from which neither could back away, each being answerable to the other.

'In't no sick boy 'ere as I know of, so yer wastin yer time.' A look of insolence appeared on the man's face as he spoke.

'Yes there is, and unless we see him we're not moving', John quickly intervened.

'Here, I'll deal with this if you don't mind. Keep out of it. I'm beginning to regret listening to you in the first place', the constable retorted angrily, and turned back to the man on the steps. 'Come on, open up the door and let me in.'

The man swore to himself and pushed the door open. The hideous noise of the machinery increased to a throbbing din as they entered the building and the overseer came across, a sickly grin on his ugly face. 'What can I do for you gentlemen?' His oily voice irritated John immensely.

'We've come to look at an injured boy. I'm Town Constable and I'm here to answer a complaint of cruelty' Thomas Smith announced.

'We've not got one', was the terse reply, intended to rebuff the enquiries.

'I have it on good authority that there is a boy here in need of help, and unless you let us see him I'm going to have to stop the machines and search the place. I'll need to question the children too.' The constable was determined not to be put off. 'This man's a witness.'

The overseer appeared to ignore John and replied casually 'Oh, you mean the lad who fell into the machine! He's only bruised — nothing that rest won't cure'. No sign of concern showed on his fleshy, arrogant face but as he turned sideways he shot an evil leer in John's direction before attempting to guide the party to the door leading to the doctor's chaise.

'Now! We want to see him now!' John spoke out hurriedly. He could see that the crafty man was succeeding in playing down the affair.

The constable was becoming irritated by John's constant interference but stood his ground, for the leer had not gone unnoticed, 'Yes, come on man — if you've nothing to hide you'll be in the clear'.

Grudgingly the overseer turned and led them to a small room which went off from the back of the main factory workroom. There, crouching in a corner, dazed and only half conscious, cringed a forlorn bundle of flesh. The doctor bent and attempted to straighten out the limbs, but with each touch and movement the child emitted groans of pain and despair. The weal's across his neck and face were still covered in dried blood and one eye had disappeared beneath a black, purple mass of swollen flesh. It was impossible to find the boy's teeth at all, for his lips were so puffed up that they appeared to cover the whole of his face.

'My God, this little chap has never fallen into a machine, he's been cruelly beaten!' gasped the doctor in horror. 'Get him into my chaise as gently as you can, he'll have to go to the infirmary.' He turned to the constable. 'And get that man into a cell' he ordered.

'It was an accident I tell you!' the furious overseer spat out venomously.

John rounded on him, 'I saw you do it and I'm going to be a witness.' He looked at the man despisingly as he went grumbling and cursing with the constable.

John helped to place the boy into the chaise with the help of the doctor, and because there was insufficient room in the carriage agreed to follow later. He hung back after the doctor had gone and slipped unnoticed by the man with the stick, into the mill, took aside the two boys who had been operating the machines next to the injured boy and spoke to them. 'Would you like to get rid of your overseer once and for all? Would you like to see him punished for what he did to your friend?' Both boys nodded in unison. The bigger one spoke out, 'Ee'll gerrus though if we say owt'. Their dirty faces were full of fear.

'He won't come back if you'll act as witnesses. All you have to do is tell the truth, that you saw what he did, and the doctor and I will do the rest.' The boys seemed to prefer endless suffering rather than risk inviting further trouble. John pressed on. 'If you don't he'll be allowed back.' He paused, 'Now, will you do it?' He waited anxiously while the boys just stared at him in bewilderment. 'I'll give you a shilling each.'

There was no further hesitancy. Neither boy had ever owned a shilling before, and both nodded in unison. 'Yes, Sir.'

There was little point now in concealing the facts from Gervase, as the whole affair would soon become public knowledge. John returned to the shop several hours late, much to the displeasure of Gervase, who was struggling to complete the orders and was in no mood to be fobbed off with any old excuse.

'Where on earth have you been? You do realise that we're way behind with the orders as it is! You've been further than the Garnett's, I know, because Tom went to fetch you. If you ask me there is more behind this accident than you're letting on.' Gervase was annoyed and the tone in his voice demanded nothing less than a frank explanation.

'You're damn right there is. I'm sorry it's taken up so much of your time but things have transpired which make it now too late to turn back the clock. I think you had better hear everything from the beginning. Sit down, if you can spare another five minutes.' Without omitting any of the details John explained fully, and finally admitted, 'I'm sorry I involved Fanny, and I didn't want any of the attention that the case is going to get, but I just could not leave the lad to die — could you?'

'No! I don't suppose you could, neither if it comes to that could I, but now your head's on the block, so you'd better watch out. You're dealing with ruffians and bullies now.' He was sorry for John. Obviously he had little choice in the course of action that he had subsequently taken, but Gervase was extremely anxious for Fanny's safety. 'You've got to keep Fanny out of this — you do understand? Not only for her safety's sake but for her social standing, as well as the adverse effect which it could have on their business. Keep away from her, if you're seen together then she's in trouble.'

'Don't worry, I'm just as worried about her as you are.' The concern was obvious in his face. 'You ought to have seen the boy — in one respect I'm not sorry because if we hadn't stopped he would still have been beaten, and perhaps died as a result. That bully should be hung for what he did, it would stop him doing it again.' He was white with anger. 'I hope he is.'

Gervase laughed bitterly, 'You'd be surprised. There's little justice about, it's the poor devils who are starving that get the hardest punishment, people like the overseer live to fight another day.' His voice suddenly became very firm, 'Remember, keep Fanny out of it. She's not to be a witness — understand!'

The case against Matthew Hines was to be held at the Sheffield Magistrate's Court within the week, and Fanny was forbidden to attend the hearing for fear of being recognised. She hoped and prayed that the man would be hanged, or at least transported. After all, if boys of seventeen were hanged for stealing trivial items, then anyone as evil as Hines must deserve no less a punishment. She had never hated anyone before, but the strength of her feelings against Hines surprised even Fanny herself.

Hines' appearance before the magistrates aroused a great deal of public interest, and sufficient evidence was given against him to warrant the case being transferred to the Doncaster Sessions. Nothing was concluded, John knew that, but at least the case was going to a higher court where he was likely to see a stiffer sentence given. John breathed a sigh of relief and left the Court House. He had not missed the look of hatred on Matthew Hines' face as he passed him on the way back to the cell.

Fanny's hand healed only slowly and there were times when it gave cause for concern. The gash had narrowly missed the tendon, but careful cleansing and binding of the wound by Gervase had prevented serious complications. However, it did leave a large crimson scar on the top of her hand, running from the base of the thumb to the wrist and Fanny was quite distressed, stating that she would never again go out without wearing gloves. John blamed himself for the accident and fussed constantly over her hand, but at the same time, took great care to conceal the bond which was rapidly developing between them. They all waited nervously for the trial and finally Gervase agreed to accompany John to the Sessions in Doncaster, but again he forbade Fanny to go to court.

The courtroom in Doncaster was full to capacity as usual; it provided the cheapest form of theatre to the poorer citizens, and consequently was always well attended. Each time the magistrate asked that 'The prisoner be brought forward', there followed an outcry and hissing from the crowd, which left John unsure on which side the crowd stood.

The usher called for Matthew Hines, who came forward, bristling with confidence, to stand before the magistrates.

'Matthew Hines, cotton mill overseer of the town of Sheffield, you do stand accused that on the second day of August you did make an assault upon one Henry Ashton, an apprentice, and with a certain leather strap, did hold him and violently, cruelly and immoderately beat him. That you scourged and struck the said Henry Ashton upon the head, neck, breast, sides, back and other parts of the body, until his life was despaired of. What have you to say?'

Hines shook his head. 'Sir, he was a troublesome apprentice, always answering back and never competent in his work. He tried me sorely.'

'Have you not been overseer at the mill for a number of years?'

'Yes, Sir. There's never been any complaints about my dealings with the children before.'

'Then you are surely aware that troublesome apprentices can be sent to the House of Correction in Wakefield, to serve hard labour, until they mend their ways.'

'Yes, Sir, but I tried to be like a father to them all, kind and forgiving.' He was interrupted by cat calls from the public.

'Quiet there! Or I shall have the lot of you removed from this courtroom', roared the irate magistrate. 'Continue if you please, Mr Hines.'

'I also thought to save the town money, and teach the lad better ways.'

'You were seen to beat the boy without mercy after he appeared to be working ordinarily at his machine. This is hardly the action of a fair and reasonable man. Do you deny this?'

'Sir, the boy tried to avoid discipline and fell onto the frame of the machine, where he sustained his injuries. I only struck him once or twice.'

'The doctors at the infirmary in Sheffield state that the injuries are consistent with a series of beatings with a strap, and not by falling into the machine. There are also three witnesses to the incident. Please be seated.' A look of defiant indignation crossed Hines' face and he remained motionless before the magistrate. 'I repeat — sit down!' A hush fell over the room as Hines angrily sat down. 'Ask Mr Andrews to come forward.'

John was brought to the stand and observed the look on Hines' face with some satisfaction for the look substantiated the allegation that he was a bully.

'Mr Andrews, you stated that on August 2nd last, you saw Matthew Hines beat the said Henry Ashton senseless with a strap which he had taken from his belt. Do you confirm this allegation?'

'I do, Sir. The boy was working quietly at his machine when Mr Hines disturbed him, and when the lad tried to run away he beat him without mercy.'

'Did you try to stop him?'

'No, Sir, I couldn't get to him.'

'Why not, if you were near enough to see every detail?'

'I was outside the building looking in through the window.'

A ripple of laughter ran through the crowd, leaving John wishing that he could have offered a better reason.

The magistrate was irritated by the laughter and said caustically, 'It seems to me to be a peculiar coincidence that you were looking through the window at this time, but no matter, there are two other witnesses who were inside the building at the time of the incident. These boys have sworn to the truth of the fact that the incident did indeed happen as you reported'. He paused, 'The doctors at Sheffield infirmary are confident that the boy could not have inflicted such injuries upon himself by falling, and Mr Hines did try to hide the boy from the constable. Would you describe Mr Hines' attitude on striking the boy, as that of a father reprimanding his son?'

'No, Sir.' John turned towards Hines who returned the look with one of hatred. 'It was almost as though he was enjoying it. He could have stopped at any time, but he just went on and on, even though the boy was almost senseless.' John shook his head in horror at the memory. 'I fetched a doctor from the town to the mill as soon as I could.'

'Thank you, Mr Andrews, you may retire.' The magistrate waited until there was silence once more. 'This case has shocked many responsible members of the public who are concerned about the welfare of working children. The boy, Henry Ashton, will bear the mental and physical scars of this ordeal for the rest of his life, and will probably be more of a burden to his parish as a result. Child apprentices can be extremely provoking and defiant and they cannot be allowed to do as they please; however, we cannot allow such cruelty to recur. Matthew Hines does not appear to be able to control either the children or himself, and I recommend that he is forbidden to oversee children in the future and serves a suitable period of time in York Castle. He should also pay a fine.'

The news which John brought back from Doncaster was a bitter disappointment to them all. Matthew Hines was to be confined in York Castle Prison for six months and to pay a fine of 6s 8d. He was to find other employment on release from the castle. No hanging, no transportation, and in six months he could be free on the streets again. John was glad now that he had heeded Gervase's warning by keeping Fanny clear of the case, for now there was a real danger that Hines would come back to Sheffield, where his family lived, when the six months were up.

Perhaps, thought John, it would be better if he emigrated to America before Hines' return, taking Fanny with him. She had always given him hope and encourgement and he had no intention of leaving her behind.

Chapter 7

The trial of *Matthew Hines* left John in a state of discontent, and whereas for eight months he had philosophically resigned himself to working hard with an eye to the future, he now found the old spirit, of defiance against suppression, rearing its head again. The time spent working for Gervase had not been unrewarding; he had enjoyed the challenge of creating a new business and found recompense in his employer's companionship, but it was impossible for him to sit astride the political fence any longer.

He observed his fellow countrymen, a people ravaged by twenty years of war, and again they were being beaten and disheartened by poverty, caused by the failure of crops and harvests after the long period of abysmal weather. Whereas the war had caused slumps in many industries, in others it had created heavier demands, especially in iron, coal and cloth production for uniforms. With the cessation of the war the roles became almost reversed and the need for cloth, iron and coal dropped severely, throwing thousands of men and woman out of work. Wartime shortages had compelled England to grow its own foodstuffs, and many a small farmer who had extended himself in wartime went bankrupt in peacetime. It was ironical that, with fewer farmers producing less food, the weather throughout spring and summer was so severe and wet, with snow falling as late as June, as to cause near famine. The crops had preferred to hide beneath the ground, and any that did appear refused to ripen, causing price increases to match the shortages and rendering the poor unable to pay the high price asked for bread.

Outbreaks of violence resulting from the hardship were becoming commonplace, ending in men being hanged for rioting, and men, women and children being transported to the colonies for crimes committed in the name of survival.

Within two weeks of the local Doncaster Sessions John made his move. He sought out the local radical fringe in the town who were endeavouring to bring about political reform. The need for change in the parliamentary system was long overdue, and now was the time to demand a free and full representation of the people in the House of Commons. The smaller, sparsely populated counties were well represented in Parliament but the large industrial counties had few members to represent their enormous populations, with the result that they had little power in the House. Taxes on essential goods were far too high, and a call for cuts in these, and for a rigid economy in every government department of administration was essential after the long waste of public treasures throughout the war.

There had been corruption. Foreign powers had been allowed to borrow millions of pounds in treaties, thus enabling them to raise armies to fight battles to promote their own ambitious projects. This money was needed at home. The Prince Regent still lived an extravagant life style, with his entourage of idle fellows dressed in their red coats, white breeches and bespangled outfits, and all enjoying their assemblies and routs. The Prince Regent was even more unpopular now for his mistreatment of his wife. An air of sullen discontentment was gathering and men were wandering from county to county in search of work, only to return disillusioned and even poorer than before. Many were resorting to violent vandalism, forcing an entry into properties and workplaces which held weaving and lace making frames, endeavouring to destroy them in order to make employers pay better wages. Others were trying novel experiments to attract attention to the plight peacefully. Thousands of colliers from Nottinghamshire decided to present a petition to the Prince, in person; they were accompanied by three wagon loads of coal, each yoked to fifty men who would pull them to London. On the side of each wagon were the words 'Rather work than beg'.

To compound the felony of poverty, the income tax which was only paid by the rich was abolished. Banks crashed and the crime rate soared. Now men were gathering together at night in barns and whispering in secret in order to plan revolution. Men were spying upon one another, and no one could ever be completely sure of the others loyalty.

The most obvious place to find like-minded associates was in the hostelries, and John had known even when in Nottingham, that the 'Blue Bell' in Sheffield was one such place where, with care, he could make contact with supporters of the radical movement. Up to this point he had considered it more sensible to avoid controversial establishments, and had kept his socialising to coffee rooms and refined drinking houses, but he had nevertheless been keeping alert for news of the movement.

In the winter months after his arrival he had spent most evenings immersed in some of the rarer volumes which were kept on the shelves of the shop. John's insatiable appetite for reading had at first irritated Tom, who wanted to talk, but in the end his own curiosity as to the contents of the books had made him want to learn to read. The two young men eventually came to an understanding concerning their living quarters and each kept strictly to his own area out of working hours.

95

Tom's sufferance of John changed dramatically in the light of the Hines' case and almost immediately John became subjected to an allegiance from Tom which verged on idolatry. The knowledge that the lad had a habit of hanging around ale houses gave John the opportunity of introduction, which he needed, to make contact with undercover delegates. It was not entirely without kindness that he used Tom as a means to an end. The boy worked hard and was intensely loyal; he was also flattered to be seen out with the 'local hero' and introduced John to many useful people, although his own interest in politics was non-existent.

John integrated himself slowly into the movement, and their confidence in him increased considerably once they had checked his credentials with Nottingham, a move not entirely unexpected since he had given their accredited delegates information about his past. He took great care to keep this side of his life a secret from Gervase and Fanny, but Tom was not even aware of John's past and did not realise the significance of the introductions. There were plans afoot now to rally to London in the new year to demand relief for the poor and for political reform, and it was important that all meetings were held in secret.

One evening John was completely taken aback whilst in deep discussion with another radical in the parlour of the 'British Tar' to see, standing across the room, the rough-looking fellow who had barred his entry to the cotton mill in August. Instinctively he held himself back in the shadows, hoping that the man would not see him. The incident unnerved him considerably and he resolved in future to visit only hostelries which he felt were safe. Occasionally, when walking home late at night he imagined that he was being followed, and started taking different routes to and from the shop. In the morning he would laugh at himself for being foolish.

The November evening was cold and Tom chose to laze about in the warmth of the back room of the shop, rather than go with John to one of the local inns. The novelty of learning to read was beginning to wear off as the words got harder; his friends ridiculed him for wasting his time and he wondered sometimes why he was bothering at all. He was bored and restless, but the dog, which was in the outhouse, was even more restless than he was and barked constantly, much to the annoyance of the neighbours. One in particular had threatened to throttle the dog if it didn't stop howling. The dog was generally well-behaved and Tom had grown extremely fond of him, feeding him on whatever scraps he could find, and leaving him to forage for himself in the daytime — he slept in the outhouse at night.

Tom was mystified by the dog's persistent growling and went out into the back yard to investigate, but found nothing unusual out there. Later, the barking became suddenly frantic and Tom turned out the lamp, terrified and rooted to the spot. There was a heavy thud and a sharp yelp, then silence — and he knew that the dog was dead. He wanted to prise open the window to call to the dog but there was a scuffle of feet by the door and he wished John had not forgotten to put the shutters up to the windows. Instead he crawled under the bench and stayed there until, cursing the neighbours, he finally fell asleep.

The brisk walk in the evening air was exactly what John needed after the thick atmosphere of the inn. He never used the shop door for his own personal use. The back door, however, was accessible only from the alleyway which ran at the foot of the backyards and gardens, at the rear of the premises, and in spite of the moonlight, much of the alleyway was extremely dark. John had never liked this walk in the dark and nervously swore that in future he would carry a lantern, in spite of the inconvenience carrying it would cause. He hesitated instinctively, thinking to have seen a shadowy movement up ahead, but heard nothing to substantiate his fears and pushed the thought to the back of his mind. A further twenty yards on and there was a sound, this time from behind, but there was nothing there. He reached a spot completely illuminated by the moonlight where the hedge parted, and felt quite safe. Then he heard it again and spun round.

There was a second sound, this time from the front, he could run neither forwards nor backwards, trapped between two dark chasms from where black shapes came at him on all sides. Four figures seized him and thrust him up against the wall of one of the outhouses. He had no time to scream, the sickening rain of blows came down without mercy, first to his nose, then his head, his mouth, until everything swam. He tried to shout for the dog as a fist winded him and another struck him violently in the stomach. A low voice hissed menacingly, 'That's for Matthew Hines, don't tell the law or we'll finish you'.

John sank to the floor of the alley, the taste of blood in his mouth, and suddenly the boot of one of his assailants swung viciously between his legs. He rolled over in agony and vomited. It seemed as though the vicious blows from the boots would never end, but they did, and the men left as suddenly as they had come. He couldn't move, the sickening pains seeming to encompass every inch of his body, and he sank into a black void.

The dawn came slowly, rising above the black silhouette of the roofs and chimneys, and the yellow early light of the new day aroused him. He slowly opened his eyes, which were swollen and aching from the blows, not caring if he lived or died. His limbs were frozen stiff with cramp and refused to move, and there was nothing he could do about it. The town was waking from its slumber, but all he could do was lie there helpless.

The minutes ticked by, seemingly for hours, until he was able to force himself to crawl painstakingly, foot by foot, to the opening of the yard to the shop. He bumped into something soft on the flagstones and heaved in revulsion as he realised that the mound was the dog, its skull smashed to pulp, lying there limp and lifeless. It could have been himself dead there on the stones. No! That had not been their intention, they had inflicted pain. What pain! His head ached, he ached all over. He reached the door. Unable to rise he pushed against it but there was no response.

Tom cowered with fear, not daring to open the door and wishing that either John or Gervase would come. Then he heard the moaning and gathered sufficient courage to peer through the window. His eyes bulged with fear at the sight of a pair of blood covered legs lying before the door, and quickly he went to open it.

'Get help Tom! Oh God, fetch Fanny. Don't fetch a doctor, please!' was all John could utter before he sank once more into blackness.

Unable to believe what he saw before him, Tom stared at the unrecognisable swollen and bloody face, but the voice and hair were John's. He found the key to the front door and raced round to Fanny's shop.

Sarah was still sleeping, but Fanny was almost dressed when the pounding on the door began. She could not imagine why anyone would wake them so early in the morning. She hurried to the window and hastily threw it open in order to quieten the caller before he could knock again. Tom was just about to recommence his hammering when the noise of the window opening caused him to look up. 'Tom! What on earth is the matter?' Fanny demanded sharply. 'You'll wake everyone up.'

'Please come, Miss Fanny. He's in a bad way.' She could hear the panic in his voice.

'Who, Tom? Try and be calm, I don't want you to wake mother.'

His eyes rolled frantically, 'It's John, Miss. Someone beat him up. He's in a bad way. Please hurry'. Fanny quickly closed the window, and snatching her shawl from the chair by the bed, hurried down the stairs. 'He's in a terrible state but he says I'm not to get a doctor', cried Tom when Fanny finally appeared.

Fanny's mind was in a turmoil. It didn't matter who had done it, all she cared about was that he was hurt. 'You go on, Tom — I'm following.' She pulled on the first pair of shoes she could find and ran after the boy, afraid and unsure of what she might discover when she reached the shop.

She looked down in horror at the figure on the floor. She had never seen anyone in such wretched circumstances before and fought to hold back the scream which was forming in her throat. 'Oh — John! What have they done?' she begged an answer from the bloody mess that was before her, but he did not hear her in the black sea which engulfed him. 'Tom, go and fetch my mother and then Gervase, and hurry.'

Tears ran down Tom's face, 'Will he be alright, Miss?'

'I don't know, please hurry' she pleaded, near to tears herself. When Tom had gone she knelt by John's side, afraid to touch him for fear of inflicting more pain. He was so cold. She folded up the shawl and placed it lovingly between his head and the stone floor. There was little else she could do but she took his hands gently in hers, holding them against her warm face, and wept. Tears flowed freely down her cheeks as she looked at his bruised and battered face, and then slowly she felt his hand tighten on hers until his nails bit into her skin. She didn't mind the pain if it gave him comfort.

Sarah came quickly, and gently using the hot water which Tom had boiled, they managed to soften the dried blood from his face and hair; there was little they could do about the swelling or the gashes around his eyes and mouth, except bathe them gently. He was too heavy to lift and they had to wait until Gervase arrived before they could move him.

Gervase seethed at the brutality of the attack but was not altogether surprised. Even though he was not personally involved in the incident at the mill, he had half expected some form of retaliation, but in the shape of sabotage on the shop.

Carefully, with Tom's help, Gervase got John up the stairs and placed him on the bed. He left Sarah and Fanny to minister to John while he went below in order to calm Tom and also to find out exactly what had happened. Tom was standing in the doorway to the yard, his shoulders hanging dejectedly, staring out at the bundle of fur by the outhouse. Gervase turned to the lad, placing a hand on his shoulder and said kindly, 'Leave it Tom and get on with some work. I'll go and bury him — go on, that's a good lad — it's no job for you'.

He gently pushed Tom towards a pile of papers which were ready for printing and went out towards the animal. He buried the poor innocent creature in a patch of soft earth near where they usually burned the rubbish, then returned to the shop without telling Tom of the sickening sight he had seen. He endeavoured to make some semblance of order out of the day. He felt sorry for the boy and thought about the year which had just passed, a year in which much had changed; not only had he started his own business but he had assumed responsibility for a homeless boy, a fellow with a nose for trouble and a dog which was now dead. He also felt emotionally responsible for Sarah and Fanny.

The two women removed John's outer clothing which was dirty and blood stained, taking great care not to cause him any more pain than necessary and, whilst Sarah fetched more clean water from downstairs, Fanny removed his shirt. Large areas of bruising covered his ribs but his powerful chest was still bronzed from the summer sun, and Fanny lowered her eyes modestly. He seemed to be sleeping and she gently followed the lines of his chest with her fingers. His skin was warm and silky and she ran her hand caressingly towards his neck, then outlined his lips with her finger-tips. He wasn't sleeping, merely lying there with his eyes closed, savouring the gentleness of her touch. He opened his eyes and watched her face, beautiful and full of caring, and also unaware of his gaze. She raised her eyes to his and was startled to see them open, watching her, and she quickly lowered hers afraid of what he might have seen there. The colour rose in her cheeks and she attempted to rise, wanting to get away, but in spite of the pain which the effort caused, he reached out for her hand and caught it to prevent her from leaving. His grip was surprisingly strong and he pulled her toward him and whispered softly, 'I love you Fanny. Hold me close'.

She couldn't hold him without hurting him, she couldn't kiss his bruised and swollen lips either, so she lifted the palm of his hand to her lips and caressed the moist soft skin with her quivering lips and whispered back, almost afraid of the sound of her own voice. 'I love you too.' The sensuous touch of her lips sent a warmth through his aching body and their eyes met, obliterating all around them.

Sarah returned and sent Fanny away whilst she removed his trousers. She covered him finally with a quilt and gave Fanny the job of coaxing a warm drink through his lips, before going home to make him some hot gruel. Fanny propped him up, half on the pillow and half against her body, her arm round his neck to give support, and he allowed her to pour the liquid slowly into his mouth. He laid his head on her breast and in response she pressed her lips to his brow and let him sleep.

The long night in the cold alley had taken its toll. He developed a cold which turned into a fever and for two days and nights Fanny and Sarah stayed by his bedside, taking turns to watch over him, fearful for his life. Sarah was ever careful of Fanny's modesty and made her tend to other matters while she washed him herself and changed his sweat-soaked bedding. Then the fever broke and Fanny fed him until he could support himself. He watched her admiringly as she flitted gracefully to and fro around the room, catching her hand when given the chance and, in the evenings when Tom wasn't there, she sat on the bed as close to him as comfort allowed. Tom had been allowed to sit with them some evenings to listen to Fanny's reading and he sat spell-bound by the adventures of hero and animal alike, content to be allowed into their unreal world protected from the harsh realities outside.

The moment John's strength returned, his restlessness also returned, and he began to work in spite of his aches and pains. They told no one of his ordeal, being unable to provide evidence to support his claims, and also mindful of the possibility of further trouble, but John was more determined than ever to keep contact with the Movement in spite of the risks involved.

One evening when Tom had gone out, John paced the floor agitatedly. He had not been out of the building since the night of the assault and he was sick to death of being cooped up, sick of being forced to pace the room. Fanny watched as his agitation grew and was perturbed by his churlish manner which distanced him from her. 'What's the matter, aren't you well?' she asked despondently.

He stopped suddenly. 'I'm going out tomorrow', he announced. 'I've got to go out again sometime and I'm tired of hiding in this place like an animal. I'm not the guilty one. Why should I hide?'

'If you go out in the daytime you will be alright', she offered.

He spun round, 'I'm a man, not an animal and I refuse to be intimidated by bullies. There's work to do out there. I shall just have to be more careful, that's all'.

Fanny had never seen him like this before, almost cold and aloof. 'You won't go near the Movement, will you?' she pleaded.

'I have to. The Movement needs me and men like Hines can't be allowed to get away with it. It wasn't all in vain, we must do what we can to bring about change. In fact there is pressure being put on the government right now to improve the working conditions for children. It's sad but it takes an incident like the one at the mill to make the authorities do something.'

'But why does it have to be you? You've done enough already. It's you the bullies are after.' She was near to tears now, seeing that he would be putting himself into more danger.

'We've had enough! The workers and grinders aren't going to be put down anymore — their lives aren't worth living. Most of them die young and they spend the last months of their lives in agony, their dust-filled lungs and throats refuse to accept anything but liquids. There's little or no comfort for the families who are compelled to live on Parish Charity when their men folk are dead. Think of those fatherless children you saw Fanny. The men deserve more money for their labour, and better working conditions. It's not the workers, not even the manufacturers who make the money in this town.' He slapped his hand down hard on the table, making Fanny jump.

'Well, who does then?' snapped Fanny. 'Everyone's complaining about the shortage of money.'

He raised his voice angrily. 'Yes, everyone grumbles! No one admits to being wealthy, but the factors, the middlemen are, and they are quietly soaking up the money. Have you seen the big houses springing up on the edge of town? That's where the money is, they can afford to hold on to stocks and force the prices in the market to rise before they sell. Money gets money if you know how to make it work for you, if you can get any.'

Fanny was becoming angry at the tone of his voice, 'But that's not fair! I know grinders, they're a rough lot, and they drink too much. You'd think they'd spend their money more wisely'.

He spoke sharply to her, unable to understand her reasoning, 'They drink to blot out their working day, it's something to live for. They also drink to wash the dust from their throats'.

Fanny was hurt by his sharpness. It wasn't her fault that things were as they were. 'It's not my fault' she shouted back.

John looked at Fanny. She was right, it wasn't her fault at all, he had allowed his anger to take over. He softened his tone, 'No, it's not. I'm sorry, but have you seen the conditions in which they work, and live?' She shook her head. 'It's about time more of your kind did. You artisans live in a fool's paradise. You're only on the edge of reality, cushioned from the harshness of real poverty.' He was being too hard on her, he could see that, and put his arm around her. 'It's not your fault. I just wish I could take you with me, then you would see for yourself and you'd understand why I feel as I do.'

'You forget that my father's work killed him.' Fanny felt the anger rise within herself and pushed his arm away from her. 'Why don't you show me then?' she fired at him, 'I'm quite capable of making up my own mind.'

'It's not that easy. You can't go amongst them in good clothes and a groomed face. Besides, you'd be recognised before long. They don't trust outsiders prying or being patronising.'

Fanny felt patronised too and resented his attitude. 'So I never will see for myself, is that it? You can't blame me then for my ignorance can you?' She was tired of the conversation and of his quarrelling, and stormed from the room.

'Come back Fanny' he called out in surprise. But Fanny did not return. He strode to the top of the stairs. 'Damn and blast the woman,' he said as he slammed the door angrily.

She stormed out of the shop banging the door to behind her, unaware that Gervase and Tom had returned and were in the back room. Gervase breathed a sigh of relief as the door closed and looked at Tom questioningly. 'I wonder what all that was about?' He winked at Tom knowingly. 'Take heed, Tom don't ever invite a woman's wrath. I don't know what's got into those two, but I'm glad not to be in the middle of it.'

Moodiness was not something which Sarah was used to in her daughter, and she was puzzled as Fanny stood fidgeting by the sink. She wasn't sure what had caused the dark mood but lately there had been a change in Fanny. Perhaps the harsh realities of the past months were beginning to take their toll. The fidgeting began to annoy Sarah, 'For goodness sake go and read a book or something, I can't do with all this tonight' she remonstrated with Fanny.

Fanny lay on the bed but did not see the words in the book which she held. It had been a long time since she had quarrelled with anyone but tonight John had been insufferable. Normally she would have followed him to the ends of the earth, but tonight she hated him. He had made her miserable, his obsession with the Movement made him detatched and withdrawn from her, leaving her shut out. He had kept his promise to Gervase, keeping her away from trouble; in fact he had taken it to extremes and would not allow her to be seen in public with him. She hated her hair too, for the colour of it made her so conspicuous. She tugged at it, pulling the strands as if to tear it out. If only she could disguise herself, as Rosalind had done at Shakespeare's hands, but then there was no way she could hide her ample breasts.

Such was Fanny's determination next morning to put John from her mind, that she set out to spring-clean the shop. She swept with such vigour that the woodlice fled before the onslaught of her broom, and the spiders retreated back to their tangled webs. Young Bryce was quite amused at his sister's pique but knew better than to intrude on her in this mood. His own wife was also prone to such carryings on, more often than he cared to admit. He found it impossible to put even a comb down before it was immediately tidied away, until in the end he could stand it no longer.

'I don't know what's got into you today Sis, but it's certainly put you in a frenzy.'

'Just because someone works hard, instead of listening to town gossip, doesn't mean they're in a frenzy' Fanny almost screamed, jabbing the broom so hard that the head came off the stale. 'Oh no, now look what you've made me do to the poor broom' she shouted at him.

'Me?' He asked mockingly.

Fanny looked down at the broken broom and realised just how much she had made it suffer instead of John. She stared at it in disbelief, then caught the twinkle in Bryce's eye and her venom evaporated immediately.

Sarah, who was soaking the salt from the herrings in the kitchen, smiled to herself at the sound of laughter, Fanny hadn't laughed like that for ages.

In a happier frame of mind, Fanny carried on with the cleaning, determined to find some means of accompanying John about the town. The old chest hadn't been moved since the previous Christmas and Fanny lifted the lid more out of sentimentality than thoroughness. The wigs were still there and she recalled her father's joy when he had watched his grandchildren squeal with delight, as they put them on. The memories also saddened her, for she missed him so much. Her favourite wig lay in the bottom. Fanny lifted it out, and for fun, whilst Bryce was outside putting up the shutters, she put the wig on and stood with her back to the doorway, awaiting his return.

Bryce could not recall anyone entering the shop, or even being passed in the street by a woman, but nevertheless he had a customer. 'I'm sorry madam, but we are about to close.' Fanny turned slowly without smiling, or speaking, and looked directly at him. 'I'm sorry Mad . . . Oh, it's you Fanny! You are a card, for one moment you had me fooled. What are you messing about at? I've got to get off home.' He took another look at her. 'Quite remarkable you know — you could get away with a deception like that.' He saw a light suddenly appear in his sister's eyes and then found himself in a crushing embrace as Fanny whispered, 'Thank you', into his ear.

After Bryce had gone she looked into the glass, and knew that she could do it. If she wore one of her mother's old discarded dresses, even though it would be on the short side, the effect would be realistic. Surely John would take her with him now.

John was not impressed by her childish idea and didn't hesitate to tell her so. 'Look, Fanny, it's not a game for petulant girls, I don't want to take you anywhere if there is danger, nor do I want to lose my job through my own stupidity.' There was no sign of him weakening. 'No, I won't take any chances.'

'You mean you don't want to take me!' Fanny stormed, and dug her heels in, determined to make him change his mind. She knew her idea was a good one and there was no way that she was going to be stopped now.

It was no surprise to John that Fanny could be so determined, and he knew also that she would not let the matter rest. He set out to deflate the situation as tactfully as possible. 'Listen, there is a meeting at the Town Hall tomorrow about sending a petition to London. Why don't you put the wig on and meet me there?'

Fanny was not a fool and didn't like to be appeased. She was going to prove her point, she would show him.

The meeting at the Town Hall was set to begin at eleven in the morning, and, despite the extreme inclemency of the weather, the crowd gathered early outside the building to ensure their admission. Fanny slipped out of the house when Sarah and Bryce were suitably occupied, having already informed them that she wished to call on Miss Ashton in the Haymarket, to view the latest consignment of fashionable hats which had just arrived from London. Before making her escape she put on the wig and slipped a hooded cape around herself to keep out the rain. She could hear the murmurings of a large crowd even before she reached the corner of Castle Green, but on turning the corner, the size of the multitude took her breath away.

There was really no necessity for a disguise. People huddled beneath shawls and sacks in an effort to keep dry and it was quite impossible to single out the identity of any one individual. Fanny looked everywhere for John but he was not to be seen. Suddenly the doors of the Town Hall opened and the crowd surged forward, filling the place to suffocation point, and yet still leaving thousands outside clamouring to be allowed in.

Within the hall, Mr Rawson was called to take the chair, but the people inside the building were unable to hear one word of his speech, and the crowd standing outside in the rain began to feel that they had been abandoned by the meeting. A lone voice shouted, 'Adjournment', then another voice took up the cry 'Let's have an adjournment,' until the crowd began chanting in unison and it became impossible for any speaker to be heard above the uproar. Mr Rawson gave up, and it was announced that in spite of the weather the meeting would reconvene in Paradise Square.

The cheering crowd trudged, ankle deep in mud, through the pouring rain to the square. Fanny could not have left the crowd had she desired to do so, for by now she was hemmed in and was being dragged along with the mass. There was an atmosphere of excitement in the people, a comradeship which had no barrier, and a woman as rough in her dress as her speech linked arms with her. 'Ee luv I avn't enjoyed mi sen s' much fer years.' She gave Fanny a knowing wink and squeezed her arm. There were almost ten thousand people gathered together now in the old square, spilling out into the adjacent streets, climbing onto windowsills and clinging to the iron railings in an almost festive mood.

This time, in order to be seen, Mr Rawson stood in the open window of an upstairs room and beckoned for silence. A polite hush fell across the assortment of human faces. There was no class distinction here today, and all evidence of rancour between the two classes had evaporated as all eyes were raised in the same cause, to seek social and political reform.

'I congratulate this meeting on assembling so numerously on this very important question.' The jubilant crowd cheered and Mr Rawson lifted a hand once more for silence. 'This is the only way by which tyranny must receive its death blow. The public voice will now reach the constituted authorities and with the united efforts of our countrymen, exercised in prudence, in a steady and manly manner, such as becomes freemen and Britons, we must in the end succeed.' A roar from the multitude endorsed his sentiments. A voice from the crowd cut through the silence when the roaring had ceased. Fanny watched in amazement as the crowd parted to let the owner of the voice through. The fellow climbed onto the railing beneath Mr Rawson's window.

'Let him speak!' clamoured the crowd, eager to hear one of their own kind.

'Fellow workers! I am but one of the multitude here today, and am but one who has felt the great pressure of the times. It is with zeal that I urge my brother workers not to relax in their honest endeavours to support the cause of parliamentary reforms — which must in the end relieve people of their distress.' He found the position perched upon the railing acutely uncomfortable and slithered down to the floor. A tumultuous roar expelled itself from the crowd, and John felt himself being propelled over the heads of people. Mr Rawson rang a bell to obtain further attention, and John was lowered to the ground a mere ten yards from the point where Fanny stood. Slowly she inched her way through the throng until she stood by his side. He was totally unaware of her presence and she stood patiently as the speaker continued his oration.

Mr Rawson announced that he owed it to the people gathered in the rain to hear the petition in full, so that they would understand it and give it full approval, before it was submitted to the Prince Regent. Slowly the lengthy proposals, each one approved with a hearty cheer, were read out, and a Mr J. Manners moved that the resolution be passed. Fanny had stood by John's side observing him, as every fibre of his body listened to the words of the speaker, she kept her secret whilst he concentrated on the proposals. The passing of the resolution brought a gasp from the crowd which was immediately followed by an enormous cheer and John let out a yell of victory.

The people were in an exuberant mood, hats flew high into the air, and people danced merrily with complete strangers. Fanny slipped her hand into John's hand, he took it and spun her into a dance, just like all the others, and it was several seconds before she spoke. He imagined that he could hear Fanny's voice and looked round. She spoke again and he looked directly into her face. It seemed to Fanny to take forever before the truth dawned on him, then all at once a look of astonishment appeared on his face. 'It's unbelievable, Fanny, is it really you?' he asked laughingly.

He picked her up, tossing her up into the air, and caught her, then spun the pair of them into a whirl. He stopped just as suddenly and took her into his arms, kissing her so passionately that the surrounding crowd cheered with approval. The kiss was sweet and earthy, unlike any other that they had shared and in spite of their damp clothing, they clung to each other, unable to let go. She looked deeply into his eyes as she clung to him, and he kissed her again, lost in the burning warmth over which he had no control. He loosed her roughly, took her hand and led her away from the crowd.

Gervase had been higher up in the Square, observing the mood of the crowd. He was in complete agreement with their sentiments, but had been taken aback as John pushed himself forward to speak. He admired the lad, but again he was pushing himself into the public glare. Would the fellow never learn? Gervase observed how, afterwards, the jubilant throng had tossed John across their heads until the speaker's demand for silence made them lower him to the ground. The gaiety of the crowd was infectious, encouraged on by the cessation of the rain and the lightening of the skies, and as Gervase attempted to cut through the crowd towards John he saw him take the dark haired woman into his arms and kiss her. He fell back, suddenly feeling the loss of his youth and then, for him, the gaiety of the square lost most of its glitter. He blended with the crowd and left them all to it.

The wig was wet and needed drying, as did the cloak and dress. Fanny, not anticipating wet weather in her deception, was forced to hide the wig in the corner of the outhouse, where it could not easily be found. As Sarah was not about, Fanny slipped in unseen through the backdoor and hurried upstairs to her room. She leant back on the closed bedroom door with a sigh of relief at not being discovered, and knew that in future she would have to have a better plan of campaign if she wished to go undetected. She found her concentration constantly wandering throughout the rest of the day; her thoughts turned ceaselessly to John and to the passion that had been in his embrace. The memory of it caused a warm tingle in her breasts, and a tinge of pink coloured her cheeks. Every task took her twice as long and she became so distracted that she became careless in her work, until in the end Bryce asked if she was sick.

John was just as disconcerted. His lapses of concentration caused spelling mistakes and wasted valuable time. The atmosphere between Fanny and himself over the past two weeks had bewildered him, they had sparred with each other, spat at each other, wanting to cause each other pain, yet neither knew why. His love for Fanny had not been waning, but intensifying, until neither had known how to deal with the situation. The depths of his feelings had frightened him.

The lack of concentration in John did not surprise Gervase at all, for the excitement of the morning had spread over the whole town, and even he had little inclination for work. He pondered on the woman that John had kissed with such abandonment, and found himself strangely envious of their deep feelings.

Due to the constant disturbances of the day, there was still work left to finish at closing time, and the three men were compelled to work later than normal into the evening. None of them heard the tap on the door, nor did they hear the lift of the latch, but instinctively both Gervase and John looked up at the same time and saw her there. Gervase drew his breath at Fanny's radiant face and soft eyes, and suddenly felt clumsy. John met those same eyes with his own, which emanated love and admiration, and yet all three were bound by an inexplicable spell which none of them fully understood.

Tom was sick of work today. At the first sign from Gervase that work could cease, he grabbed his coat and left. He wanted a jar of ale more than anything else. It had been a strange day and he was glad that it was finally over.

Gervase however was reluctant to leave the shop. He had a secret fear which had niggled away at him since the night of John's attack, a fear that Fanny's involvement with John might put her in danger. However, he took comfort in the fact that John was publicly involved with the woman in the square and that would take attention from Fanny. He turned out most of the lanterns and bade them goodnight.

In the softness of the remaining light Fanny stood, watching John as he came towards her, and she allowed him to take her shaking hand in his and lead her up the stairs to his room. He closed the door and took her in his arms, kissing her passionately, demandingly, until the room spun and she returned his kisses softly and lovingly. He loosened the buttons at her throat and his lips reached the valley between her breasts, he lifted her up in his strong arms and carried her to the bed. He was young and strong, eager and virile, and she was shy and worshipped him, and gave him the love he asked for. She would have given anything — she willingly gave him everything. Their passion spent, they lay wrapped in each others arms, sleeping like children and forgetting everything but themselves.

John woke up with a start. It was later than he had imagined and he knew that Tom would be returning shortly. He gazed down at Fanny's naked body and kissed her softly until she awakened.

John walked Fanny home, and the short distance seemed to take forever, so wrapped up in each other as they were. They paused in the back yard while he kissed her again, this time without passion, but softly on her hair, her eyes, the nape of her neck, and she ran her hand through his curly hair adoringly.

The episode in the square served to increase John's confidence, and seeing the upsurge in public support for reform, he slowly allowed himself to relax back into the easy going manner which had been his before the incident in August. Fanny's interest and understanding in John's plans developed and although she had no great wish to leave England, it was obvious that she would be compelled to do so in order to share his life. They kept their love and plans to themselves and it was agreed that John would sail to America first and send for her when he felt that he could provide sufficiently well for her. He was determined now to take Fanny out, providing that she wore the wig and never became engaged in close conversation with friends or acquaintances who would see through her deception.

The dark winter nights and fierce weather restricted their movement mainly to walks, but the thick mud made even these outings difficult and unpleasant, and Fanny became tired of their deceit. She particularly disliked deceiving Gervase, a thing which she had never done before, but John was adamant that no one, especially Gervase, should know of their relationship.

As time passed the pretence became less of a masquerade and more of an instrument for showing Fanny the true conditions in which the less-fortunate lived. John took her into their back yards, homes and workplaces, until she was left with the conviction that the people were right to demand reform, but she was not convinced that they would succeed merely by sending petitions to the Government. Relief would never come, unless the blinkers were removed from the eyes of the ruling classes and their consciences pricked sufficiently to make them care for others. Fanny felt that it would take more than scraps of paper to change things, but the feelings of resentment were increasing daily and the authorities must have been blind not to see that trouble was brewing.

Chapter 8

Presenting the national petitions to the Prince Regent proved far more difficult than at first imagined. Obstacle after obstacle was put in the way, causing exasperation and further public rioting. The English ruling classes had never lost the fear of a rebellion on English soil, after the example set by the French Revolution, and even minor riots caused them much anxiety, but unless the powers-that-be accepted the fact that the views of the people would not go away, then there would never be peace. The Prince Regent could not accept a petition directly, it had to be presented at a levee, but pinning him down to holding such a reception was far from easy.

For the public to receive a report on the progress of the presentation of the petitions to the Prince, a meeting was arranged to take place at Spar Fields, in London. On the same day on which the meeting was held, four unfortunate men were hanged after trials at the Old Bailey, for taking part in riots. This incident sparked off another enormous riot with resulting consequences throughout the land.

On this December day Spar Fields had the appearance of a fairground; it was thronged with people and packed with stalls selling fruit and other edibles, until by mid-day a crowd of fifteen thousand people had gathered there. Even before some of the mob reached the rally they had been incensed by the execution of the four men and had entered a gun maker's shop to demand arms. In the fray one man was killed. Thus equipped with weapons, they proceeded to the Bank of England and surrounded it firing several shots. The gates of the bank were closed and the mob then marched to the Royal Exchange where a number were trapped between the gates and the buildings, resulting in many arrests. The mob then went to Spar Fields armed with bludgeons and sticks, and carrying a tricoloured flag with the words 'Protect the Oppressed' written on it.

When the crowd were told yet again that the petitions had still not reached the Prince, one fellow stood up and began to harangue the crowd.

'Fellow citizens, you want food, you want employment! Do you want a leader?' he offered, waving his flag.

The mob cheered in response, and called, 'We want a leader. We will have you!'

'I will not refuse your call. I am at your service' he replied, and instantly leapt out of the cart into the crowd, who immediately went on the rampage through the streets of London. By one o'clock the alarm had been raised across the city and shutters to shop windows went up along Cheapside, Fleet Street and all the main streets as a protection against the mobs.

Sheffield might well have existed in a backwater, but nevertheless, the indignation of its citizens was just as highly charged, and it didn't take long for sympathetic feelings to come to the fore. A menacing looking mob, some with naked swords, met in The Wicker, then adjourned across to Portabello, carrying a loaf, smeared with blood, on the end of a pole. In spite of their threatening noises and a few broken panes of glass they caused nothing more than a general nuisance to the town. However, a growing fear of local riots caused great concern amongst the magistrates, who decided to act immediately by squashing and preventing riotous gatherings.

The restrictions of their Riot Act prevented more than twelve people from gathering together for longer than an hour. If they did so then the participants would be guilty of felony. The same applied if, after dark in the evening, more than twelve gathered in the street or neighbourhood.

John saw the new act as an infringement of his liberty, and ranted and raved continuously to Fanny about it. He also had heated discussions with Gervase on the matter, until in the end Gervase thought it wise to offer him some sound advice.

'Look John, I'm all for reform, in every aspect of the word, and I don't blame you for your enthusiasm, in fact I admire you for having the courage of your convictions, but I want to get something quite straight. Keep your views and activities away from this business, and don't involve Fanny in any more good causes.'

'That's not a very progressive attitude. Fanny's quite capable of making up her own mind, and she has a social conscience, which is more than most women seem to have', replied John belligerently.

Gervase restrained his growing anger, 'It's not acceptable for women to delve in politics, even if they want to. You'll turn her into a social outcast if you don't take care. Unfortunately strong-minded women are not accepted in our society, and Fanny is strong minded enough, if you don't mind. We could do with allowing women of her calibre to have more influence, that I admit, but that is not the point I'm making. Leave her out of it'.

John interrupted, 'Well it's about time they were permitted to voice their opinions more forcefully'.

'Don't interrupt. It's not acceptable and that's that.' Gervase paused, quite unused to losing his temper, 'I pay your wages, I subscribe to the relief of the poor of this town, and I press my points of view home to many influential people, who listen to me because I'm not a rabble-rouser. First and foremost, I'm a businessman. I give you work and try to set an example by being fair. You bring trouble to Fanny, and her family will suffer; moreover, I don't want saboteurs attacking this shop.'

A sullen tone crept into John's voice. 'You're all alike in this town. Frightened to upset the centuries-old traditions. Before long you'll be left behind. It's taken you years even to get round to building yourselves a canal.'

'My lad, if you go on at this rate you'll never see a ship, certainly not one bound for America. You say you stand with all the others, wanting change. All half of them really want is to go back to being comfortable. They don't want the real change which the future is going to bring — no matter what you do! Science, education and industrialisation are moving forward — you can't stop that, or the effects it will have on industry. The men have got to learn to make use of machinery, not destroy it.'

John changed his line of thought. 'The ruling classes of this country are blind to the poverty of the ordinary people. They're not just negative, there is a callous indifference to the people's suffering.'

Gervase pressed his point again. 'Real progress and improvement takes time, standing still without upheaval will never bring prosperity. Bread is not the only answer to this problem; but raising man against master, like the grinders are doing here right now, doesn't help anyone.'

'We've got to motivate the people somehow.'

'I agree, but in spite of the short-comings and faults of the parliamentary system in this country, Great Britain still has the best Government in Europe. We've got to change it by getting more representatives of the ordinary people into the Government, men who can speak with first-hand knowledge of our problems. Rabble-rousers aren't good enough. The virulent language of the flysheets and pamphlets only incenses the people against injustice — find me men who will fight the Government from within, on the Government's own level. The power must come from men dedicated to the welfare of the people, not those interested only in self-advancement.'

'And where do we get these men from — will you stand and risk your business interests?' John jibed hurtfully.

'You are young and full of ideals. I was brought up in different circumstances', he refused to be goaded by the younger man's passion, and asked matter-of-factly, 'Why don't you, instead of shouting at other people?'

John defended himself, 'I'm doing my bit. You know you can tease a lion until he becomes desperate, and we're fed up of being teased by ludicrous popinjays.'

'Yes. Then when the lion has been teased into retaliating what are you going to offer him, the gun? You've got brains and ideals and yet you're going to take them to America, instead of giving England the help she needs.'

'And you'll do nothing at all, just carry on paying all the duties on paper and taxes, without complaint' said John unjustly.

Gervase was becoming tired of the rhetoric. 'Don't be so bloody dogmatic, John. I feel just as strongly as you, but politics is not my line. I can do my bit by building a business which gives you work, and a fair wage. My club is full of men who are just as bigoted as you in their way. All I can do is express ideas and try to plant seeds. This country needs a strong backbone, we can't all be on the march, someone has to keep the jobs going for the men to return to.'

'I'm not after running away. I want to raise a family in a land which is not hampered by prejudices, and the future is there to be enjoyed.'

Gervase turned and looked him straight in the eye. 'Who's behind this grinders trouble now? Not you I hope!' John was non-committal. 'If you get arrested you'll lose all your credibility, and liberty. Stop mixing with the riff-raff and don't incite the grinders into getting stroppy. You need men with experience to run a country, not orators who couldn't even organise a coffee-shop. Publish words for the man and woman in the street to read, newspapers with truth in them instead of sanctimonious opinions.'

The argument was leading nowhere and Gervase concluded that the time had come to draw it to a close. They were arguing like enemies instead of the friends that they were, and he guided the conversation towards more sociable topics.

Christmas approached rapidly now, and it hardly seemed possible that within the space of one year so much should happen to change all their lives so dramatically. The season of pantomime, assemblies and concerts was upon them once more, but Fanny spent much of the festive time quietly with Sarah, who was having great difficulty in coming to terms with Bryce's absence. As usual the children came, followed by Gervase who was determined to see that Fanny should not miss out on all the fun through her devotion to Sarah, and invited her to accompany him to the theatre.

John was in no position to express his disapproval at the outing, for fear of arousing Gervase's suspicions, but the sight of Fanny, so alluring in a dress of the latest mode, nearly drove him to distraction with jealousy at being unable to escort her himself. The theatre was offering the grand romantic production of 'The Wood Daemon', and Fanny was thrilled to be invited to the first night's performance, never dreaming that John would resent her going. She never saw Gervase as a threat to anything; he was her rock, towering above her, as few other men were tall enough to do, and he held her views in high esteem, treating her as an equal.

Tonight his bearing and attire were those of a successful man, self-assured and masterful, and he escorted Fanny with the attentions of a suitor, spoiling her with his compliments. Fanny was well aware that all heads were turning in their direction as, tall and elegant, they climbed the steps of the theatre together, and the heady success of their entrance caused them to almost flirt with each other as they played out their own special charade. They did not intend to set the town alight with their performance, but they did, and ladies speculated behind their fans at the carefree abandonment which they had witnessed, convinced that they had seen a romance in the making.

It was as well that the gossip never reached Gervase, for he and Fanny had been innocents intoxicated by the atmosphere of the theatre, and he would have despised himself for bringing Fanny into disrepute. The evening, however, left him with a strange feeling of emptiness which he had never known before.

John, meanwhile, had fretted the whole evening away in fits of jealousy, whilst Fanny was left breathless and unable to sleep from all the excitement which had befallen her during the evening, with the result that in the morning she awoke tired, and somehow despondent. Fanny thrived on adventure and romance, and whereas previously these dangerous preoccupations had found relief in the pens of Miss Jane Austen and her contemporaries, Fanny's love for John had placed her in emotional turmoil. During the bad weather she had been compelled to see less of John, calling at his rooms only when Tom's outings coincided with Sarah's absence from the house, as a result, the moments alone with him had been precious and traumatic. There were times when she did not see him alone for days on end, if his evenings were appropriated by the Movement, and these spasmodic romantic interludes began to leave her feeling insecure and unhappy, in the belief that John cared much more for his precious Movement than he did for her.

The Movement was also far from happy. By mid-January the petitions were still having little effect, and in Sheffield, a further, well-attended meeting, was held in Paradise Square, again calling for change.

The following week delegates from all over England gathered in London, at the 'Crown & Anchor Inn', in The Strand, but, in spite of the half million signatures that had been collected, this rally was not a success. The delegate chosen to represent the Movement refused at the last minute to have anything to do with it, because it not only advocated a vote per household, but one for each man, and that was too radical for him. Never had the reformers needed firm leadership more than they did at this time, but it was not there.

The Government had no organised police force, and often the local authorities were forced to bring in the Militia, an unpopular move, to sort out disturbances. It did however send out spies in order to defend itself, and the threat of imprisonment without trial under the new Seditious Meetings Act caused political clubs to break up when they were unable to hold meetings openly in public houses. Members now began to gather in secret at night, in private houses and in barns.

The warnings from Gervase fell on stony ground, and John continued to meet secretly with the radicals, not needing encouragement or coercion, to take part in their plans — he was all for them. Increasingly now, throughout the Midlands, but particularly in Nottinghamshire, Derbyshire and South Yorkshire, committees were meeting in secret to plan an insurrection, but Government spies were infiltrating these meetings, striving to hunt down the leaders and trouble makers. In 1815 John had escaped from Nottingham without apprehension, and being a small fish, his name soon lost its importance. However, the Matthew Hines' case had brought it once more to the fore, and intelligence sources, within the region, were gathering material on all men of radical leanings, awaiting the opportunity to make arrests. Some known sympathisers were deliberately being allowed to roam free in order to give the authorities the chance of closing the net on the ring leaders, and in some cases were unwittingly being used by spies extracting information.

Gervase continued to warn John again and again to keep away from trouble, fearing not only for his employee's welfare, but also that the authorities would believe that his printing works were connected with the distribution of the seditious pamphlets which were circulating in the town.

John's involvement with the radicals left him little time to spare for personal pleasure, and this, combined with the inconsistency of Tom's nocturnal habits, forced him to meet Fanny, after work, in the Market Square in order to keep their affair concealed.

Chapter 9

The six months detention in York Castle served only to harden Matthew Hines. The harsh, brutal man with his bullet-like head and thick-set shoulders demanded nothing short of complete revenge. Having lost his employment, he had little other choice after his release but to return to his own parish, to ask for relief. His cowering wife and five children had been evicted from their mill-owned house, and their misery and poverty increased when they had been installed in a damp and dilapidated house in Solly Street. His conviction had at least given his wife a temporary reprieve from the beatings and bullying which she regularly received at his hands.

Most of Hines' possessions had been sold to support the family during his absence and the house was so sparsely furnished on his return that his desire for revenge was immediately re-kindled. The organised attack on John Andrews had only given Hines temporary satisfaction, and the knowledge that Andrews was now almost a local hero, added to his impatience for satisfaction. The bitterly cold winter had caused Mrs Hines to burn most of the unsaleable furniture in order to keep the children from freezing, and the first task Hines had to do on returning was to scour the surrounding woodland for firewood. He had lost a good deal of weight during his long months in prison and he looked upon his pathetic wife with less than a sympathetic glance, as she endeavoured to scrape together a morsel of food from the near-empty larder. The one upstairs room offered little comfort either, retaining only the matrimonial bed and a couple of blankets which his wife, out of fear, had not dared to part with. He liked his comfortable matrimonial bed and all that marriage to a docile wife offered in it. The children, however, had to sleep on palliasses of straw on the floor, with coats for covers.

Within three days of his return he had gathered a gang of ruffians to his home, and as there was only one chair left, he sat firmly upon it whilst the other men squatted on the large stones which he had brought in for the children to sit on. His wife retreated upstairs, away from his scowl, taking the children with her.

Matthew Hines eyed his friends. 'You've all helped my family as best you could whilst I was away, in spite of your own difficulties, and I owe you all for that. The beating you gave the Andrews fellow was no more than he deserved, but it's not enough'. His eyes blazed with hatred,

'I've been rotting for six months and there's not much to come home to, is there lads? I'm ruined'.

The oldest of the ruffians spoke up quickly, 'There's not much else we can do, except finish him off. We don't owe you that much, it's too darned risky'.

'Frame him, lads, that's what I want. Get him hanged or transported. They go by the hundreds from York, dejected and without hope to the hulks — that's what I want for him, hanging's too good.'

'We know his movements, he's got friends, and fights for the grinders. It's not going to be easy. We've kept an eye on him and he meets at Adam Brown's in Scotland Street these days, and he's got a woman in the market.'

'Right, get him shopped for sedition against this new act.' Hines stopped, having decided he had the answer and stood to dismiss the matter.

The older man spoke again. 'Hey, hang on a minute, they're with us these grinders. Shop him and you shop the lot. The Movement's had a hard time this past six months, and what with this uprising in the offing we'd be cutting off our noses to spite our faces. Some of 'em think he's a good fellow.'

Hines sat down angrily and winced. He rubbed his knuckles to ease the pain in his joints. 'That bloody cell's given me rheumatism lads, that's another thing he's going to pay for.'

A young, lanky, gormless-looking lad put forward his idea. 'We could plant a letter on him from one of their leaders, that Cartwright fellow in London', he tittered gleefully.

'Oh, shut up, you great lump', interrupted another. 'None of us can write that well, and we don't want to give 'em proof against the Movement.' The lad sat back, sulking. 'Use your brains next time, that's all. He's right though, we could plant something on him.'

Hines thought for a moment. 'No one knows that we're all connected with each other. Do you think he saw any of you that night when you duffed him over?'

'No, it was dark in the alley and Lanky over there hit him such a blow first time round that he keeled over like a babe. Who'd have believed him anyway?'

'Right. Bennett, you got that damn fancy watch of yours still?' The older man nodded. 'Here's what you do!'

The dimly lit stalls were being packed away as Fanny approached the market place, and all that remained of the dwindling crowds were a few shrewd housewives hoping for bargains as the traders carefully replaced their wares into carts or onto mules. John was later than usual and Fanny stood in the shadows of their usual meeting place, feeling safe beneath the wig and hooded cape, as she observed two urchins squabbling in the gutter. They were mere babes of not more than six years of age, scratching amongst the market waste in hopes of finding food. Fanny shuddered. There were so many of them running wild and no one seemed to care.

As a child she had found the market a place of fascination, especially at dusk when the stalls were illuminated by oil lamps, but she had been a well-fed child who could mingle excitedly with the throng, not needing to steal, or forage for food. It was surprising that the poorly-clad children were not ill from being out in the cold and damp all day, but then she did not envy the traders either, for they had been standing there since early morning. She too was cold, and still John did not arrive, until in the end she wondered if she should return home.

Suddenly John was there, breaking into her thoughts and she watched him stride towards her, blocking out the view of the urchins. To Fanny he was an impressive sight, with his powerful body and sturdy legs, and she waited impatiently in the shadows, longing for him to take her in his arms. A drunk lurched suddenly sideways, losing his balance and causing a collision between John and himself. Fanny recoiled in horror as she recalled her own experience with a drunk. John seemed as if to prop the fellow up before disengaging himself from the drunk's intoxicated body and Fanny remained in the shadows and waited.

A piercing yell rent the air as the drunk fumbled around frantically in his pocket. 'Mi watch!' he screeched accusingly 'Mi bloody watch's gone.' He almost fell over in his fit of fury. 'Some thief's nicked it.' He looked at John, 'It's 'im, the young scoundrel' he yelled, pointing a drunken wobbling finger in John's direction.

All heads turned towards John who stood motionless and unable to grasp the meaning of the accusation. Two burly men quickly emerged from the crowd which was already increasing rapidly. 'I saw him do it when he struggled with the silly old fool' said one.

'Me too' added the other, 'search his pockets and see!'

John laughed back, 'What on earth do I want someone else's watch for — I've got a good one of my own'.

'Here let me search him', added a market trader. John stood indignantly protesting his innocence but allowed the man to rifle through his pockets. 'Here, bring that lantern over — he's got a watch alright!' The man held the watch up into the light, 'What's your name? Not Samuel Bennett I'll be bound!'

John protested wildly. 'No it's not, and I've not handled the damn thing.'

The drunk lunged forward. 'I'm Samuel Bennett — it's mine I tell you.'

The second burly man added convincingly, 'I saw him take it. I'd say he was as guilty as hell'.

A woman broke in, 'That's Samuel Bennett mister, he lives round the corner from my mother'.

'He wants hanging for stealing from a broken old man' added another. 'Fetch the constable. We'll make sure this one never steals again.'

Fanny stood paralysed within the shadows, fearing her movements would be seen, as a man was despatched to fetch the constable, then suddenly, in a moment of desperation, she tipped over one of the empty stalls and screamed. The crowd, startled by her sudden outburst, turned, distracted momentarily from the excitement in hand, and started towards the demented Fanny.

John seized the opportunity, sprang from the grasp which held him prisoner and ran for his life. Immediately the crowd lost interest in Fanny and with a hue and cry, set off in pursuit of their victim, leaving her to slip away from amongst the stalls as quickly as she could, hoping that they would forget her. She had barely gone twenty yards when a voice rang out. 'Where's that female gone? She's in league with him — get her as well!'

She heard the call, heard the footsteps change direction; then in desperation she lifted her skirts to allow freedom of movement and fled from the Market Place in the opposite direction to that which John had taken. She darted down alleyways, twisting and turning through the familiar labyrinth of passages and gardens which had been her childhood playground, until, exhausted, she reached the house. She paused by the out-buildings to regain her breath and was greatly relieved to find that there was no one following.

Suddenly, without warning, there was a movement behind her, and she froze as a hand fell across her mouth stifling the scream which formed in her throat. She knew that all was lost.

A voice whispered urgently, 'It's me, Fanny — keep your voice down.' John kept his hand tightly against her mouth until he was sure that she would not cry out. 'Oh, John, you escaped!' Fanny sobbed with relief.

'Yes, but only just. How can I go back to the shop now? Someone may have recognised me.' He paused, waiting while she fought to regain her breath. 'I didn't steal anything. Why would I be foolish enough to steal a watch?' he said, his voice filled with disbelief. 'That's the funny thing; most watches have names engraved on them so it's not worth being caught with one.' He fell silent, immersed in thought, and when he did speak his tone was hesitant and unsure. 'Where can I go? I can't stay here and implicate you. I just don't know how it got there unless the drunk put it there. But why would he do that?' She could hear anger rising in his voice.

'Shush!' she interrupted, as the sound of feet approached. They held their breath but the footsteps neither hesitated nor stopped, and Fanny lamented dejectedly, 'I wish Gervase was here; he'd help us if he wasn't away, I know he would'.

John pulled her closer, 'I wouldn't have got away if you hadn't acted so quickly' he said, attempting to comfort her.

'They'll never find you here.' Fanny protested wildly.

He stopped her. 'Listen Fanny, I've got to hide somewhere until daylight. I daren't even go back to the shop to get my things, can you think of anywhere safe and I'll try to get away tomorrow?'

Fanny clung to him in fear, 'Where will you go? I'll never see you again — please stay and we'll prove your innocence'.

'Yes, and if we don't prove it then I've had it. If I can get to the coast and catch a ship for America I'll send for you. Would you come?' He kissed her, more for reassurance than pleasure. 'Can you think of a place?'

She pulled herself together, trying desperately to think of somewhere safe, somewhere away from prying eyes. There was nowhere, only the old crumbling barn across Allsop's Fields, where she and the boys had played when they were children. There wasn't much of it left now and it would be cold and dark, but what choice had they, at least no one would be there at this time of year. 'There is only the old barn where we used to play as children. I think I could find it in the dark.'

'It may be muddy – how will you explain things to Sarah?' he asked, concerned for her safety. 'Gervase was right, I should not have involved you in my life.'

Fanny covered his mouth with her cold hand. 'Hush — don't say that, we didn't fall in love deliberately and we're not the ones in the wrong.' The light from the house window disappeared as Sarah closed the curtains and they were left standing in the dark shadows of the outhouse. 'We're lucky' she added, 'there is a little moonlight to help us find the barn.'

'Yes, and that means we shall have to be more careful lest we be spotted. I don't like to involve you. Fetch me a blanket and try to explain where I am to go. This is my problem not yours.'

She shook her head firmly. 'No. How could I rest, not knowing what was happening to you? Stay here and I will fetch a lantern and a few necessary items, though I will have to wait until mother goes to bed, but she goes early these days. I'll get some things together and take you to the barn.' She took off the wig and exchanged the cloak for a shawl which hung in the outhouse.

Deceiving her mother was no easy task, and each chore Sarah performed seemed to take forever until Fanny wondered if she would ever retire.

The prospect of spending a cold night out in the open did little to calm John's shattered nerves, as he recalled the hours which he had spent in his uncle's cellar, and he knew that it was all happening again, the fear and the torment. He fretted, wondering why Fanny was taking so long, then suddenly the door opened and he saw Sarah framed in the light of the doorway; but she went only as far as the midden and back again. Finally, Fanny came out with a bundle in her hand and locked the door quietly behind her as John took the bundle. She put the wig and cloak on once more, taking care to conceal any evidence of her own identity.

The searchers had abandoned all hope of finding their victims for it was impossible, in the dark, to see further than the light of their lanterns. Nevertheless, at daybreak they would certainly renew their relentless search for John and leave no stone unturned until they caught him.

Fanny and John kept to the back alleys in spite of the difficulties and were prepared to put out their lantern if anyone approached. Then, on reaching the edge of town, they had little choice but to extinguish the light for fear of attracting attention as they approached the dark open field. They struggled on, keeping close to the perimeter wall which Fanny knew would end up at the old barn, aided only by the light of the moon which cast strange shadows that frightened Fanny, and she knew that she would be unable to return home by herself in the dark. When finally they reached the barn, Fanny took a tinderbox from her pocket and struggled to light the lantern, John took it from her and quickly succeeded. 'You are a marvel Fanny, what else have you brought?' he asked admiringly.

Carefully unwinding the bundle, Fanny revealed another blanket, three candles, a flagon of water, bread, cheese and fruit. 'I'll go back for your things in the morning.' She was tired now and in the cold of the night air, the stark reality of John's plight began to sink in. She shivered, overwhelmed by the upheaval of the past few hours. He seemed to read her thoughts and drew Fanny closer, comforting her in spite of his own fears, and they sat huddled together in silence round the pathetic little flame, in a barn that had no door and where half the back wall had collapsed. Most of the roof had fallen in, excepting at each end where the corner stones butted together, still supporting the end beams and blocking out the moonlight.

John broke the silence suddenly. 'You can't go back on your own Fanny, it's not safe for you.'

'I know, I was afraid of that and left the bed crumpled so that mother will think I've gone out early. I don't want to go, I want to be here with you.' She laid her head against his shoulder, fearing to lose contact with his body.

He shook his head. 'I can't work it out. How else could his watch have got into my pocket, unless someone put it there? He must have done it.' Then his voice became angry, 'Perhaps Gervase was right. Hines came back from York two weeks ago; maybe he is still out for revenge'.

'But how do we prove it — it will be even harder because he will have covered his tracks. Oh John! What are we going to do?' He heard the sob in her voice and kissed her wildly, trying to stop her from crying, he tasted the salty tears as they ran down her face and pulled back.

'I just don't know' he sighed. 'I've got to go away from here. I hated the place when I first came but now it's grown on me, I've made friends, especially you, and Gervase. I was really beginning to enjoy working with him. He's wise Fanny, do listen to him.' Fanny heard regret in his voice and wished too that Gervase would hurry back. 'You won't be able to fetch much for me, I must travel light but I've got to have my papers, my indenture and some warm, useful clothing. My money is hidden under the floorboards behind the washstand. I have enough saved for my passage and sufficient to make a start when I get to America.' He drew her close, protecting her from the cold.

'How will I manage without you?' Fanny whispered.

'You are the bravest woman I've ever known, if I could be sure that you were safe and happy, then it would give me hope. If I don't get away — God forbid that they catch me, then don't waste your life over me; what makes it worse is that I didn't do it.'

'Hold me', sobbed Fanny. 'Don't talk about failure.'

'Dear, sweet Fanny, where is that spirit of yours? I don't want to leave you either but I have no choice.'

They fell silent as the cold night dragged on, and huddled together for comfort beneath her shawl and the blankets, clinging to each other in desperation until, exhausted, they drifted into a fitful sleep.

With every fox-cry or owl-hoot their fear returned and they finally woke cold, cramped and miserable. Fanny did not touch the food which she had brought, for John would need every morsel throughout the long day ahead and she could eat at home. Fanny knew also that she must leave before the whole town awoke, in order to minimise the risk of being seen.

'Poor Fanny', he said. 'It's been a long uncomfortable night for you and I'm sorry to have brought you to this. I've been thinking. Don't go or come back in the wig, that way if you're seen no one will connect you with me, they will think that you are just out walking.' He clasped her to himself, afraid to let go.

Reluctantly she left his arms and promised, 'I'll be back as soon as I can so that you can slip away before it gets too dark.'

'Oh, how I need you, dearest Fanny. Take care of yourself for my sake, and don't come back if it means them catching you.' Fanny sped across the field and was soon swallowed up by the buildings of the town.

Chapter 10

*A*nnie *Hines had returned* from the market the previous evening, pleased that she had been able to obtain a few meagre vegetables for her family, even though they were damaged. She had lingered patiently amongst the stalls until closing time, in the hope that the left-overs would be sold off cheaply — and she had been rewarded. Just as she was leaving the market a skirmish broke out, but she was afraid that if she stayed to see the outcome of the affray her husband would scold her for being late. Since his return from prison, Mr Hines had been even more unbearable than usual, and she had not been alone in bearing the brunt of his harsh tongue and quick temper, for the children had suffered too, and they now kept well out of his way.

Arriving home, she hastily placed the bruised and battered root vegetables into the iron stew pot, together with a few old bones which she had bought from the butcher, and prayed that the fire would remain alight until the broth was cooked sufficiently well to placate her husband's hunger. He was late, and she knew that the later he returned the more mean-tempered he would be, until in the end she began to hope that he would never return.

It was, therefore, something of a surprise to Mrs Hines to find him neither drunk nor bad-tempered when he eventually did return, and he even smiled at her. It was not a warm smile, but one which seemed to hide a secret satisfaction and she was uneasy, wondering what lay behind it.

Wasting no time, he greedily ate the broth which was placed before him, then, having finished, he lay back in the chair and belched noisily. 'I needed that, gal!' he pronounced, as he loosened his trouser belt, and watched his wife's body as she arched it over the fire. Six months in prison without a woman had nearly driven him crazy and the sight of her ample rounded thighs stirred his blood. 'I'll eat more later' he muttered, as he reached out and fondled her buttocks suggestively, causing her almost to drop the ladle which she held. She was weary of his constant attentions, knowing full well what he wanted; she slowly put the ladle down and accepted that it was better this way than when he was in one his rages. 'Come on woman, the kids are in bed!' he urged impatiently, pulling her up and forcing her round. He seized her skirt as he did so and pulled it upwards. 'I missed you when I was in

York Castle, that's near all I could damn well think of! Come on woman!' he said roughly.

There was little point in protesting; if she wasn't already with child again, she soon would be. Not that he would care about that, until it was over and he had another mouth to feed. Then he would blame her and give her the rough edge of his tongue. 'I'm tired' she sighed, 'can't it wait?' she asked hopefully; but he wasn't even listening.

With his passion spent, Matthew Hines was a contented man. Once again the proceeds of his daily poaching had provided his starving family with enough to fill their bellies, and himself with sufficient ale to blot out his miseries. Even his enemy would be safely behind bars by now. He chuckled, an evil chuckle, to himself and turned to his wife, 'You go to bed lass, I'll stay down here for a while'. He watched her go. She wasn't such a bad wife, a bit docile, but then she never refused him and she made ends meet quite well.

He was sitting, musing over the possibility of John's downfall, when a quiet tap on the window disturbed him. He peered out into the darkness of the night but was unable to see anything, and had almost convinced himself that he had imagined the noise, when the tap was repeated on the door. Taking the poker from the grate, and raising it to strike at any unwelcome intruder, he swiftly opened the door. The startled figure ducked backwards and Matthew Hines recognised him as the lanky youth who had been at the house when they had planned his revenge. 'What the devil are you doing here?' Hines hissed at the youth.

'Can a cum in Mister Hines, I don't want anyone to see me?' the youth begged timidly.

Matthew Hines caught him roughly by the sleeve and pulled him into the house. He then peered cautiously out into the night, but seeing nothing suspicious, closed the door. 'I thought I told you not to come here again' he snapped.

'They sent me', the lad spluttered. 'It's gone wrong. Andrews managed to give them the slip . . .'

'What!'

'He disappeared. Into the alleyways.'

'You bloody fools. Do I have to do things myself!' His face was flushed with anger and his eyes rolled with rage. 'Where are the others?'

'They joined the hue and cry, but they've given up for the night! Ratty sent me to ask you what you want them to do next.'

Hines shook his head, 'A fat lot of help you lot have been. Did you watch that shop? — If not, it's too late now, he's not daft enough to go back there. We've got to get the Militia out after him, he'll not have got far in the dark.'

125

The lad stood dumbly watching Hines, afraid to speak.

'Well? Did you watch the shop or not?' bellowed Hines.

'No', answered the lad meekly. 'We never thought he'd get away in the first place.'

'Somebody's got to tell the constable that they recognised him. We've got to give them a good reason to search him out, and it will look suspicious if anyone tells the constable now. 'Go and fetch Ratty, and make sure you're not seen — you hear! Tell him to bring some paper and ink, and something to write with.' He pushed the bewildered youth towards the door. 'Go on then, and be quick about it.'

After the lad had gone he paced the floor impatiently for half an hour, until finally Ratty came; by this time he was thinking clearly and had a solution to the problem worked out.

The sharp sound of shattering glass woke Constable Smith from his pleasant dreams, and left him feeling disorientated. He stared around the blackened room in disbelief, until he became aware of the draught of cold air which caused the curtain to flap about, and he realised that he would have to get out of bed to investigate.

By the time he had set his candle alight and reached the window, there was nothing unusual to be seen below in the dimly-lit street. He let out a yell as a piece of glass cut into his foot, and as he lowered the candle to examine the wound, saw a ball of crumpled paper lying amongst the broken glass. He hobbled back to the bed and lit the lantern. Blood streamed from his foot and he knew that he would have to go downstairs and see to it. When he eventually returned to the bedroom to tackle the offending missile he was cold and began to resent the interruption of his sleep.

The paper concealed the real cause; a large jagged stone. He ought really to have read the message earlier but the pain had been enough to claim his full attention. However, the meaning was clear enough. 'The thief in the market is a radical stalwart. His name is John Andrews.' John Andrews — the name rang a bell. Suddenly the name in question gained a face. He groaned wearily; not that young trouble-maker again! All he wanted to do was go back to bed and sleep. If the accusation were true then he would have to call out the Militia in order to ensure the capture of the fellow, but it was too late to send a runner to Wentworth for permission at this time of night. Earl Fitzwilliam would hardly appreciate being woken up on such little evidence. He'd send a messenger at day-break. Or should he do it now? He shook his head. 'Oh sod it!' he exclaimed exasperatedly, and went back to bed.

Sneaking back into the house was not difficult. Fanny managed to wipe the mud from her boots and change her dirty crumpled clothes before Sarah left her bed-chamber, but the prospects of lying to her mother distressed her. It would have been easy, as well as a relief, to tell someone of their plight, but Fanny could not take that risk, the merest slip would bring danger. She forced a brightness into her voice and told her mother that she was merely going out to fetch some mending of Gervase's, while he was away.

Tom let Fanny into the shop and watched her go upstairs; she appeared preoccupied, even mysterious, and he was puzzled by her evasiveness. He was in no mood for mysteries this morning; it was late and John had not put in an appearance, but had left him to do all the work.

Fanny came down after a while clutching a bundle of clothing bound up with a leather strap. 'John's not here', she stated. 'I'll take these things and wash them for him.'

Tom protested loudly, 'Gervase won't like it if John's not set up his new type by the time he gets back. Where's he gone anyway? He's been out all night and I'm not doing all this work by myself!' Fanny did not reply, and he looked at her keenly, demanding an answer.

She hesitated. 'Don't worry Tom, you carry on. I'm sure he will be back soon — it's not really like him you know.' She didn't wait for his reply but left him to sort it out for himself. He continued to grumble and mutter long after she had gone, and wished that Gervase would hurry back.

Bryce was listening excitedly to local gossip when Fanny returned, she was not surprised that his news was often inaccurate, for he never checked out the real facts by reading the newspapers. It was true that his rapidly growing family took up most of his spare time, but his father had considered it his duty to check that he had got the correct version. He turned as she entered, eager to impart his news to her. 'Hey, Fan, guess what! They've got the Militia out looking for a thief, apparently they chased him and some woman through the town last evening. What's more they think he could be a spy', he concluded excitedly.

She almost dropped the bundle in horror but managed to conceal her dismay. 'Oh!' she uttered, then dared to ask more, 'What's he like?'

'Some say he's small, others that he's big. They'll end up apprehending the whole town before they've done. Gossip has it that the woman's a gypsy, but you know what they're like for embroidering a story.' His voice held an air of authority, 'They'll get him!'

Fanny looked at him; he was becoming as big a gossip as the rest of them. If it were true and they were scouring the town for John, then there was little time to spare. If they thought him a spy as well as a thief they would never give up. But why should they think that of him? Perhaps Bryce and his cronies had got that wrong too; for the war was over now, and the authorities would never search for one of their own hirelings. She remembered the time when her father had been in the Volunteers, and how sometimes they had searched for days until they found their victim.

It would be too late to escape if she waited until the afternoon, she would have to go immediately. 'I'm sorry, Bryce, but I have to go out again — please don't tell mother, will you?' she pleaded. 'I'll make it up to you — I promise.'

He spun round to protest but Fanny had already disappeared, leaving him to cope with the workload alone and he shook his head in disbelief at her behaviour.

Fanny snatched a basket as she ran through the kitchen, and hurriedly hid John's papers and money in the bottom of it, beneath the oatcakes and bread, which she had prepared earlier. She then hastened back across the town.

There seemed to be evidence of Militia, men in bright red jackets and grey trousers, everywhere, just lying in wait for her, until in the end all Fanny imagined she saw was crimson. Slowly she crossed the field, picking the odd flower here and there to allay suspicion, until she was able to reach the barn without raising alarm. She called softly, 'It's only me' and slipped inside.

John hurried towards her gratefully. The tedium of inactivity had eaten into him as he waited for time to pass and he began to wish that he had left already, but he needed papers and money; without them he stood little chance of getting anywhere. 'Fanny, you're early' he said. 'I was beginning to think the worst.'

'There is hardly any time left, the Militia are looking for you now. You must go as soon as you can, they're everywhere.' Her face was white and drawn and he could tell that she was frightened. 'Please hurry.'

She was in danger, he no longer cared about himself, if they found them together with the wig it would be too late. 'If they find you here now they'll know who you are.' He took her in his arms, 'I've been aching to hold you all morning but you must go. I will miss you and your wild spirit, you and I will make good partners in America.' He nibbled her ear as he whispered into it.

Suddenly the spell was broken. The distant sound of men's voices, strong voices, instructing voices, came closer. 'They're coming!' she cried.

'Put the cape on, Fanny.' She stood rooted to the ground and he put it on for her. He put the basket into her hand. He too was afraid but he dared not let her see it. He felt the sweat trickle down his neck, icy cold fingers of terror. He had to get rid of her so that he could make a run for his life. The voices came nearer. 'You've got to go, Fanny, it's me they want not you. Walk slowly down the edge of the field with your hood up, then go through the break in the wall and run for your life. You'll have a head start and I'll have a chance to slip out of the back of the barn.

'I won't leave you now. Don't make me go', she pleaded, crushing his hand with hers.

'You've no choice, I can't run fast enough with you, please go!' He took her face in his hands and placed his hungry lips on hers. 'Now, Fanny, please.' He put the wig on her head, gently pushing her lovely hair beneath it until it had vanished completely, and then he pushed her through the doorway out into the open field.

She couldn't go back now, she must draw them away from the barn when she was far enough away. She walked casually, her heart pounding and her hands shaking, and then quickened her pace but Fanny had not quite reached the gap in the wall when there was a shout.

'It's the same woman. After her lads, she can't get far. He must be up here somewhere — you lot, get that barn surrounded.'

She was now the fox, terrified, cornered, she ran over the fields, her skirt constantly getting in the way, she climbed a fence and crossed an orchard. They were closing in on her and she knew that the nearer the town she got, the more chance there was of someone stopping her, but equally there would be more opportunities to hide. Fanny could hardly breathe, her throat burned and she was slowing down. She cut through an alley and reached her own churchyard, knowing that if she could slip in through the gates she could escape from the far side into Pepper Alley. She rounded the corner.

'Stop that woman!' shouted one of the Militia in a voice she imagined the whole town would hear. Too late. She saw the figure ahead look round, she weaved and ducked as the man tried to block her path.

God, it was Gervase!

His hand shot out to catch her arm and he seized it firmly. She had to get away! Fanny bent her head to avoid him seeing her face and bit deeply into his hand.

The bitch! He let go of her arm in a moment of surprised pain, and then he saw the scar on her hand. His mind reeled. It was Fanny! The voices were almost at the corner now, he could hear their heavy footsteps but Fanny was disappearing down the alley that led to his shop. He made as if to stumble and dropped his bag to the ground.

'Why didn't you stop the woman, you bloody fool? We've been after the pair of them since last night. Where the hell is she now? Didn't you hear me call out, are you deaf or something?' The man's face was as red with anger as his uniform was red, he looked scornfully at Gervase, then turning to his men shouted, 'Space out men, she can't be far! It's like a maze around here.'

Gervase stalled for time. 'The bitch bit my hand and I lost my balance', he lied. The man looked with contempt at Gervase then hurriedly followed his men.

What the hell was Fanny up to now? He'd only been away three days and there was trouble. It had to be something to do with John, he was convinced of that. He wished he'd never set eyes on the fellow. That bloody wig! What did she think she was doing. He knew where she was heading alright — back to his shop. By the sound of it she had managed to get away and for the moment he would leave her to her deception, but he would talk to her later; he owed that much to Sarah and Bryce before she caused them further grief.

Before Fanny reached the back yard she tore off the wig and realised that she still carried the basket with the entire contents intact, she raced into the printroom opened the stove and thrust the wig into the fire. There were no footsteps now and she knew that she was safe. Gervase had not followed, much to her relief, but she was still not sure if he had recognised her or not. She had bitten his hand instinctively, as a cornered rat would have done, and now she was sad to have brought him pain.

The longer the silence outside lasted the more convinced Fanny became that all was well, but she must return home quickly. Slipping off the old dress to reveal her own beneath she became aware of Tom eyeing her in amazement as he stood in the doorway. Her strange behaviour never ceased to bewilder him, but he had learnt the futility of questioning Fanny's motives in the past.

'Tom, John's in trouble. He is being blamed for something he hasn't done and you mustn't tell anyone that I've been here, do you understand?' she pleaded, hoping that he could appreciate the desperateness of her request. 'You don't want Gervase to get into trouble as well, do you?'

Tom was even more confused when Gervase arrived back, his hand all wrapped up in a handkerchief. The bite had gone deep into his flesh and he had been compelled to stem the flow of blood. 'I've been bitten Tom — by a bitch.' Tom panicked as he remembered the stories of people bitten by mad dogs and immediately rushed to put on the kettle for water to wash the wound. Gervase shook his head, smiling to himself, for he knew just how Tom's simple mind worked. He felt the throbbing in his hand and decided firmly that he would tackle the little minx before the day was out.

With Fanny safely across the field, John quickly climbed up what was left of the back wall of the barn and dropped down onto the rubble which had piled up on the other side. In his anxiety for Fanny's safety and the need for him to escape the barn, he had never checked to see if anyone was coming up the hill from the rear, and as he jumped he realised, too late, that he was trapped. Three Militia stood waiting, muskets raised in anticipation of his move. They took no chances, they tied his hands behind his back and marched him at gunpoint back to the town. They were pursuing Fanny, that he knew, but he was powerless now to help her and could do no more than wait for news.

Within the hour, rumour reached Bryce's ears that there had been yet another chase across the town and that a thief had been caught; the woman accomplice, however, had given them the slip. They had got John! Fanny braced herself as she faced the customers, while her mind fought the nightmare which seemed never ending and to which there seemed no solution. What could she do now? Fighting back the tears which were stinging her eyes she mumbled an excuse and ran out to find Gervase. It did not matter now if he had recognised her, the truth would be out soon enough. Gervase, however, was not at the shop, he had been summoned to the town gaol by the Parish Constable.

John stood dejectedly in the gloomy cell, his face chalky-white with shock and already resenting the isolation of the cold unfriendly tomb. At the sight of Gervase his hopes were momentarily raised until he saw the stern look on his face.

'Can you get me out of here?' he rushed forward, 'I don't have to tell you that I'm innocent, do I?' he asked questioningly.

'No. Of that much I am sure. You'd better tell me the whole story, I've already had the constable's version and he's more or less condemned you out of hand. Why the devil did you run away?'

'Sheer panic I suppose. I was meeting someone in the market.'

Gervase interrupted sharply, 'Yes, and we all know who that was! The pair of you have been playing some stupid game'. John drew back in alarm realising that Gervase had guessed of Fanny's involvement, but kept silent. 'You young fool, I told you to stay away from Fanny if you had to continue with your other activities, but you never seem to learn.' He was angry now, trying to keep a tight rein on his feelings in spite of a growing desire to blacken the other fellow's eye.

'I suppose you know that we love each other!' retorted John unashamedly. 'I didn't mean her any harm and we are both innocent.'

'Fanny doesn't know that I'm aware of her involvement but it is most important that you forget her now. If anyone else finds out then she is in as much trouble as you are.' He waited. 'So, go on, what happened?'

Gervase listened, his brow furrowed as he digested the details, most of which confirmed the constable's story of the incident and yet Gervase had sufficient faith in John to realise that at least he wasn't fool enough to steal a watch. 'I did warn you to keep low. You've been falsely accused but how the hell we're going to prove it beats me.' John's crestfallen face moved Gervase to soften his tone, 'Don't despair, I'll do whatever I can.'

'Listen, will you please go to Nottingham for me. I realise it's a lot to ask, but if my uncle could come and speak for me I think it would help. He knows I'm not a thief. Please Gervase, if I don't get help then my life is ruined', he pleaded, suddenly seeing in the imposing figure before him the stalwart friend that he had become. 'Please!'

'God knows how I'm going to manage the shop with you in here and me dashing off to Nottingham but I don't suppose I can do anything else', Gervase stated gloomily. 'I can but try.'

John put his hand on Gervase's arm, hardly daring to ask, 'How's Fanny?'

'You might well ask' retorted Gervase 'the last time I saw her she had that damned wig on and bit my hand'. He saw the look of disbelief cross John's face and decided to leave the matter there. It would give the fellow something to ponder on while he languished in the cell. Then relenting somewhat added, 'Look, I'll try to bring her here, as a friend of mine for cover, so just act as though she's nothing more than a stranger'.

There was little time for Gervase to dwell upon his own feelings and he felt himself to be like a log pushed along by the current. He was losing a damned good worker in John, as well as a friend, and he was convinced from John's explanation that the Hines' case was at the root of it all. He could ill afford the time to go to Nottingham, but he could do nothing less for the lad. If he prepared some galleys of type Tom could be running off two of the larger orders in his absence, and Fanny could mind the shop. Fanny! He would have to call and tell her what was happening, but first he'd better tell Tom of his plans.

Fanny was waiting for him in the back room; she was frightened and distraught, her hair dishevelled, and where she had rubbed the tears there were streaks down her face. Gervase had never seen Fanny so miserable and his heart went out to her; he found himself wanting to wipe away the tears and to shield her with his arms.

'Oh Gervase, what have they done with him? It wasn't his fault!' she sobbed.

'Come upstairs, it's quieter there.' Gently he took her arm and led her to the stairs. What a fool he'd been not to notice that something had been going on between the pair of them, and the woman in the square must have been Fanny. He was glad that she couldn't see his face as she climbed the stairs ahead of him, for he was not sure himself what she would see there.

Once they reached the room Fanny turned to face him. She was puzzled by the look on his face. He was tired and drawn but there was a look she'd never seen before, a sad lonely look and something else, but her mind was racing. 'I've got to help him. You've always been my friend and I have nowhere else to turn . . .' her voice trailed off as her mind seemed suddenly to go beyond the room. He watched the forlorn figure before him and wanted desperately to ease her pain.

'I know how serious the matter is, and I will go to Nottingham to try and enlist his uncle's help.' His voice was kind.

She was fighting back tears now. 'Oh thank you. He didn't steal anything at all, it's because he stood against Matthew Hines isn't it?'

Gervase nodded, 'I believe so'.

'It's not fair. You know sometimes I feel ashamed when I go out in good clothes, knowing our families feed well because the rich indulge themselves. Every time there is a ball or concert we feed their vanity, Bryce and I, we get richer and the poor get poorer. All John wants is to help the poor out there.' Her impassioned voice held a sob.

He was uncertain what to do. He stood there helpless, sharing her passionate grief, and wanted to hold her, to protect her from the heartache which lay ahead. He wanted to enfold her until she transferred her pain to him. He wanted. What did he want? He stopped himself, horrified and unable to cope with the strength of his feelings for her and realised too late that he adored her. He looked shyly into her trusting eyes with a tenderness which she did not fully understand. He took her hand kindly. 'Come, I'll take you to see him, but don't let them know that you are anything to him other than my friend. I've told John to treat you the same way or else I wouldn't take you. They must not suspect who you are.'

Fanny was grateful for his care, he understood, he always did. When no one else understood her, he did. She leaned across and lovingly kissed his cheek. He pressed his large hand onto hers and she felt the comforting strength within reach out to her. He would always be there, she knew.

The meeting in the cell had to be a cautious one, for they were within earshot of the gaoler. Gervase observed the two as their eyes met and his heart sank as he saw the love that passed between them; they were oblivious to his presence and he wished that he could be elsewhere. His overwhelming desire, in the upstairs room, to hold her and protect her had progressed beyond his intentions. He had worshipped this child all her life, had suffered her tantrums, indulged her whims and endeavoured to protect her from the world. He was shocked now because he saw her suddenly as a woman, a beautiful woman, something soft and warm and he needed to touch her, crush her to him as he had never wanted to with a woman before, but she was not his to hold.

There was such little time allowed for this visit, and Gervase stood as if in a dream, a veil covering his mind. Words were spoken but they had hidden meanings and he was torn between his love for both of them and his need to detach himself from his own emotions. A summons from the constable rescued him from his misery. He left the pair, with a whispered word of warning for them to be cautious, and followed the messenger back through the building.

It transpired that there was going to be very little time between the arrest and the Petty Sessions, leaving Gervase with little option but to go to Nottingham on the next coach. He had to act quickly, for if the case went further, then the Quarter Sessions were only two weeks away. He dragged the reluctant Fanny away from her lover, with the promise that he would go to Nottingham, and Fanny for her part agreed to help in the shop.

There was a Nottingham coach at eight o'clock tomorrow morning, passing through Chesterfield and Mansfield but there was so much work to prepare that Gervase despaired of there being sufficient time left to catch it. He led Fanny home, endeavouring to reassure her that all would be well, yet he knew deep down that in spite of everything the law had its own idiosyncrasies and could be manipulated to suit the establishment.

Gervase worked on through the night in order to leave sufficient work for Tom to do, then hurried home to collect his things before the coach left in two hours time. He sat in a solid high-backed chair, exhausted but not daring to sleep for fear of missing the coach. During the long night he had fought off the vision of Fanny's face which had persisted in breaking into his thoughts. He kept remembering the loving kiss which she had given him and the touch of her hand on his. She had never laughed at him. She had sat for hours by his knee, listening to his adult adventures, arguing with her youthful ideas and awaiting his responses and approval. Trust had been part of that bond, a bond which he had shared with old Bryce and all the Garnetts. Now he felt that his thoughts betrayed that trust.

In the cold grey light of dawn, as he looked out of the window onto the street below, he felt drained of energy and lonelier than ever before, but his daydreams persisted, affording him little peace. He recalled the day by the river when she had splashed before him like a woodland nymph. He had nearly kissed her then. At the time he had laughed at himself, believing that the smell of the meadow and her childish pleasure had captivated him, but now, sadly, he knew that it had not been so. He was now thirty-six, a self-made man, not rich but comfortable, and to the outside world he was a confident man. It was an image which he enjoyed but in truth it hid from the world much of the real man. He could never have approached Bryce about his daughter. Bryce would have been horrified and would have laughed at him.

He was overwhelmed by the desire to bury his tired face in her soft beautiful hair and to feel again the touch of her lips on his skin. Perhaps in reality he had always loved her, placing her high on a pedestal and never realising that the day would come when someone would take her from the pedestal, away from him. His heart ached, for that time had now come, but he could also see the pain which came with it, for her and for him too. Fanny loved the boy, and Gervase knew that he must keep his own love, and the desire which was beginning to burn within him for her, to himself.

Gervase had always been a man of action; his strength had seen him through many scrapes on his travels for Montgomery and he knew that now he must put his thoughts aside, and go. He seized his portmanteau, locked the house, and left for the coach.

Chapter 11

'The Golden Fleece' and 'The Three Salmon' were hostelries to be avoided in Nottingham in the early part of 1817. Under normal circumstances Gervase would most probably have chosen to stay at either, but as they held the reputation for being radical strongholds he felt that it was advisable to lodge elsewhere. 'The White Lion' on the other hand was a favourite meeting place for the Tories and it was into this camp that he chose to go. The inhabitants of Nottingham had always had a tendency to disregard authority anyway, and he felt safer at 'The Lion', in spite of the extra cost. He had often witnessed scenes of disorder here in the Market Place on previous visits, and concluded that if such disturbances were to arise in Sheffield, then perhaps the town's officials would find their office less comfortable.

Upon his arrival, and without delay, Gervase despatched a message by runner to Mr Bailey, John's uncle, requesting an urgent interview; within the hour both men were seated in Gervase's hotel room. Mr Bailey, a resplendent figure in buckskin breeches and a fine worsted jacket, beneath which he sported a red and yellow striped waistcoat, greeted Gervase cordially. He was naturally disturbed to hear of his nephew's present situation but seemed hardly surprised. Gervase left the man in no doubt that he himself believed that John had been framed in reprisal for the Hines' case, and Mr Bailey agreed that his nephew was at least incapable of theft.

'I don't understand why the boy is such a rebel. He's never wanted for much as far as I know, except for a mother. You are right though, to believe his story — he's no thief, the suggestion is completely out of character.'

Gervase recalled that Mr Bailey was a bachelor, and although he might have been a kind and considerate uncle, it was obvious that he knew little regarding the workings of a child's mind. The lack of both mother and father for John might well have encouraged his rebellious and independent spirit, as Gervase knew from personal experience. 'I have come to look upon the fellow as a friend and to rely substantially upon his talents. I don't want to lose him, for purely selfish reasons. Can you come over and speak for him? He says that the Sheriff is a friend of yours. Do you think he could help?' Gervase asked hopefully.

'You say you're here all day tomorrow?' Mr Bailey consulted his fine silver pocket-watch and mused, 'John has a matching one to this you know. What would he need another for anyway?' He placed the watch back into his pocket. 'I'll go and see the Sheriff when I leave here. Will you be available tomorrow evening?'

'Yes. The coach leaves very early in the morning and as I worked through all last night to leave the business running smoothly, I didn't get any sleep. I mistakenly thought that I could sleep on the coach but I hadn't allowed for the appalling weather conditions. We darn near bottomed in every rut and there was flooding everywhere. I have business contacts here in Nottingham so I shall return the day after.'

'You've been exceedingly good taking the boy on in the first place. What more can I say, except that I am most grateful to you. May I buy you something to eat?' Gervase hadn't realised until now that he was indeed hungry and accepted gratefully.

The two men chattered as they descended the stairs, speaking in low voices so as not to be overheard, and Mr Bailey continued, 'I thought that getting him away from this town would rid him of his crazy notions, but it seems that I was mistaken. There's a lot wrong with this system I don't mind admitting, but I'm too long in the tooth for fighting'.

'He's become like a son to me', Gervase replied. 'I've tried to warn him but he is so single-minded. The irony of it is that England needs men of his calibre if we are to make progress in the future. Too many artisans have lost their spirit or have left our shores.'

The two men reached the foot of the stairs, relaxed in each other's company and Gervase observed how alike Mr Bailey was to his nephew, in mannerisms and appearance.

Turning to Gervase he said, 'Many an employer would have abandoned him by now. It was fortunate for him that you took him under your wing'.

The food was hot and adequate but Gervase toyed with his meal, unable to appreciate any of it through his exhaustion from lack of sleep and the tedium of travelling. The emotional disturbance of the past forty-eight hours had also drained him and his mind began to wander. He was desperately in need of sleep and Mr Bailey, observing the other man's fatigue, tactfully excused himself the minute the meal was consumed.

'I will come again tomorrow evening, whatever happens. You say the Petty Sessions are in three days time! If he's not freed then I will have to come to Sheffield myself.' He shook hands with Gervase and made to leave.

'I think you had better be prepared for a fight. I must take back nothing less than a letter of reference from you, although I think a personal appearance would add more weight' Gervase added pointedly, disappointed that the uncle could not be more positive about his action on behalf of his nephew, but he was too tired to remonstrate with Mr Bailey.

So deep had been the sleep from which Gervase awoke next morning that he was left completely disorientated. He had seen one rumbling coach wheel after another flit through his dreams, until when he did finally open his eyes he was unable to fathom out where he was. It was already eleven-thirty and he felt almost guilty at his unaccustomed slothfulness but he had no actual commitments for the day and stretched out in a luxurious sprawl. The indulgence in day-dreams was also a pastime foreign to his nature, but as he lay beneath the warmth of the bedclothes he found his thoughts constantly turning to Fanny. Her bubbling simplicity and intelligent mind were a stimulus to him, and he knew that if he lost her company, which he acknowledged he had come to take for granted, then his life would be the duller for it. Her face, with it's infectious smile, surrounded by that golden hair, tormented him, and the memory of her youthful figure which had blossomed this past year into a desirable body, began to obsess him. Most of all it was her eyes, like an open book, revealing her moods, her sadness, happiness, expectancies and trust which stirred the deep feeling of love in him. Trust, he sighed, what was the point of this torture when she loved John. To Fanny, Gervase was a good friend. The pity of it was that they were all good friends, bound up in a wretched situation.

That evening, Mr Bailey returned to the hotel carrying two letters of reference, one from himself and the other from the Mayor who promised to do all in his power to uncover any plot and assured the court of John's good character. Gervase was extremely disappointed in Mr Bailey who, in spite of his offer in writing to act as guarantor for his nephew's future behaviour, had practically abandoned the fellow without giving a credible reason. He bade Mr Bailey goodnight, and was greatly sobered by the prospect of the problems which were to face him on his return to Sheffield.

Fanny had been waiting all day for his return, hoping for nothing less than a miracle, and when at last he did appear she ran with a sob into his arms. He held her gently, smoothing her sweet-smelling hair as she clung to him. He loved her clean hair, most of the population had hair which stank, but not his Fanny. Her distress disturbed him deeply and the desire which he had to protect her kindled a tenderness as he felt the warmth of her body against his. He entwined his fingers in the back of her hair and pressed her head comfortingly against his breast, but she was unaware of the tender touch of his lips in her hair or of the burning desire which forced him to close his eyes lest the world should read his thoughts.

He could not scold her nor condemn her for the part she had played in the charade, for neither she nor John were guilty of more than naive innocence and he was saddened by the knowledge that the harsh reality had removed the scales from their eyes. Her painful distress was more than she deserved.

The local magistrate listened intently, and with a good deal of interest, as John made his statement; this case was at least different from the usual string of confessions, complaints and denials brought before them. These same two gentlemen had heard the Matthew Hines' case previously, and although they had appreciated that the bullying of children had to be stopped, they were nevertheless unhappy about the uproar which had surrounded the case. The letters of reference from Nottingham, together with Gervase's testimonial of John's character, were impressive, and the account of the beating also added conviction to his claim of innocence. However, there was still the sworn evidence of witnesses to contend with. These could not be ignored.

Hines' men persisted in their claim to have been present at the incident in the Market Place, and John could offer no better explanation as to how the watch got into his pocket, except that he was convinced the timepiece had been put there in order to discredit him.

There was, however, more at stake for the town than a mere case of theft. The magistrates were well aware that the Government held a list of potential radical plotters and pamphleteers, and the name of one John Andrews, was on it. The Government spy, William Oliver, was presently infiltrating all the radical strongholds, and had already sized up the Sheffield contingent, thus enabling him to furnish London with names of men to be watched. The Government was poised ready to strike out against these men but felt the time was not yet right. However, the two Sheffield justices concluded that the town needed ridding of potential trouble and passed John's case to the Lent Assizes in York, which were to take place the following week.

A hushed silence followed the announcement as a sense of disbelief struck deeply at the hearts of John's friends who felt that such a miscarriage of justice should not have happened.

Fanny's knuckles were white with tension as she gripped the rails in front of her, and Gervase restrained her as she made to stand and protest as John was pulled unwillingly from the room. 'I'm innocent' he shouted in anger back at the magistrates 'I'm an innocent man!'

Blind faith in justice had not prepared Fanny for this outcome and the speed at which the system moved, when it chose to do so, made Fanny angry. It was harder to prove someone innocent than guilty, and she wondered just how many other men and women had been wrongly convicted, or too harshly punished, for crimes committed out of desperation. Some stole in order to keep their families from starvation, and others had been hanged for a principle. There were children whose fathers were doomed to years of harrowing work and miserable separation on the other side of the world, and for what? Men had the right to food and work. The years ahead suddenly looked empty and futile to Fanny, the high hopes and ideals of youth were being crushed by harsh reality and her dreams stolen before they had time to come to fruition.

Fanny could not openly admit her love, nor cry out to the world in his defence, neither would anyone know that she had been loved, for she knew that she would never love anyone again.

Gervase travelled alone to the York Assizes and was filled with a sense of foreboding which was difficult to suppress. The constant disruptions to his work schedule were creating problems, and at the back of his mind was the knowledge that if things went badly wrong for John today, then he would be compelled to find a suitable replacement. It was not a prospect to which he looked with enthusiasm; the two of them worked well together and Gervase felt guilty at his negative thinking. What a mess they were all in! He hated injustice and despised the men of power for shamelessly using the weak and vulnerable, but most of all he saw no possible excuse for the cruelty which the inhabitants of the world practised upon each other.

A look of relief flooded across John's gaunt face as he greeted Gervase. Life in gaol was sobering, and the pent-up anger was beginning to consume him, causing him to talk with great agitation. 'Gervase, it's darned good to see you, there's not one intelligent soul to talk to in here. I hate this filthy place and everything about it, they've no right to keep me here.'

Gervase tried desperately to advise him yet again. 'Calm down. If you go to the Assizes talking like that you'll only arouse their resentment of you.' To his relief, John appeared to regain his self-control. 'I think you should try to think carefully about your options', offered Gervase, in a bid to raise the other man's hopes.

'What options? My life is at an end!' cried John.

'Nonsense. Hopefully you'll be freed, but if you are I think you may have to go to America straight away, for your own safety.'

'And the other option?' he quipped back disdainfully.

'If you are convicted there are three roads down which you could go; you could spend time in prison, you could be transported or, heaven forbid, they could hang you.' Gervase bit his tongue, wishing that he had not uttered the words that until now had only been in his mind.

'Thanks for nothing.' A bitterness crept into John's voice. 'I'm innocent and I resent the suggestion that I'm otherwise.'

'We believe you, but we can't offer cast-iron proof. You don't realise just how this is affecting all of us. We're doing everything we can, but for God's sake don't annoy the magistrates or you'll increase any sentence.'

'You don't think they'll clear me — do you?' Gervase didn't answer. 'Do you?' John repeated.

Gervase sighed deeply. 'I only wish I knew. Fanny has sent you a note, please read it then give it back to me. She hasn't signed it, I don't want anyone else to get hold of it.' He handed John the letter, wondering over its content whilst John read on. He turned away, lost in his own thoughts, until eventually John spoke in a softer tone.

'I'm sorry. You are the last person I should take it out on. Thank you for all that you are doing for me, I fear I have been ungrateful.' His anger had subsided with the reading of the letter and he seemed contrite as he folded the letter and returned it to Gervase. 'If anything happens to me, will you take care of Fanny? She has great trust and affection for you. I fear that I shall be of no help to her if the outcome is bad.' The fighting spirit had deserted him now, and suddenly Gervase saw in his face the look of fear and defeat.

'Don't lose heart, we're doing all we can to help', Gervase heard himself utter in spite of his own misgivings. 'I will be in court with you, just keep your temper mild and show them your integrity.' He took John's hand in a gesture of solidarity and hope, then left the cell to go to the courtroom.

The courtroom was filled to capacity with the usual array of officials, jurors and sniggering public, the latter appreciating less of the seriousness of the cases than the opportunity to see a good play unfold before their eyes. It was cheap theatre with the prisoners merely actors who came and went, leaving the audience eager only for another performance.

It gave Gervase little satisfaction to sit there watching the stream of humanity brought to its knees, pleading their cases before the court. The unnecessary severity of some sentences alarmed him and his heart was full of pity for the young offenders, many of whom were merely victims of the system. The simple-minded accepted the inevitable, whilst the unrepentant hurled abuse at the bench, risking further punishment. He had been sitting in court for almost two hours, saddened by the sights he had seen, and physically cramped from lack of movement and the hardness of the wooden benches, before he heard them call John. By this time, Gervase judged that the jury had become tired and were in a mean mood, becoming meaner with each verdict they pronounced. He wondered how they could justify the sentence of transportation for stealing a pair of kid gloves, when they had given Matthew Hines only six months for such viciousness against a child. It appeared to defy human decency. A sentence of public flogging in the town centre for one felon, had pleased the crowd enormously, and Gervase was beginning to become despondent by the time John appeared.

The voice of the court usher bellowed, 'Call John Andrews!' A hush fell across the bloodthirsty crowd. There hadn't been a hanging so far in this Session and they were feeling cheated.

John's obvious bearing was not that of a common thief, nor were his handsome features concealed by the stubble which he had not bothered to remove from his face. It was little wonder that Fanny had fallen in love with him, his fair hair and fresh complexion awakened the interest of the women in the courtroom. They sensed that this particular case was different, and leaned forward, eager not to miss any of the proceedings. He'd had the world at his feet, connections, talent and good looks, but what had it achieved?

The accusation was read out, along with the two letters from Nottingham, and Mr Rogers, acting for the prosecution, energetically addressed the court.

'Two witnesses have sworn under oath that they witnessed the accused, John Andrews, push the defendant Samuel Bennett violently, causing him to fall almost to the ground. The latter feeling the act to be more deliberate than accidental, felt into his pocket for his watch and money. He discovered to his dismay that his silver pocket-watch was missing and promptly called out in alarm. The two witnesses, realising that the accused was more than likely the guilty party, apprehended him in front of several witnesses, and held on to him whilst a market trader searched him. They found the pocket-watch, inscribed to Samuel Bennett, in the accused man's pocket. He appeared to have a woman accomplice waiting in the shadows, the same woman, it is said, that he has been seen with on several occasions. This woman, realising that her companion had been caught red-handed, caused a commotion sufficient to distract the crowd's attention.' Mr Rogers paused and blew his nose, much to the amusement of the crowd. He continued, 'The accused took advantage of the situation and made off at great speed into the surrounding alleyways, finally concealing himself in a barn until he was captured by the Militia. No innocent man ever runs away, but stays to defend himself. I understand that he refused to implicate the woman, instead of calling her as a witness in his defence'. He paused. 'I would like to call Richard Taylor as a witness'.

Richard Taylor, ruffian that he was, stood in the dock whilst Mr Rogers questioned him, his coarse features contrasting sharply with John's fine proud face.

'Richard Taylor, is it not true that on Saturday February 22nd last, in the Sheffield marketplace you witnessed the aforementioned incident? Will you please tell the court exactly what happened.'

In a harsh rough voice the man repeated his version of the incident. Gervase watched John, fearing that he would lose his self-control, as his obvious agitation at being unable to speak up for himself began to show, Gervase recognised the familiar sign of twitching in his cheek-bones whenever he was tense. Things looked black for him. Why had the silly pair run away in the first place? Until now Gervase hadn't re-alised that John had refused to name Fanny, and he was grateful that at least she would be safe from whatever consequences were to befall John.

The second witness, and the market trader who had searched John, both repeated their versions, and all claimed that Samuel Bennett was well known around the market place. The watch was a familiar sight as Bennett often displayed it with pride. Each man flatly denied any con-nection with Mr Bennett, other than having seen him in a frequent state of intoxication in the area, and stressed that he was quite honest.

At least John's uncle had engaged an eminent solicitor, named Burton, to defend his nephew, in spite of the fact that he had been un-able to attend himself. Mr Burton began his eloquent plea on behalf of his client.

'My client, John Andrews, is a hard working, honest man, who cares very much indeed for the welfare of his fellowman. He has no need to obtain goods by illegal means, having sufficient funds and a regular wage. He also possesses an excellent silver watch of his own, and has the intelligence to realise that most time-pieces are inscribed and easi-ly traceable. He denies stealing the watch and claims to be the victim of a malicious conspiracy of revenge. In August last year he witnessed the brutal beating of a child and, as a result of fetching a doctor immedi-ately, saved the boy's life.'

The voice of Mr Justice Batty interrupted. 'I presume this has some bearing on the present predicament, in which the prisoner now finds himself?'

'Yes, my Lord. My client was responsible for the conviction of an overseer, a Mr Matthew Hines, for that assault, and Mr Hines subse-quently served six months in York Castle for the crime. Matthew Hines was heard by several witnesses, to threaten my client with the words

'I'll get even with you'. Some weeks after Mr Hines was confined to York Castle, Mr Andrews was viciously beaten up late one night in an alley behind the printing shop where he works. One of the men responsible for the attack threatened that if my client reported the incident, he would be 'finished off' and that it had been done 'for Matthew Hines'. Two weeks ago Matthew Hines was released from prison. He returned to Sheffield, where we believe this plot to ruin Mr Andrews was planned, as further revenge.'

The intrigue pleased the crowd, who began to mutter and nod amongst themselves. Even Gervase found his hopes being raised by the growing assent of the public.

'What proof have you that these witnesses are in any way connected with Mr Hines or Samuel Bennett?' Mr Justice Batty asked.

'Unfortunately, after many painstaking hours of enquiry, all that we can prove is that the two witnesses frequent the same alehouses as Mr Hines and are friends of his associates. We feel that a great deal of care has been taken to cover up any evidence. Mr Andrews has an uncle, a respectable and wealthy merchant in Nottingham, to whom he could turn for anything he needs; you also have a letter from the Mayor of Nottingham stating similar trust in Mr Andrews.'

The two learned men considered the letters yet again, along with a third which was not offered to the rest of the court. This additional piece of paper appeared to arouse great interest, and was in fact a letter from the Lord Lieutenant of the County instructing that all radicals on their list be apprehended. The radicals were tired of futile petitions, they were ready to abandon these in favour of an insurrection in order to seize their rights by non-peaceful means. The spy, William Oliver, was doing his job well, the Government was ready to start ridding themselves of trouble makers and here then was an excellent opportunity to shorten the list.

Mr Batty lowered the papers and peered at Mr Burton over his ancient spectacles. 'You say you have the accused man's employer here as a witness. Could we hear him now? I would like to question the gentleman myself.'

Gervase welcomed the opportunity to stretch his cold stiff limbs and took the stand, catching John's eye reassuringly as he did so.

'Now Mr Webster, how long had the accused worked for you?'

'Approximately fifteen months.'

'In that case you must have become acquainted with Mr Andrew's thoughts and actions?'

'Yes Sir, he is very intelligent, honest and industrious,' Gervase replied with great sincerity. 'I have come to rely upon his work.'

'Is it not also true that in caring for his fellowmen he has become involved with the radical movement in Sheffield, and did he not make a stand in Paradise Square last October, making his feelings known?'

Mr Burton endeavoured to intervene 'Sir, I object.'

The interruption gave Gervase precious moments to collect his thoughts. This line of questioning had surprised him. It had no connection with the charges aimed at John at all, and he sensed a hidden motive beneath the questioning.

'No, Mr Burton, I'll ask these questions', returned Mr Batty firmly.

Gervase could feel the heat rise beneath his collar and sweat gathering on his brow. What right had they to ask such questions? They were waiting for his reply. 'Please go on, Mr Webster.'

'I don't know that he is involved with any movement at all, and as for his action in the Square, he reflected the thoughts of the people, and was carried away by the excited atmosphere of the crowd.' Had he satisfied them? He was grateful now that he had not gone into great details with John about his movements.

'So you think he is soon carried away on impulse do you? Isn't it possible that he also took the watch on an impulse?'

This was a devious and conniving line of questioning which Gervase had not anticipated and he protested quickly. 'No I don't think that's what happened at all.'

'That will be all, you may sit down.' Gervase was bewildered, he felt that he had been used, led into an awkward corner only to be dismissed. He was sure now that there was more to it. They wanted John out of the way and he knew that the third letter held the clue. He sat down with the feeling that John's future had already been decided.

'Bring John Andrews forward.'

Gervase could hardly bear to watch as John stood before the court answering questions which were clearly a mere formality. He could add little more than that which his solicitor had offered, and simply explained his flight as one of panic. He held his head high, without arrogance, almost accepting that the watch was not the true cause for his being there, but insisted constantly that he was innocent of theft. He was dismissed back to his seat. Both solicitors summed up their relevant sides of the case and Mr Batty cleverly offered his conclusions and recommendations which Gervase considered were more than biased against John.

The verdict, when it came, was not unexpected. Gervase sat with bowed head and listened, choking back his anger.

'Guilty. Transported for seven years. It is ordered by this court that the said John Andrews be transported, as soon as is conveniently possible, to one of His Majesty's Colonies, to be computed from the time of his conviction.'

When finally Gervase lifted his numbed head, John had gone. There seemed little left to motivate him now and he remained in his seat stunned, aware too of the mortifying and painful task which lay ahead — he must tell Fanny.

Chapter 12

In the weeks that followed, Gervase watched anxiously over Fanny as she hung despondently about the shop, almost as if hoping that by some miracle John would reappear. Time had taken its toll of her liveliness and he was worried by the peakiness in her face. The shock had devastated her, but he had expected that within a couple of weeks she would at least have begun to accept the situation.

It had been a particularly difficult time, for neither Bryce nor Sarah knew the truth. Sarah acknowledged that Fanny was sensitive and, naturally, shocked at the loss of a friend though she did wonder if her daughter had secretly admired the poor young man. Bryce was preoccupied with his own plans for he was looking to expand into new premises. The town was growing rapidly now, and as it enlarged its boundaries, there was a need for trade to spread out with it. The pleasant new houses on the Moor, with their gardens and larger windows, appealed to him. His growing family demanded a bigger house, and there was only Sarah and Fanny to accommodate. The old shop was drab now, new premises would please the customers and perhaps bring in more. He passed his hours in dreams of the future.

With great care, Gervase had concealed from Fanny the fact that John had been forced to march, in a crocodile of chained prisoners, from York, passing through Doncaster, onto the old unseaworthy prison hulks in Langstone Harbour, to await transportation to one of His Majesty's colonies. The gossips in the shop, however, did what Gervase omitted to do, and the thought of him chained and dirty, humiliated and unhappy as he would be, driven from town to town, gave her great pain. At least they hadn't got his money or his papers, for in the haste and panic that fatal day at the barn, she had failed to empty the basket. One day he would need them and she would keep them as a security for his future. He was at least alive and for that she must be grateful. She tried so hard to occupy her mind with other things, but the pain returned constantly to distract her and now there were other fears to beset her.

The moment it became obvious that there was to be no reprieve for John, Gervase was compelled to advertise yet again for a qualified assistant. This time he sought an uncomplicated being, one well trained and with simple aspirations, perhaps dull but reliable, for Gervase had suffered enough from idealism. Joseph Swift fitted the bill exactly; he was shy to the point of being timid but his work was good and he posed a threat to no one, in fact he had few faults and came from a stable background. An air of sadness hung over the place now, for with John gone, so also had the happy banter of the past year, and work was more of a toil than it had previously been.

The new fear which crept over Fanny inspired disbelief, mixed with the fervent hope that her suspicions were unfounded. One half of her knew the worst, the other clung to a childish naiveté that it could not be happening to her. As time passed and the sickness started, her hopes began to fade and she knew that she would also have to carry her humiliation through the streets. There was nowhere to hide and nothing she could do to stop its progress. She could no longer hide the truth from herself — for she was with child. With neither a prospective husband nor even a suitor to blame for her predicament she would be classed as a woman of the streets. She would be a social outcast, a target for gossip and dependent upon the Parish for charity. Her baby would be a bastard. She shuddered at the thought of her child, their child, shunned and tormented as she knew other such children were. She was haunted by the faces she had seen in the old cotton mill, of children unloved and unwanted, and she shut her eyes to the shame she would bring to her mother.

With every twinge she hoped, with every heavy thing she lifted she wished, but nothing happened and it didn't go away. The panic increased and she told no one of her shame. She had almost given everything away the day Gervase had nearly caught her being sick in the back room, but he had been preoccupied and seemed not to notice. She wanted to sit by his knee as she had as a child, and tell him everything, but he would despise her for her weakness.

She was alone and afraid, and fell asleep at night hoping to wake up with the nightmare gone. How long could she hide it, this disgrace of hers? She wept into her pillow, for herself and for her child, as the nightmare increased.

Gervase was not entirely surprised, on answering the door, to find Fanny there, for somehow he had known that she would come to him. He had hoped and prayed that his suspicions were falsely founded, had hoped that his imagination had been playing tricks with him, but Fanny's paleness of late had worried him, and when he had found her in the back room frantically trying to hide her nausea, he was almost certain that his fears had foundation. He had noticed too a sudden maturity about her and a fullness about her breasts that he had seen in other pregnant women.

'Come in Fanny, what brings you here? I didn't expect to see you today!' he said as he held the door open wider for her to enter the house. She smiled faintly and entered the tiny entrance hall. 'Go through, there is a fire in the grate, find a chair and I'll join you in a minute.'

Fanny entered the cosy little room with its candles brightly lit ready for the oncoming dusk. He had obviously been reading, for a book lay on the chair by the fire, and she guessed that the room had changed little since the days when his mother had been there. It was neat and tidy but a little bare of useless ornamentation. She drew the chair from the other side of the fire closer to the warmth and drew her pelisse closer around herself for comfort, although the room was quite warm. She felt cold, as though the April winds had followed her into the house, and she stared into the flickering flames, not knowing how to tell Gervase of her secret. He would be disappointed in her she knew, he would think her wanton and cheap. Her heart was heavy and she brushed a tear from her cheek.

He observed her from the doorway, saddened by her appearance. He was allowing her time to compose herself, and her thoughts, before he went in. He feared that if he left her too long she might become uneasy and so he entered the room, removed the book from the other chair and sat opposite her on the other side of the enormous fireplace. 'Come, Fanny, what ails you? It isn't like you to be so serious.' She found it difficult to meet his gaze and couldn't speak. 'Things can't be so bad that you can't share them with me. You have always been so frank before, and I've never betrayed you.' His voice was soft and coaxing, endeavouring to ease from her the confession which he knew was to come. Had he not known her all these years, and loved her enough to understand how she must be feeling.

She sobbed, 'Oh Gervase, I'm going to have a child, what am I going to do? No one knows that I have been seeing anyone — they will think me a slut, or a witch, what can I do?'

Gervase kept his smile gentle and looked closely at her body. He was grateful that there was no obvious swelling yet, for until then no one shared their secret. He looked deeply into her eyes which stared with fear into his, and he held out his large hands, shyly, inviting her to come to him as she had as a child. Fanny stumbled forward from the chair and knelt before him. He opened his arms and tenderly drew her towards him until her head lay softly on his huge chest. He cradled her comfortingly but she did not see the tears which welled up in his eyes. What did he care if the child were not his, it was part of her body, her flesh and they both needed help. The warmth of her body stirred his emotions and he fought off the desire to kiss her. His body burned with love for her but that love made him gentle. Fanny clung to him and sobbed, sobbed until she shook, and he felt her go weak with exhaustion then slip from his arms. He caught her and picked her up before she fell into the grate, then carried her to the sofa where he sat quietly holding her limp form.

Fanny's face was ashen but she was breathing lightly so that all Gervase could do was hold her until she came round. He lovingly stroked her hair back from her eyes. All these years he had placed her upon a pedestal and now she lay broken in his arms.

For a week now he had been tormented by the possibility that she was with child. He knew that it would be John's child and not his, but he loved children and he was in a position to offer them both a home. People would be bound to talk, but what the hell, life was short and tragic, she meant all the world to him and she needed his help.

Fanny stirred and slowly her colour returned. She snuggled unknowingly deeper into his arms until finally she became aware of where she was. Fanny opened her eyes, startled, but there was no rebuke in his eyes. 'Oh Gervase, I'm sorry, it's not fair of me to burden you with my problems. I don't know what to do!' She didn't struggle to leave the comfort of his arms but lay there deep in contemplation. 'I thought of running away.'

Anger rose in Gervase against John for his irresponsibility, but he kept his anger well hidden. 'Don't be a little goose, you cannot run away because your problem will go with you. You would hurt your mother more that way. Listen to me, I know you don't love me, but let me marry you and I'm sure we can give the child a secure home. I have this home with a garden, a business and respect.' He stopped to give her time to think.

'But they will blame you — you'll lose their respect too. You don't love me and might find someone else when it's too late.' Her head fell dejectedly.

He spoke firmly but not unkindly, 'Would marrying me be so difficult? I'm not handsome but I'm not unkind nor uncaring either. We could have our own rooms, I wouldn't force you to do anything you found unacceptable. As for other people, it would be a seven day wonder for them, you could go away until it was over'. He looked around the room. She fitted the place well and he felt a deep sense of contentment as they sat together in the firelight.

She nodded, grateful for his strength and wisdom. His eyes were soft and in a way she did love him. In return she could make him an industrious wife, but what if John were to return? He never would she knew, they'd made sure of that, but the child needed a home and she was frightened to be alone any more.

'Do you know when your time is due?' he asked simply.

She lowered her head in shame, 'November, I think'. He raised her chin with his hand and searched her face.

'You'll make a fine mother, don't hang your head in shame. If you marry me no one will ever know. Does your mother know?'

'I don't think so, she lives in the past these days. What should we tell her?' It did not seem strange to talk so intimately with Gervase. He had always been there, this big reliable man, and if she never loved him she would always revere him.

'The truth, Fanny — but only to Sarah. I could not live with myself if I let her think that I had lied to her or had taken advantage of her kindness and friendship. Thank God that it will be wintertime when the child comes. Few people will see your condition if you wear a pelisse later on, then if you go away when it really shows, and stay longer, people will have a hard time working it out. I have a blind aunt who lives near Gainsborough with my cousin. They will be glad of some young company around the farm, I will take you there. They need not know just how long we have been married. The journey will not be easy, but you are strong enough.'

She whispered, half afraid to express her thoughts, 'You know that I still love John, I don't want to hurt you'. He looked into her anxious eyes and she added, 'but I do care for you very much'.

'I know that you are more than a daughter to me and I have no one else to care for. We will have to face the world as man and wife, because to all intents and purposes that is what we will be, but we are sensible enough to keep our private lives from prying eyes.'

'But what if you should fall in love with someone else? It would be too late then.' He was touched by her honest concern.

'Fanny, all these years I have never wanted to marry. Why should that suddenly change? You too may fall in love again, but life is short and we have a more pressing problem right now. Will you marry me?' Fanny nodded shyly and gently kissed his cheek in silent gratitude. 'Stay here by the fire while I go and see your mother!'

Sarah was in the back room when Gervase called. He gave her a friendly pat on the shoulder as he always did, and was thankful that she was alone. Normally there was only Fanny with her in the evenings because her other children were with their own families, and tonight was no exception. He had never lost the boyish frown which creased his brow whenever something bothered him, but he was also hesitant in his speech as he sat at the table and begged her to sit down too.

'Sarah, I want to talk to you in great confidence because I love and respect you, and I want you to promise that even if you find it difficult to accept what I have to say, when you have thought about it, try to realise how sincere I am.' He paused unsure how to begin. 'I dearly love Fanny' he stated bluntly.

Sarah gasped at the suddenness of his outburst, then said knowingly, 'I have often wondered . . .'

He broke in, 'Hush, Sarah. That is not the problem. I would never have spoken out, for I know that I am too old for Fanny and that she is not in love with me'. Sarah sat puzzled and intrigued by his passionate outburst. 'I don't want you ever to tell her about my feelings. If ever the need arises then I will tell her myself.' He leaned over and placed his hand tenderly on hers. 'Fanny fell in love with John. I didn't know it at the time, or perhaps I could have been more protective of her, but they were besotted with each other. They were only guilty of being innocent and in love, but Sarah, Fanny is going to have a child.'

He saw Sarah blanch suddenly, and he realised how much she had aged since Bryce's death. Sarah spoke in a shocked, panicky voice. 'Oh my God, what are we going to do?'

'Hush, it won't be so bad. Fanny is going to marry me. We shall marry as quickly as possible, by license, I have the money. She will conceal her condition as long as possible then go away on some pretext, to a relation of mine. If she remains there after the birth no one will quite know what has happened.' Again, he placed his hand on her shaking one across the table, and his eyes rested on her greying hair and motherly face. He fell silent whilst she wrestled with her thoughts. Seeking to ease the pain he added, 'Fanny and John were so in love, she may be wild but she isn't wicked. I promise to look after her and the child. I didn't understand until it was too late that she was seeing him, I feel I should have known'.

'Oh Gervase, if only Bryce were alive' Sarah lamented.

'Perhaps it is as well that he isn't, Sarah.'

Sarah sighed a deep sad sigh, for she missed Bryce so very much, and now her beloved Fanny had spoilt her life almost before it had begun. They sat together at the table, sharing a silence, busy with their thoughts. Gervase got up to poke the fire and put on more wood. He turned when Sarah asked, 'Where is she now? Is she alright?'

'I left her at my place, staring at the fire just as we are doing. You can't show her your anger Sarah, she is too hurt and bewildered. She knows already the disappointment and shame that your are bound to feel. That is why I said I would come.' His eyes held hers endeavouring to reassure her.

Finally Sarah spoke, as a mother would to a son. 'Son, you love some-one who doesn't love you. You deserve something better, the sacrifice is too great. Do you really know what you are doing?'

'Sarah, I'm tired and weary of thinking. I have suspected this for over a week now, and my decision is not a hasty one. I've made up my mind and I want to do it. Will you give us your blessing?' he begged.

'I wish to goodness that I could give you more than my blessing, for I think you'll need it.'

He bent and kissed the top of her grey hair lightly. 'Thank you Sarah' he whispered, 'I'll be good to her, you wait and see.'

The private little marriage was simple enough. With money available to buy a licence no time was lost and the couple pledged their troth in the old Parish Church. That he should have won for himself such a pretty young thing left the men of the town quite envious and their women-folk quite astounded, in spite of the fact that many of them also had husbands of greater age than themselves. Their husbands were men who had established themselves before committing themselves to mat-rimony and then had often done so for social reasons and not for love. Only the poor could afford to marry for love or from the results of im-propriety, and it was lucky if love and social prestige came to the 'ladies' of the town in the same package. Nevertheless, speculation kept them amused for a little while, but the poor were too busy surviving to care.

It was much easier to live with a friend than with a lover, for emotion did not stir its spoon quite so often and left a good deal of room for re-spect for one another. When Fanny's rounds of sickness and lethargy were over, she worked hard keeping the books for both shops and turning his house into their home. In sharp contrast to the previous wet summer this one was warm and sunny, and in the balmy evenings they would stroll together on familiar walks, discussing the world at large. She fed on his knowledge, marvelled at his gentleness and when in the evenings he stood silently reading, propped by his elbow on the mantel-shelf, she found herself studying him, pondering, pondering on her feelings for him. He took her to concerts, for rides in the gig, he bought her little treats, but he never displayed anything more of his inner emo-tions than a look in his eye, which she found difficult to understand.

Towards the end of July, when her condition became too obvious to conceal and the heat prevented her wearing a coat, they informed the world that she was with child, and she remained close to the house. The nodding, winking and calculating began, and by the end of August Gervase pompously announced to his friends that he wanted the child to be born in the clean, healthy air of the countryside. His wife would leave in September to stay with relatives in Lincolnshire until her time came.

Trade was now picking up all over the country. The better weather had provided good, healthy crops and there was relief from the abject poverty of previous years. There was hope for the future and the threat of insurrection, even revolution, was receding with the promise of work and cheaper provisions. The Movement had been crushed and the masses no longer needed to march. The insurrection scheduled for June 10th had been a complete flop; and a mere four hundred men and boys set off from the villages, only to find that the expected thousands of revolutionary supporters had failed to turn up. The Government spies had done their work well, resulting in the leaders being arrested prior to the uprising, and in the end three men were hanged, fourteen transported and six jailed for their involvement in the affair.

Gervase's business, too, shared in the upturn and allowed him to keep his promise to send Fanny away.

As the time drew near for Fanny to depart, she found that not only was she afraid of the forthcoming ordeal but that she did not want to leave Gervase. Everything had been so carefully arranged to save her social face, he had taken such care to protect her and now, for his sake too, she must go. She watched him as he worked at his desk, his dear head so deep in thought. If only he knew how much she cared for him, hung on to his every word, and longed for him to hold her gently in his arms. She seemed always destined to lose that which she loved most dearly, her father, John, and now she was to leave Gervase and her mother. She had to be strong, this was the way he had planned it, to save her. If only he loved her, but she knew that it was only a dream.

Gervase for his part was having great difficulty in keeping his side of the bargain; her nearness was disturbing him to a state of distraction, and he hated to send her away. He had not allowed for his own weakness in his offer to marry her. He had believed himself capable of great fortitude and tenacity, but he had been foolish, for he was merely a man. A man with desires both physical and emotional. He had never needed that kind of love before, he had supplanted that need with other interests, but he needed it now, he needed her tenderness, her devotion, and more than that, she had awakened in him a need for a physical fulfilment.

The months spent together, so close, had changed everything and now he felt himself to be sitting on a powder keg. He doubted his ability to handle the situation anymore. He was a tormented man. She could have all that he owned, everything could be hers and he knew that she would not abuse that trust. Without her there was nothing any-more. He wanted most of all to bury his head in her breasts and feel her respond to his touch. He found himself constantly dragging his mind back from the brink of ecstasy and knew that the time had come, she must go away, go now, now before he spoilt all their plans and he would lose her. When she had gone he could forget her and drown himself in his work.

Chapter 13

he chaise, which Gervase had borrowed in Gainsborough, came to a halt in the yard behind the prettiest farm Fanny had ever seen. Ivy almost completely covered its frame and clung around the mullion windows. Gervase came round to help Fanny down the steps. It had been a long uncomfortable journey for her, first by stage to Worksop and then on to Gainsborough. He had been acutely aware of the discomfort the excess weight she was carrying had caused her. In the past seven months he had seen her blossom before his eyes. Her full pregnant body, far from dismaying him, filled him instead with a protectiveness which in turn lead to a sexual desire of such strength the likes of which he had never felt before. He longed to see her naked in her motherhood, to touch the swelling of her belly and breasts, and longed to gently cup those proud breasts to his lips so that he could kiss the nipples. He wanted to run his fingers through her hair and close her eyes with his lips. He burned with a mixture of desire, love and guilt. He was glad that he had learned how, as a boy, to hide his true feelings, and wished to God that it was his child which she carried.

Fanny caught her foot on the edge of the steps in her weariness, and slithered into his arms. He managed to catch her, his arms slipping under her flailing ones. The passion which had possessed him all day as they had been pressed together in the cramped coach still gripped him, and he pulled her tenderly against his heaving chest. His warm mouth sought hers and his senses reeled as he poured his heart out into that kiss.

How long it lasted he never knew, for time stood still while he swam in a sea of warm sensations. She moved. He stopped, horrified at his actions. 'Fanny, I'm sorry' he choked, then turned from her lest she see the passion and adoration in his eyes, or the pain on his face. Fanny looked at his dark head, turned from her, and her hand went out to touch him. She could not touch him, she had no right, how many times she had wanted him to do that; but he had given her a home and taken care of her, even holding her when she had been too sick to hold her head up. She loved him to look at her, she loved his strong brown hands, and she longed for him to touch her. He had kissed her in haste, in pity and now he regretted it. He was going to leave her here until her time was over.

She wanted him to stay, to take care of her as he had always done, but she wanted far more of him than that. She was ashamed and hung her head for she knew it was wrong to allow her thoughts to stray in such unholy ways, and she put her hand to her mouth but still could not erase the tingle of his lips. Tears ran down her cheeks. At least the blind old aunt would not see her face, and the cousin would think her tears to be tears of sorrow at their parting.

Gervase couldn't face her, he had let her down. He had promised so much, asking little in return and now he had hurt her this way. He turned and saw the tears on her face and murmured, 'Forgive me Fanny, that wasn't part of the agreement. I don't know what came over me — I'll be gone tomorrow and after the baby comes please try to forget what happened'.

He took the bags. Her heart sank, he was sorry and tomorrow he would be gone. She didn't want him to go. He had always been her strength and she needed him more than she had ever needed him before, but he was leaving her here to forget and she must endure it. Why hadn't she realised it before it had become too late? She tried to think of John and knew deep down that she hadn't thought of him like that for a long time now. Yes, she had worried about his ruined life and wondered if he was well, but she found it hard to picture his face any more. She felt that she was betraying him with the fading image.

Looking down at the bulge that was her stomach she was overwhelmed with sadness to realise that the past was gone and the future lay as a jumbled mess.

Mary, the cousin, opened the heavy wooden door. She was short and plain, but with a ready smile which widened with delight at the sight of Gervase, for it had been some time since he had visited them. He had changed little in her eyes, but he noted the grey flecks in her hair and the wrinkling of her brow, for she was many years older than he was. The responsibility of running the large farm and caring for her blind mother had taken its toll. She had devoted her life to her mother, refusing to marry, but perhaps never having found a man persuasive enough to encourage her to give up her independence.

She saw Fanny standing there, subdued and pale, and thought how young and pretty she was, in spite of the tearful look in her eyes. Mary longed for company. The farm was some distance from the village and for all her mother's sweetness she looked forward to having a young woman around the place.

Aunt Meg sat by the window, unable to see out through the opening but still appreciative of the familiar smells of the countryside. Her grey hair was wound up into a plait on the top of her head; she was dainty and frail but her face was alive and animated, and Fanny was amazed how clear and fine her unseeing eyes were. Gervase bent and kissed the old lady and took her hands into his own. 'It's been a long time, Aunt Meg, I shouldn't have left it so long between visits. You don't look any older.'

'I feel it, lad. The old rheumatism gets worse and I don't go far now, just as far as the doorway to sit in the sunshine.' Her head inclined as if searching for something. 'Come, child, where are you? Where's your wife, Gervase?'

Gervase caught Fanny's shaking hands and gently placed them into those of his Aunt. Fanny watched his face as he bent closer and marvelled at the gentleness which flowed from his huge body.

'Come child, I won't bite. Just because I can't see doesn't mean I can't feel your presence.' Fanny kissed the old lady on the cheek and as she did so noticed the smell of the flowers coming in through the open window. 'Why, child, your hands are trembling', observed Aunt Meg.

'It's very kind of you to have me', Fanny murmured shyly.

'You sound weary, my dear. I think perhaps you had better have a lie down after such a hard journey, in your condition too. Mary, take Fanny up to her bedroom. We can talk later when she has rested and we're having a meal.' She paused. 'Run along you two, I want Gervase to myself for a little while', she chuckled.

Wearily, Fanny climbed the stairs, following her hostess almost mechanically. She was too tired and confused to think straight and she lay immediately upon the bed, allowing Mary to remove the shoes from her feet. She had barely time to utter her thanks before a deep feeling of drowsiness overtook her, and she was soon sleeping peacefully.

She awoke slowly, unsure of where she was in her sleepiness, and the delicious aroma of cooking filled the room which was illuminated by the light of a lantern. In the mellow light she was surprised by the loveliness of the room. She lay in a luxurious bed of soft feathers and was covered by a brightly coloured quilt. The four-poster bed enveloped her with its rich chintz hangings and green fringe. By the window stood a dressing-table on which was placed a vase of autumn flowers and a gilded dressing-glass. The lantern stood on an old bowed chest by the side of the bed. Fanny marvelled at the sight. She had never seen such a beautiful room and felt loath to leave the warmth of the bed. A fire flickered in the ancient grate, causing her to ponder on the people who had previously lived in such an old house, with its elegant furniture, for it was, after all, only a farm house.

The room wasn't large but the deep casement of the window gave added space to its dimensions, and she realised suddenly that the curtains were open and that it was dark outside.

Reluctantly and with great effort Fanny lifted herself from the depths of the bed and dangled her feet on to the rug beneath. Her poor ankles were swollen and she had great difficulty as she attempted to pull on her shoes. On the washstand hung a clean linen towel and she took pleasure in washing the dirt of the journey from her face before going below, for the smell of cooking was making her hungry.

Slowly descending the stairs, Fanny noticed the paintings which hung on the walls. They were mainly portraits, of people dressed not in finery but in the garb of country folk. There was one in particular which drew her attention; it was of a woman with soft, hazel-coloured eyes, set in a fascinating face of the dark Grecian style. Fanny lifted up the lantern so that she could study the face more clearly and realised that she had seen the look before, in Gervase's face.

There was no one about when she reached the foot of the stairs and she called out softly, not having noticed the tall silent figure in the half light by the window. He spun round, taken by surprise, for he had been deep in thought staring out into the darkness of the night, and the softness of her slippers on the stairs had not disturbed him. For a moment, when he turned, Fanny saw the face in the painting turn towards her and she gasped.

A look of concern appeared on Gervase's face, 'Are you well? You look pale, here let me help you.' He advanced towards her.

Fanny shook her head, 'I'm well enough now. I slept so soundly and I didn't realise that you were standing there. What a beautiful house this is. Who owned it before your aunt came here?'

'The story is a long one but I'm sure Aunt Meg will tell you about it when you sit with her. She is a good storyteller.'

'Who is the lady with the dark hair in the portrait?' whispered Fanny, almost as though she was afraid that if she spoke too loud the face in the picture would hear her.

'My grandmother. Her life was quite tragic, but aunt will tell you that too, I don't doubt.' He paused. 'Dinner is almost ready. We waited as long as possible to give you time to rest. I was supposed to be coming to wake you.' He took her elbow and led her into the kitchen where they were to dine.

Fanny had never seen such a large kitchen before. The Garnetts had always been used to eating in the cramped back room. Aunt Meg sat by the handle of a spit and occasionally turned the large piece of pork which roasted over the fire, while a tin beneath, caught the fat as it dripped from the meat. When all was ready they sat at the huge farm table, and Fanny realised just how hungry she really was, when she saw the platter of succulent pork laid before her, accompanied by roast parsnips and potatoes.

They conversed amiably, but every so often Fanny glanced at Gervase, unable to catch any sign of emotion on his unusually stern features, and she wondered if perhaps, after all, he now regretted the liaison which he had so generously entered into with her. It was a stranger that faced her now across the table, and Fanny no longer felt sure of his love for her; she didn't want him to love her from a distance, as he would a child, she wanted to be his wife. He was leaving tomorrow, leaving her here alone until it was over, but what would happen after the child was born? She had never really considered life after the birth, a life without love and affection. She lapsed into a silence which the other diners put down to fatigue.

Her face, to him, was an enigma. He found it difficult to read the look in her eyes. They were soft and misty, but things had changed and the strength which he had considered himself capable of, had gone. He was no longer sure that he could live with her this way, or if indeed he could live without her. He wanted to leave, to be alone with his thoughts and to sort them out.

It was arranged that one of the farm hands would wake Gervase at five o'clock next morning without disturbing Fanny, so enabling Gervase to return to 'The White Hart' in Gainsborough in time to catch the Post Coach. Aunt Meg explained to Fanny that they all rose at six o'clock in order to see to the animals, Fanny was horrified to think that she too might have to do the same, but they warmly assured her that this did not include her.

Much later, when the fire had died down and peace had settled over the farmhouse, Gervase faced yet another problem. The bed had been prepared for the pair of them, he hadn't given much thought to the possibility of such a predicament and it never occurred to Fanny until they reached the room and Gervase closed the door behind him. With a look of bewilderment they both eyed the bed and then each other. He spoke in a low whisper 'Don't worry. I'll sleep in the chair with my feet on the bed'.

It would have been impossible for her to sleep anywhere but in the bed, yet she was concerned because the chair looked dreadfully un-comfortable. 'It's so hard and you have to be up so early, can't we do anything better? We could put the bolster between us, like Bryce and I had to when we all lived at home.'

Gervase smiled at her concern. He'd often wondered how they'd all managed in such a small house. 'What with my huge body, a bolster and you in your condition, we'd all end up on the floor. You sleep well, you need it, I'm used to managing.' He turned away to allow her to undress, until finally he heard her struggle into the high bed.

'You can turn round now,' she whispered shyly. He looked at her precious face against the pillow and wished he could touch her lips. She watched him arrange the chair. He was kind and loving and she felt sorry for him there. He didn't undress for it would save him time and noise when he rose in the morning. He reminded her of a sentinel, watching over her, as he stretched out with a shawl and blanket over him to keep out the cold. She remembered then the feel of those arms, and of the soft passion in his lips, out there in the yard earlier, and longed to snuggle up to him.

Sleep did not come easily to either of them. Fanny's earlier sleep had refreshed her and her mind churned constantly on the happenings of the past months. She thought of the morrow when he would leave her to her fate, and panicked with fear that something might happen to him and that he would never return to fetch her back. She sighed a deep sigh and tears ran down onto the pillow.

Had he imagined her sob? He listened while she tossed and turned restlessly for what seemed hours, until finally she fell asleep, and then he relaxed, not bothered so much about his own sleep but about his fears for Fanny.

It seemed as though he had only just managed to go to sleep when he was awakened by a light tapping on the door, and he heaved his stiff, aching limbs from the chair. Drawing one half of the curtains back slightly to allow a chink of light into the room, he gathered up his things and went to the bed. The quilt and covers had slipped from Fanny's body and he stood looking on her lightly covered form, stifling the desire to kneel and draw her to him. He gently covered her and whispered, 'Take care, my love'. Why did he have to leave her? If anything went wrong he would never see her again. A lump came to his throat. He paused at the door to steady himself, giving one final glance at the figure in the bed and spoke out loud, huskily, 'I love you, Fanny'.

It was mid-morning when Fanny awoke. She half hoped that Gervase was still there, but the chair was back in its place against the wall and he had left no trace that he had even been there. The day ahead seemed empty, long and black as it stretched before her and she swallowed the lump which came into her throat, fighting back the tears. She dressed slowly, not really caring about her looks, and longed for her mother. On the stairs she studied the portrait of the woman again, noting the similarity with Gervase's features, and traced the line of the woman's cheeks with her fingers, as though the face were his. The eyes seemed to follow her, steady and clear and the beautiful garnet brooch at her throat added a touch of warmth to the otherwise cool features. The noises from the kitchen below were loud and numerous, and she plucked up her courage and went down.

The kitchen seemed to be alive with people; the long, scrubbed table was surrounded by men, friendly-faced men, all wearing shirts with rolled-up sleeves and leather jerkins, their neckerchiefs peeping from the open necks of their shirts. They ate heartily, pausing only to nod to Fanny as she entered the room before they returned to their meal. Mary and a girl served the men, and Mary beckoned Fanny to sit on the stool that Aunt Meg had used the night before. The men soon disappeared, doffing their caps as they went, until the kitchen was left in a peaceful hush.

Mary had a kindly face and eyes that crinkled when she smiled. 'They've got a lot of hard work on today. It's the last of the harvest and when they've finished they will go home or leave the area until next year. Did you sleep well? Gervase had to rush because the farmhand overslept.' Fanny opened her mouth to speak, but the words wouldn't come, and Mary noticed how pale and drawn she was, and the tears in her eyes. 'He is very lucky to have such a lovely young wife. His mother would have approved of you, we thought he would never marry. He must be very happy.'

'I do hope so, Mary. I'm going to miss him so much', she managed to say.

'Look, help me wash up when you've eaten and I'll show you around the place, then you can sit and talk to mother.'

In the brightness of daylight the farm looked small as it nestled against the rolling low hills. It reminded her more of Doncaster than Sheffield. The men were busy, coming and going within the yard, with the harvest, which was a good one this year and was doing much to alleviate the plight of the poor. The carts rumbled noisily in and out of the ruts, sending the hens and pigs in all directions only to return to devour the husks which fell from the corn. Fanny cringed when she looked in the bottom of the drays, for black rain beetles and spiders scuttled everywhere. Mary explained that the hens laid their eggs all over the farm and when Fanny bent to pick one up they both giggled, for Fanny could not bend down that far. 'I can wash, cook and sew though, if that will help', laughed Fanny helplessly.

'There's enough mending here to keep you busy all winter — you go into the parlour and talk to mother. She gets lonely in her little world and I have such little time to spare in the daytime, especially at this time of year.'

Aunt Meg sat in her usual spot by the window, not seeing but knowing that Fanny was there. 'Come, child.' Fanny took a seat by the old lady who reached out and took her hand. She also felt the cord that fastened the lightweight pelisse across Fanny's bodice, and its cool silkiness seemed to hold her fascination as she twisted it between her fingers. Fanny watched her as she did this and wondered what it must be like to sit forever in darkness, although the old lady's spirits were far from dark. She had a knowingness that was almost uncanny. 'Gervase has gone my dear, and we are to take extremely good care of you or he will never forgive us', she said, intuitively knowing that Fanny wanted to talk of Gervase.

Fanny raised her head and asked questioningly, 'Did he say that? I wished he hadn't had to go'.

The old lady cocked her head slightly at the wistfulness in Fanny's voice and asked, 'You don't doubt his love or devotion do you, my dear?'

Fanny clutched the frail woman's tiny hand. 'Oh Aunt Meg, please can I tell you a story? A long sad one, but you mustn't tell anyone, not even Gervase, or Mary, but especially Gervase!'

'This house has many sad stories to tell my dear. I never break a promise. I'm not going anywhere and we have a long wait on our hands before your time comes. I'm a good listener. You tell me.' She squeezed Fanny's hand gently, encouragingly, until Fanny poured out her heart. Aunt Meg listened devotedly, as though she had never heard it before, just as she had listened to Gervase's story the previous evening when Fanny had been sleeping. She had never broken a promise, but for once in her life she wished she had never promised so lightly not to tell, and knew that only time would unravel the story for these two unhappy people. She could hear the pain in the child's voice and remembered Gervase's helplessness.

When Fanny finished her story the old lady remarked, 'I'm sure if we all try to love one another, in the end God will see that we get what we deserve. I have a strange feeling deep in these old bones that everything will work out fine'. Fanny gently kissed the old woman's hand in a spontaneous outburst of emotion. 'Go and help Mary now, and tomorrow I will start telling you about this house, and the people who lived here.'

The first day was the longest to bear, for her mind constantly turned to Gervase and then to her mother. Before, when she had gone away to the academy, things had been different; the whole world had lain open before her and she had left no one behind, apart from her family, to fret after. The first night at the farm, after Gervase had gone, she slept in the room with the chair by the bed in the hope that she might wake up to find him there. She found herself wishing the time away until his return, but then she dreaded that time too, for then she would part with the child. The fear of the unknown and the fear of childbirth haunted her, and she longed for Gervase to come back, to hold her, and take her in his arms away from this isolation that was fear.

That first day Fanny sewed and sewed, until she ended up with blisters on her palms, for the harsher country materials were meant to outlast the rigours of hard work. Fanny was only used to working with fine materials and linens, and these new materials played havoc with her tender fingers, but it was the one task which she could do for Mary without any physical risk to her or the child. She cooked and tidied as best she could, when the effort did not exhaust her, and she seemed to grow bigger with each passing day, until even sitting for any length of time became a chore. Each afternoon, after dinner, she rested in the parlour. Mary made her lie on the sofa with her legs up whilst Aunt Meg told her the history of the house and the people who had lived there, as far as she could remember.

Fanny sat spellbound, each time learning more of Gervase's family until she felt that perhaps he was not so very far away. Each time they sat together the old lady fingered the silken cord, which Fanny deliberately wore, for it seemed to form a bond which cemented the two women together. Aunt Meg kept the story of the Grecian-looking lady until last, perhaps deliberately unfolding a tale each day to keep Fanny's interest and because the last was the saddest story of them all. Each time Fanny had asked about his grandmother the old lady would reply, 'Patience child, the best always comes last'. Fanny did not mind being called 'child' for she found comfort in the affectionate term.

Then, finally, one dull rainy day, Aunt Meg announced 'I've saved the story of Isabella until last. It is a romantic but sad story of my grandmother who was beautiful and wild. Many years ago, when there were many more trees around than there are now, gypsies would come for the hiring fairs and horse fairs, and camp beyond the wood that has almost disappeared. They were dark swarthy people, who kept themselves to themselves, except when they were selling their wares, or helping with the harvest. Each year the same ones would come back. They didn't cause as much trouble in those days and their children would come to the farm for eggs and milk in exchange for some of the work their fathers had done at the farm. The children sometimes stayed to play here with Isabella, and other times she would go back with them to their camp, sitting by their fire until they brought her back exhausted.

The years went by and no one thought much of it. Isabella would disappear for hours until, in the end, her father quarrelled with her for neglecting her duties about the farm. One summer, some of the gypsies stayed behind after the others had left, because one of their old folk had become too sick to travel. Isabella became wilder and more defiant, spending most of the time in the camp, until her father locked her in her room, unaware that she was climbing down the vine by the window, in order to go to the gypsies.

When eventually he found out, he fetched her back and whipped her. He told the gypsies not to come again. They never did come back, but Isabella had a baby, a dark beautiful child whom she called Becky after the gypsy's horse. When they did not return the following spring Isabella tried to run away to find them, but her father locked her up again and put bars to the windows, threatening to give the baby away. I don't think that he would have done that, for he spoilt Becky terribly, but he never forgave his daughter. That's where the dark strong features came from. Becky apparently looked like her father.'

'Did the gypsy never come back?' asked Fanny, intrigued by the sad story.

'Someone in the neighbourhood said that it wasn't one of the boys, but a handsome married gypsy. They say that's why Isabella never married, because she couldn't forget him. In the end she became catty and spiteful, and envious of her beautiful daughter. Becky was my mother. She was kind and gentle but they say she would have had a wild streak in her had her grandfather not crushed it. Isabella made her marry a rich farmer, who wanted to own this farm, even though she did not love him. She was a dutiful wife and died giving birth to her last child, my sister, Gervase's mother. The portrait was painted just after her wedding.' Aunt Meg fell silent, then added, 'she would not have had any more children but she wanted a son.'

The first month passed pleasantly enough for Fanny, although it seemed an age since she had left home, and she took great comfort in reading the two letters which arrived, one from Gervase, and one from her mother. Fanny was finding it difficult to walk now and yet there were still three weeks left to wait. No one seemed unduly anxious about her health, the local woman who delivered all the babies in the district had a good record for live births and took a look at Fanny from time to time. Fanny was astonished by the woman's comments which were made during the visits, and wasn't sure whether she liked being told that she had childbearing hips. 'Just send for me when the time comes', she said. 'And Mary's quite used to delivering animals', were her parting words on another visit.

Fanny often took to standing in the field by the gate, looking towards the woods where the gypsies had camped so very long ago, trying to imagine the wild Isabella slipping secretly across the field. She was totally unaware of the man on the horse who watched her intently as she leaned her weight against the stoop, for she had not heard him approach.

He feasted his eyes on the beautiful picture as she stood before him, her golden hair glistening in the bright sunlight, and the sensual pose of her pregnant body arched back against the stoop. Her rounded breasts were raised innocently to the sun and he was afraid lest he should startle her and break the spell.

The horse snorted, causing Fanny to turn, resentful of the intrusion into her romantic thoughts, she saw the magnificent creature outlined against the sun and a powerful figure sitting astride it like a heavenly god. She felt dwarfed standing there as the figure dismounted, his back towards her, then she caught her breath as he turned towards her. 'Gervase!' She ran, stumbling blindly, unaware of herself and threw her arms round his neck.

Gently, for fear of crushing her, he held her, comfortingly, holding himself in check for fear that she would withdraw from his arms, and breathed in the heady perfume of her hair. He held her tight and soothingly whispered into her hair, 'Steady my love. I had to come, I've worried so much about you'. He didn't kiss her, just contented himself in the knowledge that she needed him.

The horse pulled against the reins in Gervase's hand, and Fanny released herself. 'Oh it's so good to see you. I've missed you so much.' He put his hands to her face and held it and looked down into her pleading eyes. She thought that he was going to kiss her, but he did not.

They led the horse slowly back to the farm, and nothing bothered her anymore now, as the peace of the countryside crept into her soul. 'Your mother kept on and on, asking how you were and I couldn't stand it either, not knowing if you were alright or not, so that I had to come. I hired the horse in Gainsborough but I can only stay until tomorrow.'

'I didn't know that you could ride' said Fanny admiringly.

He chuckled, 'There are many things you don't know about me, my pretty love.'

She looked down at herself, 'I don't look pretty now, do I? Not like this!'

'You . . .' he didn't get the chance to say what was in his heart, for Mary hailed them from the doorway.

The following day, Fanny pleaded with Gervase to take her to the old gypsy camp. The weather was unusually bright and pleasant for November, but the trees had shed their glorious yellow and rusty-brown leaves, and stood stark and bare against the clear sky. The strength of the afternoon sun was warm, and they decided, Gervase and Fanny, that it would not be in her best interest to go gallivanting in the rugged lanes with a pony and trap. Tiring though it might be, both felt the need to walk. They slowly crossed the field to 'Isabella's' wood, cutting through the clearing where Gervase told her the gypsies had camped. From the clearing the spire of the ancient village church pointed like a finger to heaven, and a cluster of houses huddled around its base.

Today there were no problems, no worries, no haste; the country smells filled the air with tranquillity, and when she tired he took her hand, to help her along. Both were loath to let go of the other's hand but neither dared confess to the other the enjoyment and contentment each felt. Occasionally their eyes met, soft and caring, and when he felt she had walked far enough, he placed his jacket on a boulder for her to rest upon.

It wasn't easy sitting down so low but she was grateful for the rest. 'I shall always love the memories of this day' said Fanny softly 'I'm so happy that you came. I wish you didn't have to go back tomorrow.'

'If we stayed in paradise forever we would find it tedious, a little taste of it helps us put up with the rest of our lives.' He put his hand into his pocket and withdrew a tiny bundle of tissue-paper. 'I want to give you something very special to remember today by. It is of no use to me, as you will see.' He took her hand, soft and warm, into his own, and placed the tissue into it, closing her fingers over it and bent to kiss her closed fingers. He felt her tremble and prayed that he hadn't gone too far this time.

She trembled at the touch of his lips on her hand, wanting to open up her fingers to touch his face but dare not. She opened her fingers to peep into the tissue and held her breath in amazement. It was Becky's brooch, the one in the painting; he had given her the deep rich red stone set in scrolls of fine gold. 'It's Becky's!' she gasped.

'It is also a garnet stone, just for you my little one.' He took the gift and pinned it to the high neck of her bodice. He was pleased now that he had not parted with it that day in York.

'Oh, Gervase, it's beautiful, I will treasure it always. I will never, ever be able to repay you for all you have done for me.' Fanny fingered the exquisite token on her bodice, unable to thank him enough.

Her nearness distracted him and he stiffened lest he should forget his resolve to maintain his distance. Fanny stiffened too. Why, why had he drawn back? Did he think her so unbecoming like this? She gazed unseeingly at the village; a tiny cloud had passed over her day. The sun was fading too, and Fanny spoke in a voice which he could hardly hear. 'It is so beautiful, it will be my most precious possession from this moment on. I will take good care of it.'

It would take them some time to walk back, and the air was becoming chilly as the afternoon drew to a close. 'Come, we have to start back — let me help you!' He helped her from the stone afraid to hold her hand now, and she folded her arms and tucked them up her sleeves to keep the chill from them.

The evening passed rapidly and Fanny valiantly fought off the waves of tiredness which threatened her last hours with him, until in the end she was forced to retire to bed. She managed to mutter, 'Thank you for such a wonderful day', before drifting off into a deep contented sleep.

He slept in the chair again that night, and was gone in the morning. His coming had made her forget, but his going left her lonelier than before and she wished that the baby would come so that she could go home. She wondered more these days about the baby that stretched around inside her. She had never had much to do with babies before. She had watched her nieces and nephews running wildly about the place when they visited, but that was all. Fanny found it impossible to imagine it as flesh and blood, with a mind of its own; she had dilemmas enough of her own and found it hard to know what to think. Would she even like this thing which kicked her so hard? There were times when it was almost as if there was a battle going on within her and then a leg, or perhaps it was a foot, or hand would suddenly protrude and she would stare in wonder and disbelief at the lump. Fanny thought of the birth itself and became frightened, feeling that she was alone, so alone, to fight this terrifying battle for life.

She would miss the farm, Aunt Meg and Mary, when the time came to leave, just as she missed her mother now, but there was little here to stimulate her mind; the books in the parlour were old and dull and sewing only served to make her brood. She spent hours with her paints until they ran out, but Gervase had sent more and slowly, with practise, over and over again, Fanny painted the farm house in its rural setting until she felt that one copy was commendable enough to give to Gervase. Fanny wrote to her mother, long letters, but the camphorous smell of the ink made her queasy and she had to sit by the window so that the fresh air would dilute the smell. Some letters were so long that she was constantly compelled to trim the quill with a penknife before she could complete them and the breeze dried the ink as she wrote, making it unnecessary to dry it with the fine sand.

After Gervase's visit, Fanny took to writing him short little notes in the form of a diary, telling him of her days, although she took care not to convey her feelings for him. Gradually the notes grew longer. It wasn't easy getting letters from the farm to Sheffield, but once a week, when Mary took their produce to market, she would leave Fanny's letters at the coaching inn in Gainsborough, to be sent on to Sheffield. She would pick up long newsy ones which Gervase had written in reply. They were encouraging ones to keep up her spirits, and Fanny tied them up with a ribbon and hid them in her drawer.

The days were becoming wearisome now, for she was well past her time and the child was heavy. The evenings too went by so slowly, even though the other women endeavoured valiantly to reassure and cheer her. With each little twinge came the overwhelming fear of the unknown, and then one night her sleep was suddenly disturbed and she knew that there was no going back. At first Fanny thought that it was her imagination, but as the pains came more often and lasted longer she lay alone in her despair.

Aunt Meg held her hand or chattered encouragingly while Mary went for the woman in the village, but Fanny felt that there was no one there whom she loved. John had gone forever, her mother and Gervase were far away, and during the lulls in the pain she stared in disbelief at the walls, not quite sure what life was about anymore. But the pain was real, searing, intensifying, driving her to distraction until she wanted to tear at herself before she would seemingly explode.

The nurse came from the village and mopped Fanny's sweated brow, whispering encouragement when she thought it was needed, but still Fanny felt alone. The pain increased and she screamed for the relief which didn't come. 'Push dear, when I tell you, PUSH' was all that she could hear. 'PUSH.' She was trying to push away the pain, didn't they understand that! She screamed out Gervase's name in her lonely battle and she thought she had got rid of the ache, then it started again. She thought she could hear a baby crying but the pain began again, again and again, yet they still appeared to tell her to 'PUSH'. She lay there confused and hot in a world that was becoming hazy and beautifully bright. Somewhere in the far distance she did hear a baby cry, or were they still shouting 'PUSH'.

The confusion went on, why should she push? The pain still wouldn't go away and the beautiful light became more enveloping. Finally she gave up and allowed it to engulf her.

Chapter 14

he child was buried in the lonely graveyard miles from home. Gervase carried the tiny coffin in his arms, held close against his chest, and wished that he could hold Fanny comfortingly too. Fanny, pale and sad, had said farewell from her bed to the little mite that had only lived a few hours, and wished him well in his long journey ahead. He was at least safe from the destructiveness of man, from disease and old age, but she would never see him grow or play, and she wept for herself as well as for him. They lowered him into the ground in that sad, lonely little box and Gervase thanked God that they had finally not needed a coffin for the mother too; it had been touch and go but they had pulled her through.

Gervase did not return straight to the farm but walked back across the fields alone, in order to hear the birds sing and to allow the crisp cold air to clear his mind, once calm again, he returned to the farm.

The boy had looked like his father, and it would have been quite obvious to all that Gervase was not he, but the child sleeping peacefully in the old wooden cradle looked like Fanny, with its long legs and golden hair. Gervase took her tiny hand in his and remembered how, nineteen years before, he had held Fanny's hand in the same manner. He raised his head and looked across at her now and wondered why the years in between had brought them all to this present state of affairs.

Fanny had finally opened her eyes in disbelief to find that she was still alive, for she had presumed that it had been death calling her into the warm, bright light. It had been a shock to realise that she had given birth to twins. On reflection, she recalled the family legend of multiple births but had never dreamt that it would happen to her. So many women died in childbirth and their children too, but she was alive, with a perfect little daughter, and for that she considered herself blessed indeed. Fanny was sad that the little boy had died, for she would have loved him dearly, but she had expected to take home only one child and she did not feel cheated. The births had been difficult, in spite of Fanny's size and strength but the last child, the boy, had refused to turn and became lodged, causing Fanny great pain and confusion. The long delay had harmed the child and he hardly fought at all for survival. Then there had been great concern for Fanny, who had torn during the ordeal, and although scrupulous attention had been given to cleanliness during the birth, they feared that infection would set in. Childbed fever claimed the lives of so many mothers, and it seemed for a time that Fanny would succumb to it also, but their anxieties were unfounded and although she remained ill and very weak they need not have worried, Fanny had no desire to leave this world behind.

Gervase had arrived two days later. Having heard nothing at all, and not trusting the mail, he could contain himself no longer but had packed a bag and set off to find the outcome for himself. He had found her pale and drawn but thankfully alive and had been amazed to find out about the twins. Fanny had been equally overjoyed to see him and begged him to take her home but he knew that the bumpy, tiring journey would be too strenuous for her to undertake. He left, promising to return before Christmas to take her home.

Fanny cried when he told her that he must leave without her and she began to believe that she would never go home.

The journey home for Gervase was difficult, due to the icy billowing wind which carried snow in its wake, and the beautiful white world, which appeared during the night, held little comfort for him back home in their lonely, empty house. The snow seemed to deepen with every hour that passed until in the end he knew that it might as well be an ocean that separated him from Fanny.

It was equally difficult for Fanny to accept the scene which greeted her next morning, for in those few hours the world had changed beyond recognition. She peered through the mullion window in disbelief; all that lay before her was a sea of white. The snow looked endless, without hedge or building, and in the distance the tops of the trees stood like statues in the wilderness. A lone gull, coming inland seeking shelter, soared hopefully over the farm, bringing life to the stillness and Fanny hoped that it would find the food which it sought.

A cry from the child drew her away from the window and she bent over the ancient carved cradle, entranced by the wonder of the tiny nose and fingers. She picked her up and cuddled her, aware of the sweet smell of newness which is peculiar to all babies. Only the nose reminded her of John and she could not help but feel deep anger that he should be deprived of seeing his daughter; he was not even aware that he was to be a father and perhaps it was best that he was never informed.

The days dragged on into weeks as fresh falls of snow continued to fill the paths which they endeavoured to clear; it almost swallowed up the house. Christmas, and half of January passed before Gervase could get through to fetch Fanny. The world became unreal. There was very little activity outside the isolated farm and only the odd determined person came and went, leaving Mary and Fanny to feed and care for the animals themselves.

A deep and loving friendship developed amongst the three marooned women and the child. Their eventual parting would be sorrowful but Fanny needed to be amongst the bustle of a busy town. She needed her mother and her own possessions around her, and as the snow began to melt away, an air of excited expectancy gripped her. Fanny abounded with life now; she was back to her normal, vibrant self again and the reappearance of the grass brought fresh hope.

Eventually they managed to get word through to Sarah and Gervase that all was well and each new day found them waiting for his return. By the time he did arrive, Fanny was almost shy and tongue tied. Suddenly she was unsure of her role in his life. He stood before her, strong and powerful, so assuredly wise, this man who had given so much for her; she felt inadequate and self-conscious before his gaze. Instinctively she tidied her hair with one hand to reassure her inner self that she looked her best.

Sarah had spent most of her life waiting patiently for one thing or another to happen, but this time things were different; the years were rapidly passing by, leaving her old body full of aches and pains and a growing impatience to see Fanny and her new grandchild. Fanny was the last link in the chain of her life with Bryce, and although she had been bitterly disappointed in her daughter's behaviour, she could no more remonstrate with her than she could have done with Bryce himself. She loved Fanny dearly, and in spite of Gervase's efforts to cheer her up during their long separation, she was completely lost without her. Sarah's heart went out to Gervase, for it was obvious that he was unhappy, and in unguarded moments she observed his deep despondency.

She heard their voices even before she heard the knock, and hastened to open the door. There before her stood her precious Fanny, radiant and beautiful as she shyly held out the child to its grandmother. The child whimpered as she took it into her arms and she longed to have Bryce by her side to see what she could see. She stole a glance at Gervase. The pride in his eyes brought a lump to her throat, and she cradled the babe to her ample chest before giving Fanny a loving kiss and begging them to stay to tea.

An air of contentment crept over the tiny kitchen, as the child lay sleeping in the drawer from which Sarah had removed the content and had lined with covers to make a crib, she prayed that the child would bring about a miracle for Fanny and Gervase.

Fanny had chosen to call the baby Becky after Gervase's grandmother and the gypsy horse, and the noise of the child filled the house both day and night, until when she was absent the place seemed strangely empty. Becky's cherubic face was a picture to behold; her little pink cheeks were surrounded by a tousle of fiery golden curls which endeared her to everyone who saw her, but she was hard work and occupied more of Fanny's time than she cared to admit. Fanny was tired but happy these days and Gervase was never quite sure whether he was living with one child or two. She fed Becky in the privacy of her own room when Gervase was in the house, through shyness and to save him embarrassment, but he was a man of the world and a suckling child had merely fascinated him in the past. He respected her wishes but would have loved to observe the natural bond of mother and child. He sighed, perhaps it was for the best, motherhood had not taken away Fanny's figure, nor his desire for her and the intimacy of it all would have been more than he could bear.

Slowly, Fanny occupied herself by exploring the house further, finding odd treasures hidden away which Gervase had stored rather than waste time cleaning, until in her way she claimed the house as her own. Feminine things now lay where once there had been the bare austerity of bachelorhood and Fanny lapsed into an almost idyllic world of domesticity.

There had not been sufficient space for a garden in Bryce's back yard, and as soon as the weather picked up, Fanny lost no time in roaming the ground that had once been Gervase's mother's kitchen garden. Over the years he had taken little interest in the garden, except to clear away the weeds which had encroached immediately around the back door and closet, and all semblance of order had long since disappeared. Undaunted by the task, Fanny slowly dug the beds, and rediscovered the tiny path of stones laid by Mrs Webster, so it was once more possible to reach the two apple trees without becoming engulfed by the undergrowth. She was creating her own small empire. The neglected earth was hard and difficult to work but with hours of patient digging, hoeing and weeding, she produced a fine plot in which she could plant her own vegetables and culinary aids. Amongst the onions, carrots, cabbages and cauliflowers which she hoped to grow, she kept a little corner for her herbs. With childish pride she would constantly show Gervase the results of her efforts and the more he admired her results and determination, the more ambitious she became.

He watched her often as she worked, her hair dishevelled and her warm face streaked with dirt, where she had pushed back the hair which had fallen down across it. He thought of his mother and the pleasure she too had received from the garden, and knew that his mother would have been pleased if she could but see it now. Until the earth settled, Fanny planted flowers, many of which she gathered when they walked in the fields, for it was seldom that they returned from these rambles without a few wild specimens as each came into season, the primrose, bluebells, foxgloves, moonpennies and poppies. In the years ahead each would provide a feast of colour amongst the vegetables.

Gervase was pleased to see her so happy and found her companionship delightful, but it was at night behind the closed door of his bedroom that he had his regrets. The nights were long and lonely, as they had never been before, and he found himself listening for the sound of her feet as she passed the door. His desire for her began to torment him and he cursed himself for his respectability, for many a man in his position would have demanded that the duties of a wife be fulfilled, but Fanny trusted him implicitly, and he needed her love no less than he did her body.

At first Fanny found that tiredness and the child supplanted her own desires. She was content to be near Gervase but as time passed by, she too began to lie in her lonely bed and think of him. Her dreams were of Gervase, so near to her that she would wake, startled by the intensity of those feelings and, unable to go back to sleep, she would tiptoe past his door and go downstairs. She found more and more that any physical contact with him was intoxicating and she yearned to touch him. The exhilaration left her edgy and disconcerted and she was careful to avoid any close contact with him.

Sensing her sudden need to avoid his touch wounded Gervase deeply, and he was at a complete loss to understand the reason for it. He had been a fool to think such an arrangement as theirs possible, for he had trapped her in his silly game. He began to realise that sooner or later, when her dependence upon his protection lessened, she would no longer need him and she would no doubt seek younger, livelier company than his and the nightmare would increase even more.

Instead of going straight home after closing up the shop Gervase took to staying away from the house. He rejoined the Gentlemen's Club to which he had belonged before the marriage. His intelligent opinions and participation in lively discussion had been sorely missed, and heads nodded knowingly on his return, acknowledging that the novelty of marriage was probably on the wane. Many of his fellow members had pondered upon the wisdom of his decision to take a young wife; some had lustfully envied him and others had considered that he would live to rue the day.

A general feeling of well-being was beginning to brighten up the town.

The coming of the canal brought with it the hope of fresh trade, made easier by its links with the coast and other towns, and it would leave them in less of a backwater than before. Gervase too was turning his mind to the future. His success had been achieved through two years of hard work and sacrifice, through determination and prudence, leaving him in a position to consider expansion. He needed newer, more advanced machinery to enable him to compete with his contemporaries; his Stanhope flat-bed handpress, operated by two men, would produce two hundred to two hundred and fifty copies per hour. There were two options open to him: he could either buy another handpress and print alternative material at the same time, or he could obtain a Koenig steam-driven cylinder machine which, operated by just one man, could turn out one thousand sheets an hour. Tom could operate the new machine and the handpress would be available for other work.

His mind raced in anticipation. He would have the edge on the printing world in Sheffield. The damnable size of the workshop was the only trouble; there was hardly room enough now to swing a cat, let alone give sufficient room to install a new machine. Gervase constantly scratched away with his blacklead pencil, arranging and re-arranging fixtures. If he extended the building at the back it would cost a fortune and the upstairs beams wouldn't stand the weight or vibration of the new machine, but he wouldn't give up.

Cautiously he discussed some of the salient points of his ideas with a trusted fellow member of the club who seemed astounded at his advanced thinking.

'Look lad, it's not really up my street but I think it's a bit too forward-thinking for Sheffield; you think long and hard about it first.'

Gervase was as much irritated by the fact that the man still called him a lad as he was about the man's opinion. 'That's the trouble with this town, half of it is still in the dark ages', he retorted.

'Don't knock it, we've had enough trouble over machinery taking away men's jobs already.' The man turned to fill his pipe having considered the matter closed.

Gervase persisted, 'I'd have to get another employee anyway to do the extra work'. He became aware of his own raised voice in the suddenly silent room and calmed down.

'Yes, then he does the work twice as quickly, putting three jobs in jeopardy. You mark my words lad, there'll be trouble.'

Gervase listened. God he'd had enough trouble already and he could hear John's voice ringing in his ears from when he had complained about the stuffiness of the town. He was beginning to sound like John himself.

'I think marriage has addled your brain. You've got a good business and a fine family, why take risks at your age?' The man persisted patronisingly.

It had been refreshing to talk to John with his progressive thinking and dreams of the future. Gervase looked around at the other members, a more searching look now; there they lounged in chairs, or stood, blustery old windbags with little more imagination than they had years ago and too cautious to take chances. They were right though, he could imagine the machine-breakers having a field day and it would certainly be a brave man who stuck his neck out in this town. Perhaps it was stupid to fight them all; he'd settle for a second-hand flat-bed and bide his time. 'I suppose I'd better settle for the conventional, no point in begging for trouble.'

'Good fellow.' The man slapped Gervase heartily on the back. 'Knew you'd see sense when you'd thought about it.'

Shaking his head, Gervase wondered what kind of future lay ahead for the town if it relied on such men. He left the club early, thoroughly despondent and called in to see Sarah, a habit which he had formed of late to delay going home. Sarah was always pleased to see him, even though it delayed her retirement to bed, for she sensed his need to talk. It was difficult these days to get through to either of them but he never complained about Fanny.

Fanny had given up any hope of Gervase loving her in the proper sense of the word, he loved her as he had always done — as a child, that was all. He was kind and considerate, but he had grown cold and distant, staying away later and later each evening, causing her to suspect that perhaps there was some other woman in his life. She found it difficult to believe it possible of him but remembered the words he had used on the farm, that there was much that she didn't know about him. That he worshipped Becky she never doubted. He was gentleness itself with the child, calling her his 'adorable little Becky'; and she found it difficult to understand why he could love someone else's child so much.

The summer came to an end and autumn brought with it cooler days. The sunshine did little to brighten up their spirits and Fanny took to walking alone with Becky, often calling to see Sarah and the shop. Bryce had his nephew working with him now, as an apprentice, but Fanny still continued to keep the books for him in order to save him a little money.

In early October a letter arrived at the shop, delivered by a stranger asking for Fanny Garnett, and although Bryce had been puzzled as to why the man was unaware of Fanny's marriage, he nevertheless promised to pass it on. He knew of no reason why anyone would contact them from Australia, except the chap who had worked for Gervase and Bryce, and he knew no cause for him to write to Fanny. The stranger had been explicit, it had to be given to no other person but Fanny, and Bryce was baffled by her reaction when she received it, for she seemed at a loss for words and greatly disturbed.

Hastily wrapping Becky in a shawl, Fanny plucked the child up into her arms and hurried from the shop in a daze. She was unsure what she wanted the letter to say and could not understand how it was possible to love two men at the same time. Each man was so very different from the other, the one full of youth and excitement, the other masterful and mysterious, yet neither gave her the fulfilment which she needed. It seemed an age since John had been exiled and she felt disappointed in herself for allowing his memory to fade into the distance so quickly. She felt that she had abandoned him. Sometimes, when she caught a look on Becky's face that reminded her of John, she was aware of the unhappy life which he must lead, unaware that he had a daughter and that Fanny was married to another. Time had changed her and she loved Gervase, but a deep sense of helplessness made her feel sick and weak. She put Becky down on the carpet, loosened the shawl which had protected the child from the cold, and sat numbed at the table.

Fanny's hands trembled as she fumbled to open the letter. The handwriting was not as neat as she remembered and she found it difficult to focus her eyes clearly through the mist of tears.

Camden February 15th, 1818

My dear Fanny,
I would have written sooner but I could not find a person suitable to trust with the delivery of this letter. I am sending this care of the Reverend Fox who will ensure that it falls into your hands only. He visited me in prison and permitted me to write through him. You will scarcely believe this to be my own handwriting, my knees being my desk and the grass my seat, having written it in the bush. My master's estate is about fifty miles from the capital (Sydney), where I am tending a flock of sheep, which are very little trouble but very confining as every day is the same thing, both Sunday and Holy Day with the exception of Christmas Day when I understand our master allows us to put the sheep in the fold a little earlier. This is his own goodness as other masters do not allow such indulgences.
I am starved of news and reading matter, and despair

for the next few years as we follow the sheep from
sunrise to sunset, often over fourteen hours.

I beg you Fanny to forget me. I feel very much injured
at being here in this state that I am in, and the Mayor of
Nottingham has forgotten his promise to me. I have been
unjustly treated as you know, and was sent with such
haste from the Old Country. The journey on board ship
defies description and I will not trouble you or bore you
with details, except to say that it was a most cruel and
miserable time and before I landed I was sick almost
unto death. If I had been in the hulks for any length of
time before sailing I fear the worst would have befallen
me, instead I was well before starting out. I could never
return to a land which treats its people so unfairly and
at the first opportunity I shall catch a whaler to America
and stay there.

I shall not say any more on the subject, but thank you
for your friendship. I beseech you to think no further of
me for I am consumed with loneliness, my flute being
my only comfort, and if my master gives consent I may
be forced to take a companion to wife.

There are many birds of beautiful plumage here
which you would enjoy, and reptiles. I have seen a bird
of prey called the Eagle Hawk, which took a young
lamb. I feel myself like that lamb. I cannot write again
for the past is too painful and I admonish you to marry
another who can care for you.

My sincere wishes to Gervase and your mother and all
enquiring friends.

Yours in despair,
John Andrews

Through the blur of tears she read the letter again and again with the
sad knowledge that it was from a stranger, a sad, lonely stranger with
whom she no longer felt a bond. She shivered as she imagined his life
of frustration in a strange, wild, uncultured land, a country which
sounded dreadful. Fanny could not rid herself of the feeling of guilt as
she sat in familiar, safe surroundings, while his life was in ruins. She
pondered on the futility and waste of it all, including the mess which
was hers and Gervase's lives. Nothing had turned out as she had
planned or hoped.

She rose slowly, sadly, putting the letter into the little box which Dr

Hall had given her and remembered the times in the old Chapel, where as a child she had been filled with dreams and mischief. She picked up John's child, and drew her close, as she slept unaware of the turmoil that raged beneath her mother's breast. The child was oblivious to the tears which fell from her mother's eyes onto her tender young face as they rocked to and fro in the gloom of the darkening room.

It was already too late to do anything when Sarah heard about the letter. She would have destroyed it before Fanny knew of its existence, had she been given the chance, for she believed the matter of John to be best left alone. She was far from pleased with Bryce, when she learned that he had questioned Gervase about the letter, of which he knew nothing at all, and although she understood why Gervase had left in a hurry, she was worried about what he would do.

Unable to concentrate and under considerable strain, Gervase returned to the house much earlier than usual, uncertain of what he would find there. Fanny was pale, but cheerful with a falseness which was difficult to hide, and anger rose within him at the ghost which had raised its head yet again.

His early arrival had flustered Fanny and she endeavoured to appear busy, hardly daring to look Gervase in the eye, but offered no news of any letter. It was obvious to him that Fanny was in a state of distress, but as the evening wore on and still she did not offer to tell him of the letter, he came to the conclusion that she was even now in love with the fellow. He could not forgive her the deceit of concealing the letter from him. He could bear it no longer and strode from the room, seized his coat and stormed from the house.

The temper which rose within him surprised and shocked him. He had never been prone to tempers, always priding himself on his own self-control but the mounting tension and his disappointment in Fanny had stirred him deeply. He was no longer master of himself, or his destiny, and he had never before been forced out of his own house, but, had he not had the presence of mind to walk out, he felt sure that he would have been tempted to strike Fanny. The atmosphere in the house of late had been unbearable and the prospect of going back was daunting. There was nowhere else to spend to the night without arousing suspicions and feeding the local gossips, unless he went to the shop after calling at the club.

His club offered little respite from the woes which weighed him down but he stayed there as late as he dared, without it becoming obvious that he had no wish to go home, then wearily he went to the shop.

With a heart too heavily burdened to care, Gervase made a start on a new assignment. He had barely been at work for ten minutes when Tom returned home, and although Tom was surprised to see Gervase there so late, he had learned not to question him when he appeared to be in a dark mood, and left him to his own company. Gervase worked on until the early hours of the morning before attempting to sleep in the chair.

Fanny waited and waited, but still Gervase did not come home. She had no idea where or why he had gone and was frantic with worry that someone had waylaid and robbed him. It was obvious that something had displeased him. Lately he had been withdrawn and sullen, and she was more convinced than ever that there was another woman in his life. The mere thought of him associating with another woman shocked her and she found herself gripped by a fit of consuming jealousy. When eventually sleep overtook her, it was shallow and troubled by the vivid recurring nightmare, of the pair of them in battle against each other.

Finally, when morning came, she found that his bed had not been slept in and there was no trace of his having even returned during the night, nor did he appear during the morning or afternoon. Suddenly, in the early evening, he appeared without explanation. His face, she noted, was clean-shaven but expressionless and hard, almost that of a stranger. He looked weary and did not raise his eyes to hers but spoke words which seemed to hold little meaning.

As the evening wore on, he sipped one glass of wine after another; Fanny had never seen him consume so much before. Then, as his mood seemed to darken, she could contain herself no longer and asked, 'Please, why are you drinking so much?'

He looked darkly across at her. 'That's my business', he bellowed.

Fanny tried again in a quieter, almost apologetic voice. 'Why did you storm out last night and not return?' He leaned on the mantel shelf above the fire and stared at his glass moodily without replying. 'Did I do something to upset you?' she begged. 'Something's wrong, please tell me what, I can't stand it anymore.'

He rounded on her and roared, 'You can't stand it any more! I can't stand it either'.

Fanny recoiled and shrank back looking at a stranger; she felt that she no longer knew anyone anymore. 'Is there another woman?' she dared to ask.

'You dare ask me that? You have no right to question me, you who conceal from me the fact that you receive letters from the child's father.' His eyes glowered at her.

She froze, startled by his accusation. How did he know about the letter and why did it disturb him so much? She knew that he had consumed too much wine, but she was sure it wasn't that, there was something much deeper. 'I'll show you the letter', she offered.

'Keep your blasted letter and your secrets and I'll keep mine.' His voice was sullen and almost menacing.

'Please don't drink anymore, it makes you angry. I've never seen you like this before.' She was half afraid of him now.

'God, woman, you make me angry. You accuse me of having another woman — what do you take me for? I took you in and asked for nothing in return, do you expect me to live like a monk. I'm flesh like other men, or hadn't you noticed? You are my wife and by God I've a good mind to take my rights.' He made a move towards her.

This was not the Gervase that Fanny had always known and she shrank back in fear, looking round helplessly as he advanced and endeavouring to push a chair between them. He was powerful, towering towards her as he thrust the chair to one side and she found herself cornered against the wall. Gone was his gentleness; his eyes blazed and she was afraid of him and what he would do. He gripped her arm, forcing her backwards and there was no escape from his body which pinned her to the wall and his mouth which hungrily crushed hers. Fanny struggled in vain to free herself from his grasp but was unable to move and she felt the fasteners of her bodice tear free under the strain. He slackened his hold for a moment seeking her neck with his burning lips and his hands sought the softness of her breasts. Fanny screamed but he covered her mouth again with his, compelling her to accept his mouth, while she tried to twist away.

Suddenly his mouth softened its demands and he slowly and caressingly kissed her, as though the demon within had burned away, and Fanny lost the will to resist. The uncontrollable tingle which she had felt before at his nearness took hold of her and she returned his kiss, slowly at first until he felt her respond and he whispered huskily, 'Fanny, oh Fanny.'

She clung to his jacket, inflamed by the caress of his voice, and kissed his trembling mouth. His voice was now thick with emotion and he almost pleaded with her, 'Fanny, I want you'. He gently tore away the rest of her bodice and looked down on her soft loveliness. The touch of his hands inflamed her and he lowered her to the floor in the strong gentleness which was familiar. As she lay consumed in the love which she had for him, he rained kisses over the full length of her body until she had no control, and quivered. He tore off his shirt and pressed his firm body against hers and she slipped her arms around his neck drawing his face close to hers.

She knew then that she must have loved him always, his kind eyes and gentle mouth, his masterful hands that made her body ache to receive him, and she lovingly kissed him again and again until he finally claimed her for himself. She sobbed with emotion while he held her close, and when she had calmed down he looked into her eyes shyly, questioningly, until she closed them.

What had he done? He drew back a little, half ashamed of himself. He had almost raped her. She lay there afraid to open her eyes and look at the man before her. Perhaps she was not the only one to receive his favours. Pangs of jealousy stirred deep within her and she had to know the truth. 'Is there another woman?' she ventured to ask.

The shutters came down suddenly on those gentle eyes and he rose and tossed his jacket over her to cover her nakedness, then abruptly, without answering, left her lying there.

When he had gone Fanny got up slowly. A feeling of despair hit her as she looked down at herself in the light. She could still feel his hands on her and wanted him to touch her again, but she thought of the other woman and shivered. He hadn't denied it, did he make love to this woman as he had done to her? She hated the woman and didn't want to be touched again by hands that touched another. Perhaps this was her punishment for her wildness. She had never intended to cause anyone any harm, and yet the spiral of confusion seemed to go on endlessly.

Fanny wrapped the shawl around her body and forced herself to climb the stairs. She passed his closed door but there was no sound from within the room and she climbed into her solitary bed and cried softly to herself.

Gervase sat on his bed his mind in a whirl. The drink was making him sleepy but he was too angry to lie down. How could she doubt him. He had given her everything, willingly, and now he had given her the key to his soul. He had worshipped her and never given her cause to doubt, yet she did. He had never been a man to use women for his own satisfaction, he was far too sensitive for that, but where had it got him? He recalled her response and the look in her eyes as she kissed him and he wanted to go to her and hold her again in his arms, with tenderness this time. He wanted to tell her that he loved her, but until she believed in him he would not touch her again.

Shyly Fanny turned from the child as Gervase entered the room. He was immaculately dressed and in control of himself, and she watched him from beneath her lashes as he went to the writing desk and busied himself with his papers. He had said little more than a couple of words in greeting since he had risen and gave not the slightest indication that anything had taken place the evening before. Perhaps he had been disappointed in her, maybe he found the other woman more satisfying. Whoever the woman was, Fanny had to find out what power she had to draw him so strongly. Fanny wanted to tell him that she loved him, and to press her lips against the back of his neck as he bent his head over the papers, but his manner forbade her.

He could feel her eyes upon him as he sat there toying with the papers before him. Never in his wildest dreams had he ever hoped that Fanny would love him. He wanted to rise from his chair, to hold her, but he needed her trust and he must be patient until that trust came back. The letter from John was of little consequence now, her response had proved much more to him than any explanation could ever have. The past eighteen months had been traumatic, soul searing, but now there was light up ahead in the dark tunnel.

Gervase left the desk and the child held her arms out to him. Fanny watched as he took her. Their eyes met over the tousled head and Fanny saw the kind, gentle friend that she had always known. She lowered her eyes lest he should see the adoration in them, but Gervase had already seen the look before it was withdrawn and he felt a renewed strength rise within him. He playfully hoisted Becky into the air and swung her round teasingly, for he adored the child just as much as he did her mother. As he left the house Fanny called, 'Will you eat at home tonight?' He nodded and went.

The day was long and Fanny could not wait for the evening to come. She spent most of the afternoon bathing and washing her hair. She put her hair up, she let it down, she curled it then straightened it, then curled it again in her efforts to make it perfect for him. When the meal was almost ready she changed into her little green dress, which fortunately still fitted perfectly, and waited for him.

The vision before him took his breath away, for there stood the little girl he had always loved and he knew the effort she had made had been for him. It pleased him to the depths of his soul, he lifted her hand to his lips as he had done at Miss Greaves' that day and said mockingly, 'You are beautiful, my dear. Come, we must eat for I have to go out again'. Fanny's childlike face fell at the news and he cursed himself for his cruelty but he wanted to be sure that she trusted him before he trusted her with his soul again. He was forcing himself to stay away from her. He had no real business in town and the atmosphere in the club did little to attract him to its doors. In truth he had to admit that he would have preferred to remain at home. He wandered aimlessly, and found himself entering the gates of the old churchyard, where without thinking he sat wearily on the old T'alli Stone. That too was a mistake, for memories came flooding back of the times he had taught Fanny to play leap-frog as a child. He stood up abruptly and headed for his club, hoping to divert his mind from the painful dilemma in which he had placed himself.

Chapter 15

Tom kissed Emily goodnight and swaggered good naturedly back across the road to the shop. Life had improved for him these days and the upstairs rooms suited him well. Throughout the troubles of the past two years, he had been loyal and industrious, learning well the things which Gervase had taught him, and now he carried himself with pride, considering his rewards well-deserved. He took off his neat-fitting jacket and hung it up; his clothes were no longer shabby and dirty and he talked in a moderately passable manner. He owed everything to Gervase, a fact which he readily admitted. He rarely objected to doing extra work for him, knowing that the harder he worked the greater the rewards, which was not the case for all his friends and their employers. His reading was passable now and his skills had grown considerably, but he knew his limitations and was content with his lot.

Tonight he was tired. Emily, the maid from 'The Blue Bell' across the street, had gone home late, but he had promised to finish a job for Gervase and he was determined to complete it. There was certainly plenty of work these days, not that it gave Gervase peace of mind, he seemed like a man possessed. Papers lay everywhere, there were invoices to be despatched, goodness knows what was on the man's mind. He had made little secret of the fact that he had stayed all last night, even though he had ceased work early enough. Miss Fanny was probably leading him a dance. Tom shook his head at how things worked out — funny old world, he thought to himself. He continued to operate the press until there was nowhere left to hang the papers to dry and he was too tired to stand. Printed sheets of paper hung like washing across the room. The fire had practically gone out and looked as dead as Tom felt tired, he decided to call it a day. He would tidy up in the morning before the others arrived. Taking his jacket, he turned out the lamp and by the light of his candle took himself wearily to bed. The old flock mattress felt like best feathers to his tired body and it didn't take long for him to lose himself in sleep.

The lamp in the back room was old, and rusting, Gervase had intended to replace it before the letter from John had arrived but, of course, had forgotten. Weariness had prevented Tom from noticing the drip of oil which occasionally fell onto the pile of papers on the bench, and the smell was hardly noticeable amongst all the other smells in the room. The drip, however, continued, spoiling the work which Gervase had done the previous night, then trickled down onto the floor and seeped between the stone slabs.

Walking along the dimly lit street, Gervase mulled over in his mind the events of the past three days, and began to regret his boorish manner with Fanny. She had made such an effort to please him tonight and he had spurned her. He had been a fool to take so much drink the other night, when in truth he normally took very little; he had little time for drunks and realised that he was now little better than the rest of them. The mere fact that she was jealous should have placated his pride, but his mind was in a turmoil these days, consumed with his own jealousy.

George Street joined High Street just below his shop and as he passed by, he noted that Tom had retired upstairs to his room. He was well pleased with the lad, and considering his poor start to life, felt all the effort had been worthwhile. He had been bored at the Club and now sought the wisdom of old Sarah; it was late but he had to talk to someone, even if he had to wake her up. It was with relief that he noted the light still on in the kitchen and he hoped that she would understand his plight.

Sarah was a bad sleeper these days and almost welcomed the visit; but she knew that it probably meant that there was trouble brewing. No one had even mentioned the letter and she knew that sooner or later the bubble would burst. It was not like Gervase to knock quite so late at night, she could tell by the droop of his shoulders that he had much on his mind, and wondered if something was amiss with Fanny or Becky. He had hardly entered the house when he burst out, 'Sarah, I can't live this lie anymore, the atmosphere in the house is stifling us, I can't go on'. He sat down heavily on the chair, causing it to creak under his weight. 'I can't keep the promise I made to you, and her.'

She shook her head sadly. 'I had hoped in my heart that you would both find happiness. Don't you love her at all?'

'How can you ask that? I am driven to distraction with love for her and it is causing me to behave despicably. I'm becoming a monster. I need her Sarah, and cannot pretend any more. I need her. I am afraid to tell her of my feelings for fear of losing her.' He put his head into his hands.

His pain, Fanny's pain, were her pains too and she felt powerless. 'Fanny is happy with you — have you not tried to tell her that you care for her? Perhaps that is all she needs to know.'

'No. I promised not to.' He could hear his voice; it sounded all so foolish put into words. God he was tired and making a fool of himself. 'I'm sorry Sarah, things have been bad these past few weeks. I think I had better get home to bed.'

Sarah stopped him by the door, and put her hand on his arm. 'Tell her, for my sake, tell her', she said softly.

He left Sarah and walked slowly down the street. His preoccupation with his own problems left him careless to the unusual activity of the numerous people gathered on the corner. The fact that it was so late did not strike him until the smell of burning, which hung in the air, suddenly hit him, and he vaguely came to the conclusion that some poor devil had gone up in smoke. He rounded the corner and would have left the scene had not an excited voice reached his ears.

'It's the back of Webster's place' the man yelled.

Gervase stopped in his tracks, stunned. He looked across to the crowd which had gathered in front of his shop window. 'My God it's the shop — Tom is up there' he shouted and sprang to life, pushing his way through the thickening crowd. 'Get out of the way, there's a lad upstairs.' A man burst open the shop door whilst Gervase attempted to keep the crowd back. 'Stand back, there are chemicals inside' he warned.

It was fortunate that the door which divided the shop from the back room remained shut. Smoke billowed from under the door and the sound of crackling became stronger with each passing moment, but Gervase couldn't understand where Tom could be, for the door at the bottom of the stairs was on the street side of the workshop door.

Half a dozen men rushed in and a youth attempted to open the dividing door. 'Don't open that door!' yelled Gervase frantically. 'With all that paper and stuff in there it'll be like an inferno now. There's a lad upstairs, we've got to get him out.'

'Oh, he's alright, he raised the alarm. He's helping round the back with the bucket gang' the youth screamed above the noise.

Gervase heaved a sigh of relief. At least Tom was safe. 'Let's dowse the shop with water while there's still time. When it breaks through at least we can stop it spreading to the other properties.' There was little chance of saving the stock or anything now, and it was pointless putting other lives at risk.

A man ran in from the street waving his arms in warning. 'It's reached the top floor at the back — you'd better get out before the door goes' he shouted in fear, before racing out again.

The flames were coming out of the upstairs windows now, licking their way to the roof at the back and sending showers of sparks down onto the bucket team below. 'Get back lads, it's too dangerous now', one man cried.

The crowd at the front increased, as more people arrived armed with jugs and anything suitable for carrying water. They formed a chain in an effort to stop the fire from reaching the adjoining premises. Four men took turns to operate the pumps, as the gang threw bucketful after bucketful of water into the shop. The Fire Company arrived and made no more headway than the crowd, but the air within the shop was hot and thickening as the fire raged against the door, consuming all within its path. 'It'll go any second now — stand back.'

Within seconds there was a thunderous roar and the door gave way to ferocious flames which illuminated the street, and then Gervase saw an oil lamp swinging in the window with the force of the blast. A faulty lantern, he was sure now that he knew what had caused it. He'd meant to replace it last week but other things had been on his mind. He'd taken so much care to prevent fire. The entire printing trade suffered constantly from the hazard of fire but he had never thought it would attack him. Thank God he'd paid the Fire Company his premium; it was hefty enough but at least they turned out to fight the fire, and there would, he knew, eventually be some compensation to cushion the blow.

The fire was checked momentarily by the dampened shop but the heat soon dried it out and flames consumed the lot. Gervase looked on helplessly whilst others enjoyed the spectacle which had kept them from their beds. All his precious library had gone, along with all his hopes and dreams, there was nothing left.

They continued to dowse the shop with water long after the fire had died down, making sure that it was out completely and the crowds dispersed, having enjoyed their break from monotony. Tom found Gervase gazing in disbelief before the shop frontage. 'What are we going to do now, Mr Webster?' he asked out of habit. 'I think I'll go and sleep at Emily's place tonight. You'd better go and tell Miss Fanny.' He wasn't even sure that Gervase was listening, and he gave him a gentle push. 'There's nothing more you can do here tonight, go home.'

Tom was right, what could anyone do? He was sick with fatigue and worry but the thought of going home held little comfort to him. He arrived at the house with his clothing in disarray. He was smoky and dirty, and his singed hair hung over his blackened face. He had no key, for in the heat he had discarded his jacket he knew not where and the key had been in the pocket.

Fanny came in answer to his banging, half expecting it to be Gervase and half expecting the constable. She gaped in horror at the sight of his blackened face. 'My God, what happened?'

He stood as if frozen in time, no longer caring if he lived or died, too weary to move. 'Gervase! What happened?' Fanny pleaded as he stood there. She tugged at his sleeve, forcing him to answer.

'It's gone Fanny, all of it. All gone up in smoke!' He dragged his leaden, weary limbs across to the sofa and sat in utter despair.

'What has? Please Gervase, tell me what has happened.'

'It's the shop, the back room, the lot. I'm finished, Fanny, I can't go on.' His voice got weaker and he said no more.

Fanny had never seen him like this before, beaten, lost. She knelt on the floor before him and lifted his face from his hands and his face was lifeless. She remembered the upstairs room and Tom. She put her hand to her mouth as fear gripped her, 'Where's Tom?' Her voice rose almost to the state of hysteria.

He nodded weakly. 'He's safe, we worked for hours, Fanny, to save it, but it's all gone.' His voice trailed off and she was sure there had been a sob in his throat.

She pulled his boots off, and he let her. She felt his arms go round her waist and his head fall against her and she realised that he had fallen asleep. She lifted his legs up onto the sofa and covered him with a blanket. She didn't disturb him, or wash his face, instead she kissed his hand and held it to her face wishing she could hold him in her arms like a child.

Sleep was impossible for Fanny, as she tossed and turned constantly, because her mind feverishly sought a solution that would relieve Gervase from the pressure under which he found himself. The most worrying aspect was not a financial one at all, but that of the despair to which he seemed to have sunk, and she was sure that the fire was only part of the problem. He had been so edgy of late, even sometimes moody and she knew that somehow she was to blame.

She was awoken by Becky's cry and hurried to quieten the child, lest her cries disturb him from his much-needed sleep. It was much later in the morning than she had realised and there was no sign of him on the sofa, nor in his bed nor indeed in the house at all. Fanny hastily saw to Becky and took her to her mother's house.

It was with great trepidation that she then went to the shop. The smoke-stained brickwork and the glassless, burnt-out windows gawped at her, like threatening caverns before her eyes, and she could well understand the deep despair which Gervase must feel. Not caring about the soot, or the smell, she valiantly tried to cross the flagstones of the shop floor but it was impossible, for charred rubbish and beams lay everywhere and there was a likelihood that the roof would fall in at any moment.

There was little point in climbing over the debris; it was obvious that he was not there, but where was he? Small piles of ashes were all that remained of the books. There was nothing left to recover, a burnt out lantern swung precariously on its metal hook from a beam which was about to collapse.

Fanny raced home, forgetting that she had left Becky with Sarah. She had to find Gervase, to tell him that she understood his wretchedness and that together they could start again, but he was not there. There was no answer to her frantic call, and there was nothing she could do but wait for him to return.

It was almost three in the afternoon when he appeared, Fanny had been expecting him to be dishevelled and in turmoil, but he stood there clean-shaven and neatly dressed as was his habit. It was only when she looked into his face that she saw the distress concealed beneath the brave exterior, and her heart went out to him.

Fanny ran towards him. 'Oh Gervase, where have you been?' she begged, 'I have looked everywhere for you and didn't know where to look next.'

He shook his head hopelessly. 'I went out early and didn't want to disturb you, I went to the shop first. Have you seen it?' His face fell. 'There is nothing left at all. The heat melted all the type and the machines are all destroyed. Even the building is unsafe.'

'I know, I went there to find you. It's awful', Fanny said sadly, distressed by the memory of what she had seen. 'What are we going to do?' He was at a loss to answer her and she asked again, 'Where were you?'

'I went to the Fire Office' he said simply. It had never occurred to her that he might go there, such was the state in which she had seen him last. 'I will get some money — not enough to cover the loss of orders and buy new machinery, or pay wages until I get started again, which means I shall have to let Tom and Joseph go. I shall get the limit for being in a hazardous trade, but it's not enough! Thank God I paid those premiums, even if they were excessive.' The gravity in his voice filled her with foreboding, yet she felt strangely closer to him now than she had for a long time.

'I've been thinking', Fanny offered, 'you do have enough money saved to buy one of those new machines which you dreamed of. Why not buy it now? Then you could get a second-hand one with the other money when it comes. You said you could earn more money quicker with a modern machine.'

He considered her proposal for a minute. 'That would take all our capital, Fanny, and I need paper, ink, founts of type, as well as money for rent and wages.' He had spent the day mulling over all the possibilities and decided in the end that there was little point in risking all his capital and their security on a selfish gamble. He would simply have to go and work for someone else.

'Don't give up, Gervase, please!' she pleaded, 'it's all you've ever wanted — to work for yourself. We'll manage somehow.'

'I can't afford to borrow money, Fanny, but I need capital before I lose Tom and Joseph to some other firm.'

'I could take in needlework, there are many of Bryce's clients who would be willing to pay me well enough.'

The look of determination and hope in Fanny's eyes was not lost on him. He had always admired her fighting spirit and it strengthened him to know that she was on his side. They were kindred spirits who responded to challenges, and it was a great pity that they were so far apart in their emotional relationship, but for that, they could achieve much. 'I know you mean well', he said kindly, 'but it would take far too long.'

She stopped him, placing her hand on his arm. 'There is a way, if you would trust me.' She ran the risk of displeasing him, she knew that, but she had to try, she raised her eyes pleadingly to his. 'Do you believe that I would never hurt you, or lie?'

Her face was an open book to him and he realised that she was in earnest. He could read her mind as he could one of his beloved volumes. She wasn't capable of real deceit, in spite of her fool-hardy escapades. He wished now that he had asked her outright about the letter from John, for he knew that she would have told him the truth there and then. Perhaps he had been afraid of losing her. 'Of course I trust you, trust is all that we have left, that and hope.'

'Did you know that there had been a letter from John?' She watched his face but he showed no sign of surprise and merely nodded. 'He is much depressed. I cannot help him, and I think that it will not be long before he takes a wife to comfort him. I cannot deny him that.'

Gervase watched her face. He had been surprised that she had broken into his thoughts but she showed no sign of devastating distress, only that of concern and compassion, but where was it leading?

'You remember the day he was captured — I had been to the old barn where he was hiding to take him things which he would need if he were to start a new life. In the turmoil I fled with the basket and his money is still here, safe from the authorities who would probably confiscate it if I sent it to him.' She hesitated, fearing that he would be angry with her for concealing the truth.

'Go on' he said impatiently.

'It would be better invested for him — don't you think? He still wants to go to America. He would need it there and I believe he would want you to borrow it, in the circumstances. As long as we pay him back when he needs it. He thinks the militia have it and I daren't write to tell him differently in case they read the letter. We could pay him back with interest.'

Suddenly his eyes flashed with anger and he rounded on her. 'What if he comes back? I wouldn't want to work with my wife's lover.' The moment the words were spoken he regretted his outburst. It was unfair of him to round on her when she was so obviously concerned for his welfare. He was ashamed of himself for allowing his insane jealousy to get out of control, but before he had time to apologise Fanny began speaking again, her voice soft and without reproach.

'We could pay him back, the money is doing nothing worthwhile hidden away.' Fanny waited patiently, while he considered her proposition, but her mind raced on. He had been jealous, intensely jealous in his outburst, just as he had been the night he had attacked her. She looked at his face, there was no anger there now, merely the confused look of a young boy, unsure and vulnerable. Why had she not realised the truth before. He *did* love her. It was plain enough to see and she had been too naive and too blind to understand why he had been behaving the way he had. She was sure that her intuition was right, he was in love with her. 'I didn't mean to hide the letter from you, it's not a happy one, would you like to read it?' she offered, endeavouring to heal the hurt on his face.

He lowered his eyes and stammered, 'I'm sorry, Fanny, I've been a fool. I have worked so hard to be a success and now everything seems to be falling apart around me!' He moved away and sat at the desk, crushed and defeated.

Fanny whispered, a sob in her voice. 'Perhaps it's me. I seem to bring bad luck to everyone I touch.' Tears welled up in her eyes, blurring him from her sight.

The emotion in her voice broke through into his despair and he realised that he was hurting her. 'Oh God, Fanny, this can't go on, this fighting is destroying us, and I have nothing left to offer you. You are not to blame at all.' His eyes were soft now, 'Come, draw up a chair and I will try to explain our financial position to you'. There was a pleading in his eyes which was unmistakable, and she could see into his soul, leaving him very vulnerable.

Fanny sat by his side and he reached out to the desk and drew from a pigeon-hole a sheaf of papers, which he laid out in front of her. They were the plans of the new machine. He seemed almost reluctant to look at them himself, for they were his dreams and he could not live without dreams. The plans were not complicated but Fanny found her mind unable to absorb their contents whilst his dark head was only inches away from her own. She watched his sturdy hand fumble through the papers, those gentle hands that had often comforted her and she trembled, wanting to reach out and cover them gently with her own.

Time stood still, and for a while neither spoke nor moved as each stared unseeingly at the papers spread out across the desk, but both were painfully aware of the closeness of the other. The air in the room seemed stifling to Fanny and her body warmed with the desire to touch him. She breathed deeply, causing a shiver to creep over her, and warm memories flooded back of the day he had taken her to the St. Ledger. She had wanted him to kiss her then, just as she wanted him to now.

Gervase seemed startled by the shake of her body and instinctively placed his arm round her shoulder. 'Are you cold, Fanny?' he asked, deeply concerned for her. He could smell the perfume in her hair and fought off the overwhelming desire to bury his face in her golden curls which were so tantalisingly near. She did not move, or answer, and he let go of the paper in his other hand and tenderly reached up to touch her face. He turned her face towards him, questioningly, and saw the tears in her eyes. He brushed them away with his thumb and pressed his hand caressingly against her cheek. The pain in her eyes caused him to cry out softly, 'Oh, Fanny, what are we doing to each other?' She was so close now, warm and soft and he knew that he was lost. The desire to kiss her was too much and he bent his head seeking her soft, sweet lips. He felt her lips move against his, warm and inviting, moist and giving and he took her face in both his hands possessively.

The tender touch of his hands unleashed in Fanny all the emotion, which for months she had kept suppressed, and she kissed him back with a passion that drained her. She felt his arms draw her to him, eagerly, excitingly, almost crushing her as though he expected her to disappear, then his lips left hers and found their way into her hair. It was all she could do, crushed so hard against his broad chest, but nuzzle her lips against his throat, working them upwards, begging him to return his lips to hers. She could not hold back the words which rose huskily from her throat, 'I love you' she whispered. 'Oh, I do love you.'

He drew back in wonderment, searching her face, her eyes, adoringly, hoping that he wasn't dreaming, then said, 'Oh Fanny, I thought I'd never hear you say those words to me!' His eyes became boyish, almost shy and he murmured, 'I've loved you for so long without hope, and when I heard of the letter I nearly went crazy for fear you would leave me'.

'But you kept so strictly to our bargain', she chided, resting her head on his shoulder. 'I hoped and prayed that you would learn to love me, but I was afraid that if you knew of my feeling for you it would make you regret marrying me.'

'When I asked you to marry me, Fanny, I accepted that you didn't love me, and I intended to keep my promise but it became so difficult. I did begin to regret it, but only because I wanted you for myself.' He paused then added, 'I thought you still loved John!'

'I can't even remember his face clearly', she said sadly. 'I think I've always loved you, without knowing it. Last night, when you were so tired, you put your arms around me and I was going to tell you then, but you fell asleep!' She accused him.

The childish reprimand in her voice made him laugh. It had been a long time since they had bantered with each other and he bent and kissed her playfully on the tip of her nose. She was his, he couldn't believe it, after all these years Fanny was his! He took her hand in his and squeezed it, lifting it to his lips. Fanny uncurled her fingers and traced his lips tenderly with them until his head swam with adoration for her.

He eased her to her feet and towered over her, his eyes twinkling now like those of an eager child and pulled her towards the door. 'Come, Fanny Garnett', he said coaxingly 'there are things I want to do to you, upstairs.'

Fanny giggled, then blushed as she allowed him to lead her to the staircase.

Chapter 16

Fanny always sang when she was happy. She was never in tune, nor did she get the words quite right, but that never stopped her. The happier she was the louder she sang, and Gervase smiled to himself as he listened, for it had been a long time since he had seen Fanny as happy as this. He was almost sure that her voice could be heard way down the street, and wondered what his neighbours thought about him having such a young wife. He wondered too, if they could guess why Fanny sang so loud and happily, when they were still recovering from the disaster of the fire, and he chuckled contentedly to himself as he watched Fanny bustle about her chores.

Fanny had enough energy for the two of them and he could not fail to be excited by her enthusiastic plans to rebuild the business. She was more to him than a wife, she was his inspiration, everything in life was a challenge to Fanny. Even as a child he had placed her on a pedestal, and he wistfully hoped that he would be able to keep up with her and her youthful aspirations.

She was right of course, the circulating library did take up far too much space and time, so why bother opening up a new one when he had never wanted one in the first place. He was better at printing and bookbinding than anything else, and the constant interruptions destroyed his concentration; he would be better without them. He watched his beloved Fanny bustle about her work, until his mind began to wander onto less worldly matters, however, a sudden knock on the door interrupted his train of thought.

Fanny opened the door to find Tom and Joseph, caps in hand, standing there almost apologetically. 'We've come to see Mr Webster', Tom announced.

'Come in both of you', Gervase called from within the house.

The two young men stood, feeling oddly out of place in the boss's house, both clutching their caps even tighter than before. 'We needs t'know what's 'appenin about our jobs, and wages, an I've no place to live either now the building's gutted.'

Gervase nodded. 'Quite right Tom — sit down the pair of you.' They sat on the sofa like a pair of bookends, caps on knees, and it struck Gervase how comical the pair looked. The situation however was far from comical, and there were decisions to be made. He might as well start now. 'Firstly, Tom, I will give you the money to replace your clothes and belongings, the Fire Office will repay me later, but can you find yourself some reasonably priced lodgings?'

'But I won't have any wages coming in to pay the rent' lamented Tom 'it's work what we need.'

'Listen will you, Tom.' Gervase shook his head at the lad's impatience. 'You won't need to look for jobs, you'll work for me. Miss Fanny and I have discussed the matter.' He turned for her approval. 'I'm going to get new premises as soon as possible, and one of those "newfangled machines" that you keep referring to. I'm going to London to find out about getting one brought here. You both come round here tomorrow at ten o'clock, prompt mind, and Miss Fanny will find you work. Do you think you can handle that horse and gig of mine?'

Tom's eyes lit up. 'No trouble Mr Webster', he replied, with a great deal more confidence than he felt.

'Are you sure you want to operate one of those "newfangled machines", Tom?' he asked teasingly.

In his excitement Tom did as he often did, he slipped back into his old way of speaking, 'cours ah do, but ah still need a roof ovver mi 'ead.'

'Look, if you can manage at Emily's place for a few days I'll see what we can fix up for you.' He looked at Joseph questioningly, 'Are you satisfied with that arrangement?'

In spite of being the elder of the two, Joseph was happy enough to let Tom take the lead. 'Yes Sir, Mr Webster, if Tom is happy I am.'

'Right, off you go then. There's nothing to do here today, but we have a lot of hard work ahead.' Both boys muttered their thanks and shuffled humbly out of the door. Immediately the door closed behind them, Tom tossed his hat into the air in triumph, and caught it with a yell of delight.

Gervase smiled to himself as he heard Tom's yell and returned to Fanny. 'Well, Fanny, there's no going back now is there? I really think we can make a go of it. First thing in the morning I will go out looking for new premises and search round the auction rooms to see what is available second-hand.'

'How long will it take to bring the machine in by wagon from London?'

'I'm not sure. It will depend very much on the weather, but the sooner I get off to London the better. Would you like to come with me?'

Fanny's eyes lit up at the thought of visiting London, however she shook her head. 'This time I think you should take Tom, so that both of you can learn to operate the machine. I must help Joseph buy the necessary equipment ready for when you return. I'll go one day, when we have the money to enjoy ourselves.'

He nodded, applauding her sensible suggestion. 'You're right. Your support and John's money has made all this possible. You won't regret it, I promise.' His eyes were once more alive with excitement and Fanny left him to pore over the plans while she attended to Becky.

It took Gervase all day to view what few premises were on the main property agents books. Both Sandersons and Bardwells had premises but most were totally unsuitable for Gervase's needs, some were too small or far too damp for storing paper, others were too gloomy for a craftsman to work in. The exuberance which had carried him along, slowly wore off as the day went on, until it soon became obvious that he was unlikely to clear the matter up quickly. There were premises for immediate occupation in Rockingham Street but he could not make up his mind if they were worth the extra rent asked for them or not. He even managed to locate a second-hand printing machine in Bardwell's auction room and began to wonder if his decision to buy a Koenig had been a little hasty.

He almost cancelled his trip to London but he was as stubborn as he was proud, and found it difficult to allow himself to give in so soon. He put his indecision down to his tiredness.

Gervase returned to the house to consult with Fanny, who agreed that they should take the dearer premises, preferring to get on with business rather than risk the chance of losing their present customers who were already anxious about their orders. He toyed with the idea of telling Fanny of his doubts about the Koenig but her enthusiasm for the whole plan held him back. The Stanhope machine and accessories had been at the auctioneers for some time and he knew that they would be quite prepared to compromise on the price, for a definite sale.

Together they compiled a list of their present customers on whom Fanny could make calls of reassurance, then they made a list of necessities to be purchased in his absence. It soon became evident that John's money was insufficient to cover their immediate needs until the Fire Office paid out. Their creditors were willing to wait until then, but there still wasn't enough.

Fanny watched sadly as Gervase extracted from the bookcase most of his precious books, some of which, all leather bound and many engraved, were quite rare. 'These should fetch a good price in London.' He lovingly fingered the leather bindings as he placed them, one on top of the other, into a portmanteau.

Fanny was horrified. 'You can't part with those', she pleaded, knowing just how much they meant to him.

He smiled at her knowingly. 'There comes a time, Fanny, when some worldly goods are of less value than others. I have read each one many times, perhaps now is the time to share their contents with someone else.'

She looked down at the brooch pinned to her bodice and said, 'But when the money comes in again, you will wish that they were still in your possession'. She touched the brooch with her fingers intending to remove it.

'No, Fanny!' he motioned at her bodice, 'Not that!' She hadn't wanted to part with his gift at all and the strength of feeling in his voice made her feel guilty at having considered the idea, for the brooch was precious to her too.

'Did you manage to find enough work for the lads, Fanny?' He enquired, changing the subject.

'I kept them busy all day, they even did work for Bryce and mother. I think I worked them harder than you do.'

'Yes, but I don't reward them with gingerbread' he quipped.

'Have you told Tom about the trip to London?'

'No, I thought you might have done. I'd better go and find him now, we may go the day after tomorrow.'

'Do you have to go so soon?' A note of sadness crept into Fanny's voice as she realised that she didn't want him to go. 'There is so little time for you to see to everything' she pointed out, hoping to delay his departure a little longer.

'Don't worry, sweet love, I shall be no longer than I have to. Wasted time however, is wasted money.' He drew her into his arms comfortingly. 'I shall be lost without you when I go' he whispered.

When Gervase finally located Tom it was almost dark, it had been a long day and Gervase was almost exhausted, but this task would be, he knew, a pleasant one. Tom could hardly believe his ears when he heard the good news, the farthest he had ever been was Heeley, a mere two miles from Sheffield, and then he had been compelled to walk carrying a huge bundle of work for his uncle. As a boy he had stared in wonder at the coaches, as they came and went, in the courtyards of local inns. He had often peered inside when he thought no one was about, trying to imagine the places beyond his world where the travellers came from. He had been filled with the usual envy and longing of all small boys, for the adventures which never seem to come their way, and now it was his turn.

A lump rose in Fanny's throat as she bade Gervase farewell, for it was a long and sometimes hazardous journey to London. Coaches were often dangerously overloaded, making them top-heavy and likely to topple over when driven at speed. They also often fell prey to attack from robbers, who cared very little for the welfare of their victims. Consequently, Gervase rarely took anything of real value with him on his journeys, thus relieving himself of the responsibility and the inconvenience of being permanently lumbered with luggage. The bulk of his money to pay for the machine was scattered throughout his luggage and person, although most was in letters of credit, and he always kept a few sovereigns in an obvious place to placate a highwayman and since hearing the story of the 'T'alli Stone' years ago he always carried sufficient identification about his person to ensure there would be no repetition of the plight of the stranger in the graveyard. However, Fanny had packed the two men sufficient food to feed an army, Gervase vowed to eat it as soon as possible, thus leaving him with just the two portmanteaux to contend with.

Tom's simple mind soaked up the newness of the journey as a grinder guzzles his ale. His eyes darted backwards and forwards, from one side of the coach to the other, missing not a tree or house as the miles went by. Gervase did his best to answer the never ending questions which flowed from Tom's lips at every new sight that appeared. The time was coming, Gervase conceded, when the country would open itself up to the ordinary man, and in so doing would become smaller, just as the minds of men would expand. Canals and railways were growing in number now, and Gervase considered that he had been fortunate in seeing so many of these miracles long before many of his fellow men. 'Well, Tom,' he broke into the lad's thoughts, 'what do you think of this wonderful world of ours?'

'I didn't know it stretched so far', was his simple answer, and his eyes shone with excitement. Gervase saw in that moment the eager innocence that he had been used to seeing in Fanny's eyes and he lapsed into his own thoughts. Marriage had changed him. He no longer enjoyed his own company, and he found himself wishing that he had a son to build his empire for, a son to mould and watch as the light of knowledge dawned in his eyes, as it did in Fanny's and Tom's eyes.

If going to school in Doncaster had taught Fanny nothing else, it taught her the art of patience, for it seemed that everything she had ever wanted must be waited for. Her only remedy for loneliness was to work, and she set out to fill every spare moment of Gervase's absence by being busy.

With Joseph on hand to help her make sure that the founts of type were exactly the kind which Gervase wanted, and that the paper, ink and other necessary tools were suitable for his requirements, Fanny felt that progress had been made. She visited each client assuring them that all was well, and took possession of the new premises. Together, they lime-washed the inner walls to give added light and Fanny scrubbed out the rooms, took delivery of the printing machine, type and equipment ready for Gervase's return. Fanny had never really got to know Joseph; she had thought him lacking in imagination, but as the two worked steadily together with purpose of mind, he revealed himself as a rather shy young man, from whom the best had yet to be drawn out.

He merely lacked self-confidence, but as Fanny drew him out with her endless chatter, she found him opening up like a flower. She had Sarah's knack of befriending people, giving them confidence by allowing each to express himself without fear of being ridiculed. Fanny told him of her love for birds and nature, about her paintings, and he in turn told her of his unfulfilled dreams, answering her at first in tongue-tied monosyllables then later, as he relaxed and realised that she was interested in him, he answered at length. She was surprised to learn that he was in fact two years older than she was. He was tall and really quite good looking when he allowed himself to smile, and as the days went by, he smiled more and more, and Fanny enjoyed his company.

Almost a week went by and still Gervase did not return, nor was there any communication from him at all, and Fanny was suddenly struck with terror. What if he never came back? She knew the journey was long but how would she know if evil had befallen him. Previously when he had left her, she had been lonely and afraid for herself, but now she was afraid for him. She waited daily for news from London, but nothing came, and slowly her enthusiasm for the venture began to wane.

Joseph assured her that he was quite capable of laying out and finally printing some of the simpler orders for regular customers, and they agreed to make a start instead of hanging around waiting for Gervase to return. It seemed to Fanny that each stage took forever, from the pencil layouts until the time when Joseph pulled a proof from the galley, and she watched with envy as his nimble fingers worked untiringly. She was impressed by his efficiency, his sleeves rolled up tight so as not to catch the type which he had so carefully set up. He was methodical and tidy and Fanny was determined to ask Gervase to allow him greater scope in future. Joseph had served his apprenticeship at the hands of a man who wanted nothing more than an obedient underling. The work had been mundane, but beneath the surface Joseph was an artist, and his skill at copying ancient illuminated script earned him Fanny's undying admiration.

There were times when Fanny could be of little help to him and in these periods she returned to Sarah and Becky. A feeling of guilt crept over her at her neglect of the child whilst she had been preoccupied, and she felt a need to prove her love. A fair came to town and pitched along the river bank, and Fanny decided, in an effort to make up for her many absences, to take Becky. It had been a long time since she had allowed herself to indulge in such a youthful pastime, and she invited Joseph along for the company. The evening air was heady with music, and the strange smells of the fair reminded Fanny of the St Ledger, and brought a sudden pang of loneliness to the day.

Becky was far too young to take it all in; the antics of a clown served only to make her yell out in terror, whereas the noise and aggression of a Punch and Judy man completely mesmerised the child. She wasn't too happy with the bustling of the crowd either, until Fanny bought her a cheap bauble to jangle.

The opportunity to laugh and be a child again for a while brought the mischievous twinkle back into Fanny's eyes, and Joseph soon became the butt of her torments and teasing, as she flirted outrageously but innocently with him. In her single-minded need for happiness and enjoyment, she was completely unaware of the spell which she was casting upon the shy young man, and by the end of the outing Joseph would have given his life for her.

She was well aware of the privilege that was hers, to be her own woman, for Gervase had always permitted her the freedom of self-expression, and to some degree encouraged her, thus the sense of achievement which she received from seeing the efforts of her hard work bearing fruit, gave her a feeling of deep fulfilment.

Finally, when Joseph was ready to go to print, he taught Fanny how to put the glutinous ink into the machine without getting it all over herself, then he showed her how to feed the paper into the machine. At first her arms soon tired at the unaccustomed hard work of operating the press and she found even lifting Becky a chore, but as the days passed and the piles of completed orders built up, she was proud of the aches and pains, knowing that Gervase would be pleased with her. For Fanny and Joseph there was no mistress and employee situation now; she did as Joseph bade her and together they worked in complete forgetfulness of everything else, endeavouring to make a success of their work. The one thing they made certain of, was that nothing which could catch fire was stored or dried anywhere near to flames, oil or chemicals.

A further week passed without a word from Gervase. Why had he not bothered to write to her? Had there been an accident? If so she would surely have heard by now; there had been time for him to travel to London and back several times over, so what could possibly be the delay? The more she brooded the less she was willing to forgive him this neglect of her, until, in the end, she felt very hurt and angry.

It wasn't long before customers began badgering for delivery of their orders, and rather than see the mounting number of completed orders stand idle, Fanny decided to deliver them herself. Joseph had never handled a horse and gig before but Fanny had. She fetched the pair and had Joseph place the orders into the gig. 'Come with me Joseph', she instructed, 'Gervase would not approve of me going alone.' Some of the firms were not in the best of areas and Fanny had not forgotten her last experience in those unfriendly streets. She had arranged the orders methodically, and planned the route carefully, in order to save time and effort because of the firms being scattered about.

After delivering the last order to a customer, who was situated out on the road leading to the paper mill, Fanny suddenly decided defiantly not to return to the works. She pulled the horse up, tied her hat firmly onto her head and cried excitedly, 'Hold tight Joseph, it's going to be bumpy'. Responding to the whip the horse eagerly stepped out along the open road, gathering speed as he went.

'Slow down, Miss Fanny, it's not a good idea!' protested Joseph, who was unused to horses. 'Shouldn't we go back?'

Go back! Where was she going anyway, back to the past or back to Gervase? The exhilaration had drained her and the jolting made her head spin, acid rose up in her throat making her want to heave and she pulled the horse up once more. 'I'm sorry' she whispered apologetically.

'It's alright, Miss Fanny, it's just that I'm frightened of horses.' He looked at Fanny, 'Why, you're all pale, are you ill?'

She shook her head slowly, 'I'll be alright in a minute. Have a look at the river if you like, I'd like to sit quietly for a while. I just can't stand all this heat'.

'Is there nothing I can do?' he asked.

'No, Joseph, it will pass.' Joseph left the gig and wandered a few yards before turning to see if she was alright. Fanny smiled weakly at him, wishing that he would go away, and when he did, she placed her arm on the side of the gig and lay her head on it for comfort. When Joseph returned she felt better, 'I think we had better go back now. Will you fetch Becky from mother's for me, but don't say I'm ill — just say I'm very busy'.

Joseph nodded, 'If you're sure you can manage her on your own'. The caring tone of his voice touched Fanny, who vowed that she would indeed encourage Gervase to make more of Joseph's talents.

'Don't worry — I'll be at the workshop in the morning. Surely Gervase can't be much longer before he gets back. I don't know what I would have done without you in his absence, and I'm very grateful for your help.' She dropped him off at the end of York Street before returning the gig to the livery, then slowly returned to the house.

As the coach turned the last bend in the road, Gervase breathed a sigh of relief, for in spite of the drabness of its buildings this town was his home, and he was always glad to return. He had never envisaged being away for so long, but driving rain and gale force winds in the south, had compelled them to break their journey. Fallen trees had blocked roads, bridges had been swept away by the torrential falls of rain which had swollen the rivers, and in the end they had arrived in London dishevelled and exhausted. Tom developed a nasty cold which laid him low for several days, hindering their plans. Had Gervase realised just how long he was going to be away he would have sent Fanny a letter of explanation, but he kept hoping that the delay would soon end.

A cold, empty house greeted Gervase when he eventually reached it, and he felt a sense of dismay and disappointment to find that Fanny was not there. Throughout the return journey he had imagined the warmth of the room and the brightness of her presence within it. He too was cold, and as he waited for her to return he found himself remembering the lonely days of his bachelorhood. He shivered, the house was like a tomb and he was hungry. The thought of being alone offered little comfort and he reluctantly retreated to his club. It was his first visit to the club since the fire and he was unsure of his reception. By now the members would be aware of his trip to London and the reason for it, but he need not have worried for there was a hum of excitement within the place. He received a nod here and a nod there, not unfriendly, but he realised that no one seemed particularly interested in his problems.

Gervase joined a group of fellow members by the window, where a copy of the *Iris* lay open on the sidetable for all to see. An immaculately attired fellow standing next to him passed the newspaper across. 'I suppose you've seen this?' he asked still casting an eye over the headlines.

Gervase shook his head. 'No, I've only just got back from London. It certainly seems to be creating a lot of interest. May I read it?' The column to which the man referred was headed 'Sheffield Police Act'. Gervase read the report intently. At last a gas company had been formed and street lighting was to be installed. Not before time, he concluded. Watchmen were to be found to provide protection, street cleaning was to be taken seriously at last, no football was to be played in the streets, no cutting up of beasts on the pavements, the list was endless. There was to be no standing of wagons in main streets for longer than necessary, no throwing of fireworks or dumping of refuge in the streets. He wondered if the Police might take notice of that too; the stench down on Shalesmoor, where they dumped their manure, was disgusting, especially during the hot summer months.

The other fellow continued when he saw that Gervase had finished reading the article. 'Things are certainly moving in this town. With the passing of this act we are going to move into a new era. It's time the darn place was cleaned up and improved. Not fit for women to walk down the streets sometimes.'

One sour looking man chipped in, 'Sounds as though we'll have to think twice before breathing now'. Then he strode off to join another group of members.

'Well, how did the trip go?' A hand slapped Gervase heartily on the shoulder. 'Sorry to hear about the fire, at least no one was hurt. Good job you'd got insurance cover.'

Gervase sighed, 'It won't cover everything I'm afraid, but I had some savings. I may as well start from scratch, and you may as well pass it round, I'm buying a steam-powered printer'. He expected an unfavourable reaction but was quite taken aback with the reply.

'So we hear. Rumour gets around fast you know!' He looked idly round. 'That wife of yours is a brick; she's been delivering orders this week. Saw her at the fair last week, with that printer of yours. Want to watch out, I wouldn't trust my wife with a good looking fellow like that.' He winked at Gervase. 'God, the heat has been stifling this week. Must go, got a new filly to see to, got her at the fair quite cheap last week. Now that you're expanding, you could do with a son and heir. Time you got your filly in the family way again.' He chuckled and walked away.

Gervase hated vulgarity of any sort and resented being the butt of the man's amusement. He merely continued to read the article until the man disappeared. So Fanny had been at the fair, with Joseph of all people! He wasn't sure that he'd ever noticed Joseph's good looks but he wished Fanny wouldn't get up to her escapades. Anyway, it certainly looked as though his venture would cause him little trouble, it was about time he had a bit of luck. The coming of street lighting would certainly provide much needed work in the town and the opportunity for men to train in new skills. He cared little now whether anyone objected to his plan or not, the machine was on it's way, he was more concerned about finding Fanny. Where was she now? He drummed his fingers agitatedly on the polished surface of the sidetable. Of course, she would be with Sarah!

At least Sarah was at home, both she and Becky were pleased to see him again, but Fanny however was at the Rockingham Street premises helping Joseph. He never realised that Fanny knew Joseph sufficiently well enough to go out with him, all he'd seemed to hear since he got back was that Fanny was with Joseph. God in Heaven, what was he thinking of, was he to be suspicious of every young swain that happened to touch their lives? He hastened his steps. How he had missed her irrepressible good humour and soft femininity, without which he no longer felt whole.

They did not hear the approach of Gervase's footsteps above the noise of the machine, and he watched them, unobserved, from the doorway as Fanny and Joseph worked side by side. The transformation within the building staggered him. The whitened walls, the scrubbed floor, and the orderliness of everything took his breath away. He felt almost a stranger standing there, as if intruding into their world. He was aware of Joseph who seemed strangely changed, taller than before and almost handsome in his youth, and Gervase was aware of the fact that their ages were far closer to each other's, than his was to Fanny's. This was not how he had envisaged Fanny either. She stood sweaty and dirty, working like an apprentice and laughing companionably with this powerful youth. Gervase felt afraid to intrude and would have drawn back had Tom not rushed passed him into the workshop.

The sudden movement caught Fanny's eye. She saw Gervase framed in the doorway. He was home. She wanted to run to him but he seemed neither pleased nor eager to see her. She tried to tidy herself up, aware of how she must look to him and unable to understand why he looked so withdrawn. Tom on the other hand stood with his mouth opened wide in amazement.

'Wow, Miss Fanny', he panted, 'you've gone and done a miracle 'ere.'

She laughed at his simple praise. 'Why, thank you, Tom, but it wasn't just my work, Joseph did most of it.' Fanny waited for Gervase to speak, sensing the strange broodiness in him which she had only seen once before, on the night of his intoxication. She glanced around the room. What could be displeasing, they had worked so hard in order to please him. 'Don't you like what we have done? We've even completed a dozen small orders for you.'

He appeared to emerge from his trance and look round. He saw them all waiting expectantly for his approval. What right had he to spoil their pleasure, and indeed what grounds had he to suppose that there was anything going on, other than the petty mindedness of a spiteful gossip fuelling his travel-weary mind. The three pairs of childlike eyes watched him, awaiting his praise and they deserved it. He forced a brightness into his voice. 'I can't believe it. Tom is right, you have worked miracles. I feel as though I have been away for years. You've both done extremely well, you must excuse me if I'm preoccupied', he lied, 'but the journey was long and tiring.' He turned to Joseph, 'There's no need to ask if you have any problems, Joseph, you seem to have coped very well.

The youth looked at Fanny admiringly, 'Miss Fanny ought to be a printer, Mr Webster, she learns very fast'.

Fanny could not contain her curiosity any longer. 'How did you get on about the machine? When will it come?'

'It's on its way, Miss Fanny', interrupted Tom. He was busy inspecting everything in the place with a childlike innocence, 'and I can work it'.

Picking up a couple of proofs from the workbench, Gervase ran his eyes critically over them, noting with satisfaction the quality of the layout. They were certainly as good as those pulled off the old machine, and Joseph had done them well, but he was puzzled. 'How did you remember the layout, Joseph? They are almost identical to the previous ones we printed. You can't have such a good memory?'

Joseph spoke up proudly, 'Miss Fanny fetched a sample back from the firms who were in a hurry and we just copied them. Are they good enough?' he asked, unsure of himself.

'They're excellent, Joseph. I'm very pleased. While I think about it, we must keep an extra sample in future of everything we do and I'll take it home for safe keeping. I think we'll keep a duplicate set of account books too.' They had thought of everything. He set about inspecting every inch of the premises but could find little fault anywhere. When he thought Fanny wasn't looking, he watched her, afraid to go to her in front of the boys yet aware that again he was building a barrier between them. He wanted Fanny to himself. He had enjoyed Tom's simple company but now he longed for more stimulating conversations, and Fanny's affection. He crossed the room and said quietly, 'Fanny, the house was cold and empty when I returned. I'm hungry too. Go and tidy yourself up and let's go home. I'm too tired to work today'.

It did not take Fanny long to wash her face, tidy her hair, and remove the smock which protected her clothing from the ink and dirt. So far there had been no explanation as to why Gervase had been away for so long, no excuse about his lack of communication and no reason for his earlier black mood. That he was tired had merely been a cover-up, she knew him well enough for that, but she too was tired after working so hard on his behalf and was in no mood to placate him. 'I'm ready!' she stated with an air of starchiness that hurt him, and she flounced ahead before he could stop her.

That she was annoyed with him was obvious. Had his face been so transparent, he wondered as he followed her. He wasn't sure whether to be angry at her haughtiness, or laugh at her childishness, but he knew that he would never fully understand women. He quickened his gait in order to catch up with her.

In the haste of trying to keep ahead of him, Fanny found the flimsy material of her skirts tangling with her legs, making it difficult to keep her balance and she found herself becoming as angry with herself as she was with the skirts. He caught hold of her elbow. 'Wait on Fanny. What have I done to upset you so?'

'You never wrote one word to let me know that you would be away so long, Joseph and I worked so hard for you and you didn't even seem interested when you arrived back. You ought to value Joseph more, he's very talented.'

At the mention of Joseph's name Gervase became annoyed. 'Really, Fanny, you shouldn't get so involved with the workmen' he said acidly 'I couldn't write because I didn't expect to be away so long. With each passing day I kept thinking I would be returning, but things cropped up.' He paused for breath as they waited for a wagon to pass before they could cross the road. 'The weather was so bad on the outward journey that it took two days extra to get there. Then Tom caught a chill which kept him in bed. Eventually, when we did get involved with the machine, it turned out to be more complicated than expected.'

Feeling ashamed of her behaviour, Fanny slowed her pace and asked, 'What was the journey like?'

'Like any other, bumpy and tedious, and the beds like all beds, lumpy and none too clean – and empty without you' he added softly. He saw Fanny blush, and was relieved that they were nearing the house, for the street was no place to sort out their difficulties.

Closing the door behind him, Gervase took hold of Fanny's hand and led her into the drawing room. 'Put your things down, Fanny', he said firmly, looking closely into her face. Now that her face was clean again he was able to observe it more clearly. She had that pinched look around the nose that he had seen before. 'Are you feeling well?' he asked, watching her keenly.

A rosy hue stole over her face and she lowered her lids. 'Why shouldn't I be?' Fanny stammered hesitatingly, and avoided his eyes whilst she toyed with the edge of her sleeve.

'Fanny Garnett' he chided 'are you trying to hide something from me?'

His eyes were serious now, but there was no mistaking the love in them or the concern.

'I've felt a little strange these past few days, but nothing more,' she lied 'I think it's been the heat. I've worked very hard and I was worried about you. I couldn't imagine why you had stayed away so long, but I'm fine now.' She wasn't sure whether she saw a sudden twinkle in his eye or not, but she had the strangest feeling that he was teasing her.

'Do you realise, Fanny, that I've been away three weeks, I've been home three hours, and you haven't kissed me once.' His head was tilted to one side as he watched her closely, invitingly, waiting for her to go to him. He opened his arms, 'Come here', he begged.

He wasn't handsome standing there, but he was powerful, rugged, and he understood her so well. Beneath that strongly disciplined exterior, lay a sensitive, loving being, capable of such deep passion that Fanny felt unworthy of being allowed into his soul. Fanny knew that she had the power to make him both happy and miserable. She went towards his outstretched arms humbly, needing to yield to his love, and offering him her gift. 'I'm with child,' she said softly 'your child.'

'I know, my love', he whispered triumphantly, 'I know.'